A Broken Boy

On a Broken Road

Journey of Healing – Volume 1

Other books by Robert G. Longpré

Through a Jungian Lens series (Psychology):
Volume 1 – Swamplands: Dark Night of the Soul, 2009
Volume 2 – Tunnel Vision: Journey on the Prairies, 2009
Volume 3 – Discovering the Hero Within, 2009
Volume 4 – Sol and Luna: On Becoming Whole, 2010
Volume 5 – Individuation and Consciousness, 2011

Journey of Healing series (Autobiographical):
Volume 1 – A Broken Boy, 2014
Volume 2 – On the Broken Road, 2013
Volume 3 – A Journey of Healing, 2018

Meditation Poetry series:
Volume 1 - By the Sea and on the Prairies, 2013
Volume 2 - At Home and in Nature. 2014
Volume 3 - She, He, We, 2015

René Beauchemin novel series:
Volume 1 – A Small Company of Pilgrims, 2014, 2018
Volume 2 – It's Complicated, 2017, 2018

Other books (Social History):
Sagitawak: Bicentennial History of Ile a la Crosse, 1977
Crazy Emigrant: The story of Nicholas Berdowitz, 1979

A Broken Boy
On a Broken Road

Journey of Healing: Volume 1

Robert G. Longpré

Retired Eagle Books

Second Edition – Canadian Edition

May, 2018

Dedication

This story is my gift to my seven living brothers and sisters who shared this story with me in their own manner, through their own unique experiences. Somehow with the exception of one brother who took his live, we have survived in our separate silences. There are no victims in this story, just a cast of unique individuals. There is no blame to be laid on anyone's doorstep. In spite of generations of family dysfunction, we remain family, unconditionally. This story is also a gift to my wife, children and grandchildren with hopes that the generational heritage of abuse has stopped.

Robert G. Longpré

"whatever reality may be, it will to some extent be shaped by the lens through which we see it". – James Hollis, Jungian Analyst, The Middle Passage, 1993.

Copyright © 2014 by Robert G. Longpré

Copyright © 2018 by Robert G. Longpré

(2nd Edition- Canadian Edition)

All rights reserved. This book or any portion thereof may not be reproduced or used in any manner whatsoever without the express written permission of the publisher except for the use of brief quotations in a book review or scholarly journal.

Retired Eagle Books

Box 423 Elrose,

Saskatchewan, Canada S0L 0Z0

ISBN-13: 978-1989019061

Introduction

So, why am I writing this book? What is the point of digging up the past, especially when a number of the characters involved in the story are no longer alive to speak for themselves? The answer began as a rather simple task as part of one of my counselling sessions. I had looked for mental help after falling into a deep depression in my late thirties. That original activity of "remembering" my past basically confirmed what I knew at that time, which was that I really did not remember very much at all.

When I met my wife, I didn't have much to tell her about my past other than I had come from a large French-Canadian family and that we were poor. I was able to tell her that I had been to too many schools as I grew up, too many schools in too many provinces. The rest of my past I kept to myself. Eventually, I did admit that I had had a hard time with my father as I was growing up, though there weren't many specifics given about these hard times. I had a good reason for not saying more – I just didn't remember the specifics; or, I didn't want to remember.

The assumption I made then and continued to believe for the first fifteen years of our marriage, was that there was nothing very remarkable about my past to remember. Throughout those first fifteen years of our married life, I had adopted my wife's family as my own family. It wasn't that I had disowned my family of birth, it was just that I found little reason to connect with them other than with visits every couple of years to see my mother and whatever brothers and sisters were still at home during those visits. Perhaps that distance from my family of birth had as much to do about geographical distance as it did with immersion into the life of my wife's family.

Whenever we did make an effort to connect with my family, we would see my father as well even though he was not married to my mother anymore.

These visits back "home" were short, and I kept a safe distance from the past, while focusing on polite small talk followed by quick exits. I knew that there had to be something behind this distancing from my father and family; however, I just didn't know what it was. And to tell the truth, I didn't really want to know as my life was just fine as it was. My real home was several provinces away where I raised my small family and did my best to be a good husband, father, teacher and reliable person in the community.

Unaware of inner workings, I began to unravel a bit at the seams, at the edges of my personality. Sleep became an issue and I was becoming more and more upset with the images that began to appear in both my dreams and in occasional flashbacks. These images left me feeling angry, an emotion that scared me. I turned that anger onto myself, beating myself up mentally and eventually physically. Ten years of trying to contain these images and memories though mental health counselling didn't work and I was left confused and almost helpless. Of course that just led to more therapy, this time with a Jungian analyst during the late nineteen-nineties. Again I found myself writing my story as part of the therapy, the story as I then knew it, a story that had grown since my first attempt at the story. There were still gaps that I thought of as black holes of memory, but they were dismissed. Cured, or so I thought, I headed back to teaching and to school administration, as well as continuing on with my small private practice as a mental health counsellor.

Unsurprisingly, the images and memories continued to emerge, always when least expected. Another dozen years later I again found myself back in counselling following the death of my mother. That was three years ago. Now, it is time for me to bring the story out for my children so that they can better understand what makes their father tick, as well as for my brothers and sisters who shared so much of my story.

Robert G. Longpré

Preface

As I began to write this book, I was in Mexico. Like a lot of other Canadians who flock to warmer climates in order to escape the winter at home in Canada, we left the Canadian prairie winter behind. Like most Canadian snowbirds, I had thought that this escape from winter would be mostly about sun, sand and sea, with the occasional *Marguerita* or *Cerveza con limon* thrown in from time to time to spice up the otherwise languid hours, when the afternoon sunshine tends to banish the snowbirds into their apartments, condos and casas. I truly had no intention of writing this book at this time. And, truth be told, I don't think I ever wanted to sit down and write it. I still find myself resisting this task. So, like any good therapist I decided to poke into this refusal, this resistance. What follows is the result of all the poking and prodding of the shadows and ghosts and scary things that go bump in the night.

This work of remembering is put into the form of a story. I have decided to change the names of the main people in the story because that is what one does when trying to tell the truth as I came to understand it, my truth without putting others into a tough situation. I have used a bit of creative license at times so that the result feels more like a story. Those instances don't suggest truths, but simply allow the story to flow a bit better. The last thing I want to do is to cause harm to anyone in the telling of this story, but to disguise and cover-up my experiences of growing up would cause more harm than any omissions, denials and sugar-coated fabrications. Like any story, even those such as this one which is a memoir of the early years of my life, absolute truth is impossible to pin down. There always will be a few facts that some would argue about and disagree with; but even those debatable points are based on something that resulted in being captured in my memories.

These memories have emerged slowly, and usually with quite a bit of surprise, and at times with shock that served to propel me into a depression. Over the years, I have approached this story a number of times and finding out that each time I come back to the story, a few more layers are exposed. I imagine that even more will be re-discovered in the years to come. With that said, I want to begin this story with a few basic facts and then let the story tell itself.

I am the first child in a family that grew to have nine children, six male children and three female children. All the records and a head count at various times would quickly and easily establish this as a truth, a non-debateable fact. It seems simple and straight forward. But, it isn't the whole truth in spite of what was assumed as the truth. Digging below the surface of this truth one finds that not all these siblings shared the same biological parents. All nine emerged into life from the same mother of this family, but that is about as close to truth as one can get.

The rest has to be taken on faith, assumption and hope; or, if one is deeply questioning the fact of "who is my father?" a DNA test can provide some sort of answer. All nine of us children grew up knowing each other as brothers and sisters and perhaps that is good enough even though biological truths and psychological truths would likely tell a different story. But, enough said for now about truths. I am the first child to be conceived, and with that conception, the story of our nuclear family began.

I will be telling this story from two levels: in the first level I tell the story as it is happening to me at that time with the feelings and understandings I lived with as the events unfolded. On the second level, I look back from the position of the present time where I bring my knowledge as a mental-health therapist and as an educator into an attempt to make sense of how the past events have shaped my present.

This story is about the breaking of a human soul and the long journey of healing, a journey that doesn't necessarily have a "happily ever after" ending.

One final word before I begin, this story is a dark story. If you are looking for a feel good type of story, then it would be better if you set this book aside.

Robert G. Longpré

Part One

The Sins Of Their Fathers And Mothers

"The LORD is slow to anger, abounding in love and forgiving sin and rebellion.
Yet he does not leave the guilty unpunished;
he punishes the children for the sin of the parents
to the third and fourth generation."
[The Bible, Numbers 14:18, New International Version]

Chapter One

Today I am a man of sixty-five. I was a teenager when I had the opportunity to be with my maternal grandfather as he talked with me about his childhood and youth. As he spoke about those things which spoke of the abuse visited upon him by his strict, Protestant father, and about the harshness of his grandfather, a harshness that was all about control and bitterness. He told me about how even the choice of his wife was one that was under the control of his father, who was still under the firm stewardship of his grandfather. As I listened to my grandfather, I heard his sadness and pain as he spoke of a loveless marriage that was filled with work and duty. I heard the voice of my grandfather as a victim, as an inheritor of his father's sins, and the sins of his grandfather before him.

I began this first part with a quote from the Bible which has children punished for three and four generations for the sins of their parents and grandparents because it is necessary for any story to have a context. This Christian truth is a way of understanding a world view that accepts suffering as deserved, regardless if the source of suffering was through one's own acts or through the acts of others down through generations of family. That family history was accepted as normal and even righteous by my grandfather who has a large role to play in this story as seems only sensible when one considers that as the father of my mother, his influence through words and deeds would then be transferred onto the grandchildren that would eventually come into existence when my mother became an adult and a mother.

Of course, there is another thread that needs to be followed, another generational thread that would leave its imprint on the psyche of my father. I knew my paternal grandfather much better simply because there was so much more contact between him and myself over the years.

By contrast, he was easier to be around, a man who was not overtly bitter with his lot in life as I experienced when being around him. He didn't have an easy life. Where my maternal grandfather had a good home, security, and pride in a family name that was associated with privilege; my paternal grandfather was poor. Home was a constantly changing address. Security was a momentary and fleeting thing depending on the vagaries of chance and perhaps even of focus and energy. And as for pride in the family name, even that wasn't present. Yet, for all of this absence, he simply adapted and shifted with the winds. Obviously, this had an impact upon the character of my father, for it is through the examples we experience while growing up that each of us cobbles together our own way of being in the world as adults, and eventually as parents.

Before going on with the story which really has yet to begin, I want to stress the importance of these roots. I have not said anything about the wives and the mothers and grandmothers but I need to acknowledge that their presence and roles were just as pivotal in the eventual fashioning of two people, my parents. Both my mother and my father were children and grandchildren, and both were victims of the sins of their parents and grandparents and great-grandparents.

Now, to begin.

~

I want to start telling my story with how I came to be born. I remember hearing the story of my parents meeting each other quite a number of times over the years. It was at the end of the summer of 1948 when my mother, Betsy Glen Schiller, a pretty girl, a beautiful dark-haired girl, who was fifteen years old, was walking down a street where a building was being constructed. When she noticed a virile young male not much older than her, but obviously very much a man, a very strong young man.

While climbing a ladder with a heavy stone lintel on his shoulder, this dark young lad of seventeen called out a compliment. Laurent Guillaume Laflamme, my father, was working with his father, Gilles, as his helper that summer in Ottawa.

It was love at first sight for my mother, as she told it. According to her, it was one of those Romeo and Juliette kind of stories. For my father, it was more like lust at first sight, a normal male response for a seventeen year old when a pretty girl flirts with him. My mother made a point of passing by the work site at least once a day hoping to catch the eye of the dark young man who had won her heart. Eventually, the "Hello's" opened up enough courage in both of them to say more than passing greetings. Laurent could hardly believe his luck in catching the eye of a girl like Betsy. It was obvious that she came from a well-to-do family, an English family. She was English and she was of a different social class. For my mother, Laurent's powerful arms and muscled torso gave the promise of him being someone who could take care of her, protect her.

~

"To protect her." It has only been in the very recent past that I have learned more about my mother's story. Betsy was the second of seven children born to Robert Schiller and his wife Heather. There were four boys and three girls in the family, well actually just two girls at the time when my father and mother met. Hidden in the Schiller family's skeleton closets was the fact that my maternal grandfather was a sexual predator. Wrapped up in his own pain and bitterness at finding himself in a loveless marriage, Robert had sexual relations, first with his eldest daughter Betsy and then with the passage of time, his two other daughters. Heather, his wife, did her wifely duties and suffered his sexual demands retreating into her head and grim silence.

The Schiller home was haunted by dark silences and secrets that no one dared to expose. The whispers hid behind doors and only slowly emerged. As I was growing up, there were times when our family would get to go to the Schiller home. Though there were still three children in the house, it was always a strangely quiet place. I had two uncles close to my own age and an aunt who was younger than I was, yet the house never showed signs of disorder, of running and laughing that one would normally consider would be the case with children in the house. If anything, I saw the house as something that was picture-perfect including an English garden which was my grandfather's proud accomplishment. Though my brothers and sisters were a rowdy bunch, we learned to sit uncomfortably still and quiet when entering the Schiller house without having to be told to do so. Something in the very air of the house dampened the spirit and weighed heavily.

~

That such a young woman actually saw him and smiled at him was enough to embolden Laurent to reach high, to perhaps taste the forbidden fruit denied by both race and class. Reason had nothing to do with the magic that swirled in the air. Laurent had noticed her staring her staring at him and flexed his young muscles to accentuate them. It didn't miss Laurent's attention that she was beautiful and petite as well as being a flirt with him.

Loving the attention and the flattery, Betsy continued to visit the work site over the next few weeks. And, like all "boy meets girl" love stories, she walked around in a daze at home. School resumed and Betsy couldn't help but steal every opportunity she could to pass by the site and spend some time with Laurent. Together they would sneak into various dark corners of the building site and explore their bodies and then talk about their dreams.

And, like all young, love-struck girls, she talked to her sister about Laurent. Betsy even told her mother about the handsome young man that had entered her life like some knight in shining armour.

It wasn't long before Betsy's father found out about the Catholic French-Canadian boy and how Betsy had been skipping classes to be with him. Robert Schiller was adamant that these meetings would have to come to an end; demanded that she never see the papist boy again. Betsy feared her father and his temper, an anger that he took out while he molested her. But, she was in love and hopeful that Laurent would save her from her father, so she found ways to continue to meet with Laurent.

In late fall Betsy became pregnant though she didn't realise it at the time, nor even think about the possibility. Her morning sicknesses had made her mother, Heather, suspicious enough to ask Betsy about her menstrual cycles, "were they still regular?" When Betsy said she hadn't had her period, Heather's suspicions were confirmed. Always the good, dutiful wife, she had to tell Robert about Betsy being pregnant.

"What? Betsy is pregnant? Heather, how could you let that happen?"

"I didn't let it happen."

"Who is he?"

"I don't know, probably that boy she was seeing earlier, that French boy."

"Betsy! Get down here immediately!"

As Betsy stood meekly before her father he issued his decrees.

"You are no longer my daughter, no longer a Schiller. Before the day is done I want you out of this house. You are a whore, a shameless woman fornicating with papist pigs. Now go, get out of my sight. You sicken me!"

My mother, pregnant with me, begged her Dad to relent, tried promising him anything he wanted, anything, if only he would let her remain a part of the family. Betsy couldn't imagine not having her mother and her sister in her life anymore.

Heather was shocked by Robert's decision. Helping Betsy gather a few things, her mother whispered that she would work on her father and make sure that Betsy would be able to stay in the family, that she would be allowed to enter the house. Heather promised Betsy that she would always be her mother and that Robert would change his mind, especially when he saw the baby. If she was lucky, the baby would be a boy. Her father would be pleased if Betsy would name the boy Robert. She would pray tonight and every night to make sure that everything would be okay in the end. Both mother and daughter spend their last hour together in tears, one crying for a lost daughter and the other crying in fear of having lost everything.

It was January, 1949 and Betsy had been declared out of the Schiller family and out of Robert Schiller's will and sent from the house. No one goes unpunished in shaming the Schiller name.

~

Of course, I didn't know this when I was a child. It is not something that gets spoken about. It took me a quite a few years of life before I realised that I was conceived before my parents were married, and few more years before I learned that my English grandfather had disinherited my mother, a fact that didn't change when I was born and given his name.

The reason given for being disinherited was the fact that she had married a Catholic, and even worse, a French-Canadian Catholic. Yet, being given the name Robert did allow my mother access back into some sort of relationship with her family.

Being expelled from the Schiller family because of my conception would have been enough of a trauma to affect my mother's ability to deal with her first pregnancy, made even more traumatic in having to deal with the anxiety of not being married, and finding herself in a strange, chaotic world that was to become her replacement home. To add to the context of my mother's situation in life at the time of my conception, one needs to remember the fact that she had been sexually abused by her father in a family situation of paternalistic oppression, and with a mother who somehow was blind to what was happening and didn't protect her as a child from her father's sexual demands. There is no question that her own short history would have added an even greater psychological distress to an already extremely stressful situation. Rather than lay blame and stoke the feeling of anger and disgust, I have to tell myself and to remind you the reader that the sins against children go back generation after generation. And through the generations, everyone becomes both a victim and an abuser. It then becomes the duty of those wounded children to grow up and become conscious, aware of their roots and their own damaging life scripts in order to bring an end to the cycle of wounding.

~

Having almost no choice in the matter, as she was pregnant and had been thrown her out of the family and her home; Betsy turned to Laurent and his family for rescue. Though he was working with his father, Laurent was still dependent upon his own family and needed their help in dealing with the crisis.

He wasn't yet an independent man with a career nor de he have the capacity for providing a safe and stable environment for a wife and child-to-be. Laurent needed his own mother and father to take on that responsibility for him.

His parents welcomed Betsy into their home that was already filled with their nine children ranging from their eldest child, a young man of nineteen, Jean, to a three year old boy, Roland. Betsy was almost the same age as their eldest daughter, Laure. They made space for Betsy and took charge of planning a wedding so that the child-to-be would be born in wedlock. In the month of February, 1949, Laurent and Betsy became husband and wife.

Betsy was a young woman in love, in love with the idea of being in love. This man she had married, though a stranger in almost every way conceivable, was her husband. She really didn't want to be a mother yet, as she was barely out of childhood herself. She knew that she was pregnant and what that meant. But somehow, it didn't seem real. Yet, being pregnant opened the door to a life she was sure would be filled with love. With Laurent, in his bed, she didn't have to worry anymore about her father coming to her bed in the darkness. Maybe this baby would be her passport to a life that would be lived happily ever after.

~

But what about Laurent, the man who married my mother? What did he bring into the psychological stew into which I would emerge and begin to develop as a baby? What sins did he bring into this mix, what of the sins of his father and mother, and the sins of the generations before? What wounds had he suffered as a child, wounds that would in turn be unconsciously passed on to his children? Each of us enter life wounded and suffer wounding from our parents who have no intention of wounding their children.

Each of us brings these wounds into our relationships where they act beneath the level of our awareness, as toxins which become part of the fabric of our relationships. My mother and father were no different from anyone else. Their conscious acts were based on the unconscious scripts that their separate childhoods had imprinted upon them.

~

Laurent was much different than his older brother, Jean who was a quiet young man, quiet like his father. Laurent was like his mother, a commanding presence who was sure of himself. He had done extremely well at school though he hated the nuns and priests who didn't seem to recognize that he was smarter than they were. He never forgave them for the beatings he received at school. Dad told me that he had often been physically punished for writing left-handed. The nuns would then force him to write with his right hand.

Laurent saw himself as a leader, as someone who would be famous and rich as soon as the world came to realise just who he was, how smart he was. There was a sense that he was owed and entitled to fame and fortune. Laurent hated being poor. The poverty that had been entrenched in his parent's house following his father's accident, an accident that had taken the life of a young female child while he was under the influence of alcohol, had kindled a fierce determination in my father to escape that poverty.

Living in the Laflamme home on 52 Marquette Avenue with many other Laflamme families nearby, and being dependent upon Gilles for work, left Laurent feeling the need to escape and find that fortune that was being denied. Seeing his father wasting what Laurent thought of as his birthright was too much to handle. There had even been a street named using the family name in 1947, just two blocks from the Laflamme family home.

In the Laflamme home, it was the females who dominated. Gilles' wife, Monique was the dominant person. Laurent had learned early that in order to unconsciously save himself from engulfment, from the dominant too-muchness of his mother, he had to find a way to move from under her shadow or he would end up like his father and his older brother, passive victims. Laurent vowed that he wouldn't touch alcohol, for it was his dad's alcoholism that had been responsible for the family losses. He hated the tensions at home between his mother and father. He wasn't aware of the history behind the tension though he guessed it was the alcohol. It helped that Laurent was an extravert and had a certain charisma that allowed him to become the masculine leader that had been vacated by his father. As he became a man, he had cultivated his appeal to what he understood as the real holders of power – women.

Yet, here he was, seventeen years old, married to a girl who had just turned sixteen; and now once again, he was dependent upon his mother and father. With the addition of Betsy into the house, there were now seven women to three men. One couldn't count the two youngest who were boys as they were too young. Laurent revelled in the new power as a father-to-be and the continuing approval of his mother and sisters, yet he knew that if he was going to truly become the master of his own fate and achieve the fame and fortune that was out there waiting for him, he needed to escape. Laurent had a plan, a dream.

~

As I wrote this part, I hadn't been aware of other things going on in the Laflamme home at that time. I knew that my grandfather enjoyed drinking and smoking cigars, but I wasn't aware that his drinking had been a problem. I only learned about this after the second re-write as I prepared this story for publication. I learned from two of my father's female siblings that my grandfather repeatedly sexually molested his daughters.

I learned of how the older girls worked hard to protect the youngest of my father's sisters. My grandfather's drinking had been responsible for an accident that claimed the life of a small girl, an accident that resulted in him losing his trucking and construction business. With further research I learned that the family home had turned into a public park in Vanier City. All of this information added to the complexity of trying to know what made my father respond the way he did in the role of "father."

~

Like all young men of his time, heard that real fame and fortune now lay in the west. "Go west young man, go west," were words that were heard in newspapers, on the radio, and in the movies. It was a dream that burned inside of him. But now, it seemed that his dream was slipping away. In this dead time of winter with no construction work to fill his hours, and with Betsy being so dependent upon him, almost suffocating him with her need, an anger was triggered in my father.

Betsy saw this anger and it triggered old fears associated with her father's anger. Knowing that if she met Laurent's sexual needs, she would be safer. Sex became the honey that would soothe Laurent's frustration and impatience. But, sex also became the poison that felt so much like a cage preventing Laurent from becoming the man he believed was waiting for him if he would only dare to reach for that future.

~

Neither my mother nor father were ready for parenthood in spite of the fact that I was making the nine-month long journey into life. My mother was too wounded and too consumed with her need for psychological survival to be able to shift out of her own needs to comprehend what she needed to do in order to be a mother. My father was as wounded by the sins of his own father, his grandfather and his ancestors down through the generations that led to his birth.

He was also as narcissistic as my mother, a self-focus that was based on illusory images of grandeur. Both of my parents were too young, too immature, too wounded, and too wrapped up in themselves. No matter which way one looks at the situation, the scene wasn't too promising for a new born who was getting ready to enter into life.

Before going on with the story, I want to add a few words from Carl Gustav Jung here, words which speak directly to the story that will emerge:

"THE PSYCHOLOGICAL RULE SAYS THAT WHEN AN INNER SITUATION IS NOT MADE CONSCIOUS, IT HAPPENS OUTSIDE, AS FATE."

This is what the world looked like for everyone going through this story, all were victims of fate; and as victims of fate, they would unconsciously wound those they loved. Though it is a dark story, no one in the story is a heartless or evil person. Every individual had dreams and hopes for a better life as they became adults. However, life didn't give them the time and the space or the knowledge to make conscious, the dark shadows that drove them as fate. They saw themselves as victims, and as such, they missed taking ownership of their own life.

Chapter Two

It's time to begin the story as told by my voice of as an adult long removed from the action of the story itself. I will switch voices when what needs to be told, can be told by the younger person that I used to be, a person not knowing the world through a philosophical or psychological lens. I was born in the morning on July 22nd, 1949 at the Ottawa Civic Hospital. I was christened Robert Gilles Laurent Joseph Laflamme. I carried the names of both of my grandfathers and my father as well as the obligatory Joseph that was awarded to all baby boys at their baptism. The honour of the first name being that of my English grandfather had been enough to grudgingly re-open the door to the Schiller house for my mother so that she regained some of the relationship with her mother and siblings. My grandfather was still angry and he remained aloof having as little to do as possible with his daughter, my mother. His attentions had shifted to his third child, another girl less than two years younger than my mother.

Following his marriage to my mother, my father returned to full-time work with his father in March, just before his eighteenth birthday. Work had slowed down when winter set in. With the wedding now over, he hated being stuck, being dependent upon his father. It was hard to feel like a man when he needed his father to give him money. Being back at work, full-time, had taken some of the frustration and anger out of his system, but he still was left with the feeling that he needed his own job and his own home. After all, he was a married man with a son.

At least working full-time, he was able to celebrate my birth, his son. He made a vow to himself to finally do what needed to be done to achieve his dreams of independence, wealth and fame.

Without realising exactly what this would mean, my mother was encouraged by this determination to finally escape the threadbare existence of poverty and living in the slums of the city. My father's plan was to first find himself a job as a ranch-hand in Alberta, where he could be a cowboy and with luck and time, become a rancher in his own right, a rancher with a huge home with everything that would speak of success and power. But first, he had to find a way to get started.

While my father struggled with being dependent upon his father for money and work, and his mother for meals and the foundation of a home environment, my mother slowly began to adapt to the role of being a parent under the guidance of my French grandmother, Monique, who I was to come to know and address as *Mémère*. With the initial rush of being a proud parent dissipating, the world returned to normal rhythms for my parents. I thrived as my mother breast-fed me and my aunts took over my care and attention in between feedings. Having to deal with the physical and psychological stresses of being a parent, my mother began to panic at what she sensed as a growing distance between my father and her. With my aunts and paternal grandmother focused on me, my mother spent her time trying to entice my father back into her arms. Her girlish figure soon returned and she used it to recapture his attention. Sex and constant flattery were used successfully to pull him back into the spell of love. At least, that is how she understood it while he enjoyed the fruits of the marital bed. In between those spaces my mother suffered post-partum depression. It took all of her energy to focus on keeping Laurent engaged with her with little energy left for her baby.

The none-too-subtle project of my mother had served to have my father realise that he didn't have to do any of the work at maintaining their relationship. He had sex on demand, he had the elevated role of being a real man, being a father.

In the family circle he became even more the real man of the house. He didn't have to do any of the work of being father with so many in his family making sure that I was a happy little baby.

In this environment of having both parents abandoning the work of parenting to others, these two teenagers lost the opportunity to develop maturity. The seeds of future abandonments of children, both emotional and relational were set in place. Both were learning by default that they didn't have to be responsible for any child that should appear on the scene leaving them to focus on themselves.

Laurent had heard of a job as a ranch-hand in Alberta, not far from the city of Calgary in the late fall of 1949. The job wanted a man to work with cattle. The pay was better than what Laurent earned as a labourer in Ottawa, especially when there was very little construction work through the winter. Laurent shared this job opportunity with my mother, after he had already responded to the job advertisement and had been offered the job. Laurent had accepted the offer before bringing the news of the job to Betsy and the family. Again, the scene below uses some creativity with the hope that it mirrors, somewhat, what was the real story. Regardless of how the scenes played out, my father did go west, did become a cowhand and did ride in rodeos.

~

As he talked to Betsy, dad spoke of how he was going out there first to set up what would be their home on that ranch. He told her that she would get to come to him as soon as he had it arranged with the owner of the ranch. He promised her that they would only be apart for only a few weeks, a month at the maximum. Then they could have their own home in which to raise their boy, a home in the clean air of the countryside.

And so he left after La Fête des Rois, January 6th, 1950. The weeks passed with no word from Laurent.

February passed, and with it their first anniversary, with still no word from him. As February turned into March with still no letter from Laurent, Betsy had sunk into a deep depression. She was abandoned by the man she had trusted, to whom she had willingly given her body and her love. No one in the house seemed able to pick up her spirits, not even her baby. It wasn't as if I was suffering for attention, not like her. I had all the Laflamme women at my beck and call with even my little uncles just five and seven years old taking some time to play with me.

One person was aware of mom's depression, Jean, Laurent's older brother who had found himself even more in the shadow even though his brother was absent. Jean reached out and listened to worries and fears of his sister-in-law. He was careful not to speak badly of his younger brother in spite of the fact that they barely tolerated each other as brothers. Laurent was stronger and simply dismissed his pathetic smaller but older brother. Laurent had all the luck with girls and had often belittled his shyer older brother calling him a fag and a homo, a guy with no balls. But now, with Laurent gone, it was him, Jean who listened and comforted Betsy.

Betsy reached back holding on to the young man who came to her in her need. There was enough of Laurent in Jean to allow her to imagine that she was again with her husband. And at night, when the household slept, they came together and filled in the holes in their hearts and souls with sex. There was no thinking, no plan. Afterwards, they both would retreat and pretend that nothing had happened. Yet it wasn't long before they would find themselves again in each other's arms, in her bed.

With the arrival of a letter at the beginning of April, from Laurent talking about the work Betsy was flooded with guilt. Laurent hadn't forgotten her or abandoned her at all. The letter talked of how the rancher was hoping to get a place for dad so that he could bring his mom and me out to live with him.

As dad wrote, this would likely happen once the cattle were turned loose onto the prairie hills where they would pasture for the summer. A big sigh of relief from the constant anxiety of wondering if he was okay, and if the dream was actually beginning to come true was felt by everyone in the family, not just mom. In the letter was a cheque with a promise that more would be coming, as well as a rail ticket for Betsy.

Laurent went on to describe cowboy life and how he was learning how to break horses and wrangle cattle. He wrote of how he was learning the ropes so that he could take part in rodeos with the prospect of earning big money quickly at these rodeos. The money and the news was enough to rekindle high expectations in the whole family. There was a belief in the family that when Laurent struck it rich, they would all share in those riches. My young uncles would ride sticks all around the house pretending they were cowboys just like Laurent, their older, famous brother.

~

It was as if my father had disappeared. No one really knew where he went. My father would return with his arm in a sling and cast following a rodeo mishap; however, in his absence, another story was taking place. My mother had become pregnant.

The discovery of Betsy's pregnancy had been first greeted with joy. But, that joy soon turned sour when they realised that my father couldn't have been the one to make my mother pregnant. Dad had been gone for two months before my mother conceived her second child. It didn't take Mémère long to root out the truth when she found out when the last menstrual cycle had happened. Betsy confessed that she had been unfaithful, but unwillingly. However, she didn't say who the father was nor how the betrayal had happened.

With not many people having contact with my mother, it left only three possibilities – my paternal grandfather Robert, my maternal grandfather Gilles and my father's older brother, Jean. Worst of all, it was all too likely that whoever had done this, had raped my mother. Both of my grandfathers had histories of sexually assaulting their daughters. In the end, it doesn't matter who was the father.

Mémère, my grandmother, was furious. Who was the father of the child growing within my mother? Since Betsy had rarely left the house other than to go to see her mother, there had to be someone to take the blame. Somehow this had to be kept quiet if possible. Laurent would be furious if he found out, perhaps so mad that he would abandon the Laflamme family. Who was blamed?

My brother grew up believing that it was his uncle, mistakenly thinking it was one of our younger uncles as we never knew about an older uncle. Our father had for too many years been cruel to my brother, telling him that he wasn't his son. As I grew up, I knew that my father was the second in the family. I never knew or met my father's brother, Jean until I was nineteen years old. It was as though there had never been an older brother until that Boxing Day in 1968 when he came to our house.

Laurent returned to Ottawa in July with his arm in a sling. He had broken his arm trying to ride a bull in a rodeo. Unable to do his job as a ranch hand, he lost his job. Regardless of the fact that he was out of work, he had returned home as if he was a hero. He carried his broken arm as if it was a trophy. He had tales to tell everyone about the biggest meanest bull ever to be part of the Calgary Stampede. He told them of how no one had managed to ride that monster, and of all those who tried, it was him who lasted the longest on the bull. He told them that he had returned to spend time with Betsy and me before returning to work on the ranch in the fall.

When he returned, he promised that he was taking us with him. All he had to do was wait for his arm to heal and be strong enough for the hard work of being a cowboy.

Laurent never noticed his brother, Jean's absence and no one mentioned it. Laurent did notice however that Betsy was pregnant, but thought nothing of it as he assumed that he had made her pregnant before he left for Alberta. All that mattered was that he was a hero to all in the family and that he was again at the centre of attention.

~

My mother was again well into her second pregnancy and, as with the first, her health was an issue. Pregnancy didn't agree with her physical or mental well-being. Yet, the appearance of Dad back into the house did animate her and she did her best to please my father in every way that she could, given the tight quarters and the general lack of privacy. My mother was learning that all she had to do was to praise and stroke Dad's ego if she was to keep his attention, and keep his fidelity. Sex was the key and sex was the answer. 'Give him what he wants and when he wants it and then give more,' was her strategy. The more she gave him, the more he gave in return, even if it was only physical. And in the process, she discovered that she needed the sex as much as he did. It was the act sex that made her feel loved, needed, worshipped.

I passed my first birthday with my all of the Laflamme family together with the exception of Jean. My father was almost back to full strength with his arm, and he had returned to helping his father on the latest construction site. Talk of returning to work on the ranch somehow had lost its intensity as the summer months passed. In August, Dad finally found out that Mom was due to deliver in December. He knew that pregnancies generally lasted nine months. Something didn't fit in the picture. He had noticed that Mom wasn't as big as she was the last time when nearing time for delivery.

By his calculations, assuming Betsy got pregnant no later than the first week of January before he left, she would be having the baby in September, or at the latest, in early October. December wasn't possible.

"Bets, when did you say the baby was due?"

"The doctor said, sometime in early December."

"That can't be right. Perhaps you need to see a different doctor."

"It's right, Laurent, the doctor is right."

"If it's true then I'm not the father! What the fuck is going on? Who is the father, Bets?"

~

My mother had been expecting that this scene was going to happen and that it would be bad. For my father, the story he was told of non-consensual sex – rape –hardly registered. What he heard was that my mother had had sex and had conceived a child with another man. Rightly or wrongly, for the truth still has a way of hiding, Jean had been cast as the villain. My father refused to touch my mother once he learned of her betrayal. At least, that is what he felt and believed. Both Betsy and Jean had betrayed him.

As my father learned of his wife becoming pregnant with another man's child, other things were happening in the world outside of the family. The news of the Canadian army recruiting soldiers because of the likelihood of war in Korea began to fill the newspapers and radio newscasts. At the end of August, 1950, my father enlisted. He needed to escape and get away from both his wife and the Laflamme family.

It was the uniform that changed things in the Laflamme family. Seeing Laurent in a soldier's uniform shifted the mood. Once again, Laurent was seen as a hero. Basic training was completed and then he took some further training as a bombardier to be held at Camp Borden.

My father had left his family. I was one year old and I wouldn't see him for a year, a long time in the early formative years of a child. Having already be separated for almost six months of my first year of life, the bonding of father and son was jeopardized. And that, would have its psychological cost for both in the years that would follow for both of us.

In November, 1950, my father left Canada en route to Japan and then to South Korea for a final round of training before his unit would engage in action. On December 6th, 1950, my brother Kevin was born. The name Kevin was in honour of Laurent's sister's husband, Laure who was my mother's best friend in the family. Kevin and Laure became Kevin's godparents. My father was wounded in Korea and spent time in Japan at a hospital during his recovery before being returned home to Canada in August, 1951. The event of his reunion with his wife and two children was captured in a photo that was published in the Ottawa Citizen newspaper. Though he was back in Canada, he remained a member of the Armed Forces until 1953 when he was honourably discharged.

~

Chapter Three

In July, 1954, my first sister, Béatrice Monique, was born. My first memories come about a few days before my sister's birth, just weeks before my fifth birthday.

~

My parents had driven from the city to visit my Uncle Kevin and Aunt Laure, who had children of their own who were younger than I was. My aunt and uncle lived in the countryside. At the end of the visit, while I was being distracted by "Tante Laure," my parents drove off. I was almost five years old, but not old enough to realise that I was staying with my aunt and uncle while my mother was going to the hospital to have a baby. I stood in front of the house crying in panic at being abandoned as the car drove off.

My parents had left and I panicked. Why? What had I done to make them want to leave me?

~

I did what all little children did when confronted with the trauma of being abandoned – blamed it on not being good enough, being bad, being responsible for their action of driving away and leaving me behind. I wasn't being abandoned; but as a little boy at the time, I didn't know that. Jungian psychologist, James Hollis explains that a child's thought process is characterized by magical thinking in which the child believes he or she causes adults to behave in various ways, both positive and negative, to the child. What I felt and believed as a child of four was that I was responsible for my parents abandoning me.

I can still feel what the little Robert was experiencing – parents driving away. It didn't matter that it was only for two weeks, as two weeks didn't have real meaning in a child's world. It didn't matter that I was left in the care of people I knew.

Like all wounds suffered, psychological wounds, by a child, an inner belief system is carved out in response to that wounding. And out of that belief system, a child attempts to control his or her outer world to fix everyone around him or her so that the wounding doesn't happen again. In psychological terms, a complex has been set in place.

In his book "The Eden Project", James Hollis, goes on to note that when a child feels powerless, the child often learns to be pleasing, to be responsive to the needs of those who have power over her or him. One of the responses to the wounding of being abandoned in my case, was to attempt to make those around me to become dependent upon me. If others come to depend upon the abandoned child, the chances of being abandoned again should cease to exist – at least this is the magical thinking that fills the head of the child. Of course, a single event would soon pass leaving a very small wound in the soul of a child. However, the wounding takes on depth when it is experienced repeatedly. Abandonment is not just the experience of having others leave physically; more often, it is a psychological abandonment.

The first four years of my life had seen abandonment take a number of forms. With my mother's retreat into depression, leaving me to the care of my aunts and grandmother, there was a perhaps a more profound abandonment than if she had left the house never to return. One feels the care and attention being withdrawn as though one wasn't worth keeping when the mother is physically present but removed in all other ways. With my father's disappearances for extended periods of time, only returning to guiltlessly break down the walls of protective distance before leaving again while being blissfully unconcerned on how his leaving was wounding the bonds between a father and his son, I learned that I wasn't worth being his son. Both of my parents were unconscious of the effects of their total obsession with their own wounds to see that they were wounding their children, that they were wounding me.

~

I remember living in a small place near the Ottawa River, a place not much more than a cheap tenement in a district of the city called Tunney's Pasture when Béatrice was born. It was their first home separate from the Laflamme clan once my father was discharged from the army. There had been a girl child born a year earlier, June 2, 1953, who didn't survive more than a few hours, just long enough to be baptised and named, a girl that was christened Elizabeth in honour of the woman who would become Queen Elizabeth that same day.

In comparison to the Laflamme home that was bustling with life at my grandparents' place where my grandmother took charge of everything, where my Dad's siblings were constantly massaging his ego; this new home was too quiet and too demanding upon both of my parents. Mom was suddenly expected to do everything to make this mean shack a home while making sure that Dad continued to stay interested in her. With a third small child in the house, a baby that was seemingly always crying and a toddler trying to discover everything there was to find and touch, as well as being insecure, unsure that Laurent wouldn't once again take flight leaving her alone with the children with no one to help her, my mother struggled. And, as she struggled, a dark anger began to surface in my father.

It was an eruption of Dad's anger that evoked another traumatic memory, a scene which has this shack in which we are all crammed into the only bedroom as the backdrop. My baby sister's crib was against the wall near the bed and my brother and I were on a small mattress on the floor at the foot of our parents' bed. My sister Béatrice had woken in the night, crying. My mother wasn't able to get Béatrice to stop crying which then woke my father who had been having trouble sleeping since his return from Korea even though it was almost two years since he had returned.

Dad began to yell at my mother to get the baby to stop crying. His anger-filled voice woke Kevin and me from our sleep. As his temper rose in a fury, Kevin huddled close to me as if I would somehow protect him. Dad grabbed the baby, Béatrice, and shook her as he screamed at her. I could see and feel his rage as he shook her and I could hear my mother begging him to stop, to put the baby down saying, "Please, Laurent. She's just a baby. Please, Laurent." As Kevin clung to me, I told him "Sh!" as I didn't want to have Dad turn his anger upon us once he was finished with Béatrice.

~

Volatile anger that would erupt without any notice, an anger that was expressed verbally or physically, was always sitting on the sidelines. Post-Traumatic Stress Disorder [PTSD] didn't exist as a condition understood by medicine or by the public. People went to war and often returned home changed, even damaged psychologically. However, for most, like my father, it was something that lurked beneath, hidden from the world. Occasionally something would trigger an irrational response such as rage leaving everyone shocked, even frightened as the rage erupted and then wore itself out. I have seen this same rage in other veterans who were in the Korean War, and how that rage caused their families collateral damage.

It was safest for both my brother and I to be quiet, or to rush to give my father an ashtray, or some other thing that he wanted. Kevin wasn't as quick to catch being just three years old and he was always getting on my father's nerves. He called him my mother's little bastard and rejected him as his son. With his return from Korea, there was no way to continue the pretense of him being Kevin's true father. It wasn't just the war in Korea that had created an immense anger. His wife had cheated on him and had foisted her bastard child on him pretending that it was his son.

It was only through the pressure from my grandmother that he grudgingly agreed to protect the family's honour, to bury his shame and go on as if everything was as it should be. Our home was a dark place for a child to develop and grow with my father's rage always simmering just below the surface.

Of course, children take ownership of all the bad things that happen to them and to those around them. A child doesn't have the mind of an adult and so can't look at the evidence in order to judge properly any cause and effect and ownership of words, moods and actions that end up wounding the child. My father's deteriorating relationship with his family was taken in by myself and magically transformed into somehow being my fault. "If I was better, he wouldn't yell at my mother. If I was quieter he wouldn't yell at Kevin, Béatrice and me. If I somehow did the right things, he would smile more." Like any other child in the same circumstances, these things went on below the surface, creating patterns of beliefs about myself that would eventually serve as an unquestioning foundation for my later life.

Not long after I got sick.

~

Mom was cleaning up the flat we lived in at Tunney's Pasture. I was in the bedroom with Kevin while Béatrice was sleeping in the crib. While we in the bedroom, my Grandmother Schiller called my mother. No sooner had my mother answered the phone than my grandmother told my mother to quickly go into the bedroom and take me to the hospital. My mother's response was a laugh as she had seen us not long before and all seemed normal. My grandmother's insistence caused my mother some distress as she was very familiar with her mother's psychic abilities. Dropping the phone she rushed into the bedroom and found me on the bed, apparently turning blue. I was rushed to the hospital.

My mother phoned my grandmother from the hospital when I had been taken into emergency. She wanted to thank her mother for her timely call that allowed me to get to the hospital in time. My grandmother took the thanks in stride and then told my mother that I had a disease called nephritis. Since the doctor hadn't yet returned with any information about my condition, there was a bit of scepticism in her voice as she told her mother, "Sure, Mom. I'm sure the doctor will be glad to know that in case they can't figure it out."

When the doctor did come out of the examination room later to tell my mother what they had diagnosed and what they would be doing about it, my mother was again confronted with her mother's scary psychic ability. The doctor told my mother that I had acute nephritis. He said that there would be a chance that I might eventually need a new kidney, and that even with a new kidney, the chances of my long-term survival weren't all that good.

~

Early childhood trauma often shows up in some sort physiological disturbance as well as psychological disturbances. As a therapist I have long known that stress in the workplace and in the home often shows up in the form of ulcers, tension headaches, heart conditions, etc. Is it that much of a stretch to see a correlation between the trauma of my first four years of life and the onset of kidney disease? In modern medicine it is accepted that psychological trauma can lead to the lowering of physiological resistance resulting in a predisposition for the development of allergies to develop. So much of my work as a therapist has seen clients present themselves not only with behavioural and habitual dysfunctions, but also with various stress related conditions. The mind is a powerful thing, both friend and enemy at times. In spite of all our science and research, so much of what makes us tick and what causes us to fall apart are still mysteries.

With the diagnosis of nephritis, the impact upon both my parents was significant. There was no choice but to shift from their self-focused narcissism to take on the role of parents giving their children needed care and attention. My illness served as a wake-up call for them. They saw their first born at risk, and they did their best to not lose me. My mother began to learn how to cook without salt leaving it as a sprinkle-on condiment for everyone else's plate. My father toned down his anger and his demands enough to hold a job that allowed us to finally move into a better house on Sunnyside Avenue just a few blocks off of Banks Street.

Chapter Four

With a new home of our own on Sunnyside, we began to have individual families visit us, Aunt Laure and her young family, and more often, Aunt Jacqueline and her young family of two children, Gabrielle and Adèle. I remember this house which felt like home, quite well. My mother would often take me for my medical checkups to the Ottawa Civic Hospital, an adventure as we would travel to the hospital by street car often passing horse-drawn wagons delivering ice and milk along the way. In the fall of 1954 with my health stabilising, I began my schooling in kindergarten.

~

I was excited when it was time to go to kindergarten at Hopewell School. It didn't matter that the other kids had been in school for a while already. I was in a hurry to learn how to read and write. My father would always be reading the newspaper and my mother frequently had her head buried in some novel or magazine. Often what my father saw in the newspaper would lead to debates and discussion with adult visitors. The newspaper seemed to be an opening to a bigger world.

Yet, when it was time for my mother to leave that first morning at the school, I panicked. The fear of again being abandoned surfaced. It was an irrational fear, but it didn't matter. My five year old child's brain felt the trigger, the abandonment trigger being pulled. It took quite a while after her departure for me to settle down. Finally, when the teacher brought a book with pictures and words after failing to calm me with a toy or teddy bear or treat, I stopped crying. The book was magic. Holding the book and smiling at the teacher, I began to read aloud what I saw in the book. It was with a mixture of surprise and at the same time worry that the teacher responded to my reading.

Seeing that I already knew how to read, what was she going to be able to teach me, especially when learning to read was to begin in grade one, not kindergarten.

"Mrs. Laflamme," began the teacher when my mother arrived later to pick me up and take me home. "Robert already knows how to read. I don't know what we will be able to teach him at school."

"Just call him Benjy, that's what I call him. Yes, he knows how to read. When he gets upset at home we give him the newspaper or one of my magazines to distract him."

"There's nothing we can teach him in kindergarten. I'm afraid Robert will get bored and become a behaviour problem."

"It's Benjy, not Robert. As for becoming a behaviour problem, I think you will be in for a surprise. He is the peace-maker at home with his brother and sister and with his cousins when they visit. If anything, he tries too hard to be good all the time."

"Hmm? I wonder?" mumbled the teacher as she worked with what my mother had told her about me, "Perhaps he could skip kindergarten and just go to grade one next year. What do you think about that idea, Mrs. Laflamme?"

"I think he needs to be out of the house. He is too quiet and needs to learn how to interact with kids his own age. He needs to learn how to play. He watches too much from the sidelines except when he is being the big brother and fussing with his brother and sister. He is always helping as much as a five-year old can help. He needs to make some friends and learn how to play and laugh."

"Okay," replied the teacher. "We'll let him stay in our classroom for now. However, if he becomes a problem for us along the way, I'm going to ask you to take him out of the class and keep him at home."

~

I have heard my mother tell this story of my first day in kindergarten over and over again to various aunts and uncles and even strangers. The fact that I could read before I started kindergarten and that I was such a well-behaved little boy fed my mother's pride, as if she was responsible for my accomplishments. And in a way, both of my parents were the catalysts for my being so well-behaved and perhaps even precocious. Being well-behaved had a lot to do with magical thinking, that belief that as long as I was super good, my father wouldn't get angry or that my parents wouldn't abandon me. Fear. Magical thinking didn't disappear with the expansion of my world through attendance at school. If anything, the same strategies seemed to be reinforced at school where I heard that I would be sent away from the school if I misbehaved or displeased the teacher. Reading and having my parents take pride in that fact served to spur me on to try and please them more and more. Reading also opened up a door into another world, a safer and friendlier world.

~

Our home on Sunnyside was a two-storey building. My father had painted the inside of the house not long after we had moved in. I was particularly struck by the wall along which the stairs climbed to the upper level, a wall that was painted in two colours with the darker colour at the bottom angling up the stairwell so that it was always at the same height from the steps. Along the other side of the stairs was a railing with round, sculpted, wooden dowels behind which I would perch and watch my parents when I was supposed to be in bed sleeping. I didn't want to miss out on anything that they might have to say, especially if there was company in the house.

On Christmas Eve, 1954, I was sitting in my usual spot on the stairs when I should have been in bed waiting for Christmas morning.

Earlier Kevin had begged me to stay in bed so that Santa would come for we had been told that he wouldn't come if we didn't go to sleep and stay asleep until morning. Under no circumstance were we to go downstairs in the morning to check out the tree and the presents before we were given permission. In spite of that threat, I just had to sneak a peek when I heard a noise downstairs. Silently, I crept down a few more stairs and stayed close to the wall away from the railing, the first thing I noticed was the tree. When we had gone to bed, there wasn't a Christmas tree in the house. Now I couldn't believe my eyes. Somehow, magically, a tree had appeared and I could see presents under the tree. Santa must have brought the tree when he brought the presents.

I heard a laugh and dared come a bit closer to the railing. I held my breath in shock. Santa was still in the house and he was kissing my mother. I was terrified that my father would find out and beat up Santa. I was afraid that he would become so mad at my mother that he would begin hitting her and then he would leave us. As quietly as I could, I snuck up the stairs and hid under my covers next to Kevin hoping that Santa would hurry up and leave before my father found out.

In the morning, when Kevin woke up, he was excited as he had gone down a few steps and seen the Christmas tree and the presents. He was begging me to come with him downstairs and open the presents with him. I reminded him of the rule – no going downstairs until Dad said we could. So, we sat on the floor outside of our parents' bedroom and waited. We didn't have to wait long. Dad was in a good mood and soon we were racing down the stairs to the tree and the presents beneath it.

~

When I began to write this story, I had somehow thought it was going to be a record of all the trauma, a horror story.

But as the words began to form as the story unfolded, I realised that such a one-sided story would be more of a lie than a search for the truth as I experienced it. Life on Sunnyside was good for the year we lived there and the images remain, mostly good ones. Life wasn't only about fear, there were times when fear was replaced with curiosity about the world. And, it comes as a surprise that my understanding of myself as being such a "good boy" had not included the fact that already at an early age, I had a shadow that had its own agenda, an agenda that overrode the intent to be good, very good. It was as if there were two of me.

~

As winter began to shift into spring, my world began to be bigger than just the inside of the house and school. I would go outside with Kevin in tow to discover the world of our street. I didn't wander far, never going so far as to not see our house, but far enough to see all sorts of wonderful things. Kevin and I would stand on the sidewalk and watch the milkman take his crate of glass milk bottles to the doors of our neighbours' houses. We would watch as the horses that pulled his milk wagon, would stand still waiting. We watched in fascination as the horse left droppings on the snow. Sometimes the horses had bags to catch the horse shit.

One day, while our cousins were at our place, Aunt Jacqueline's children, I became curious about an old car that was parked on the street near our house. Gabrielle, Kevin and I were looking at it when I go so curious that I climbed into the front of the car and sat behind the steering wheel. Gabrielle soon followed along with Kevin. The car was at the edge of a gentle incline that soon turned into a hill. While we explored the car, I felt a sudden movement and hurriedly got Gabrielle and Kevin out of the car. I followed them out and watched as ever so slowly the car gradually began to move, bit by bit, slowly picking up momentum and then speeding down the short hill before turning into a slushy pond at the bottom of the hill.

Seeing the car settling into the field pond, we rushed into the house and didn't say anything about what had happened. We knew we had done something wrong even though we didn't have a clue what that was. We all knew that if the adults found out that we were responsible, there would be hell to pay.

Gabrielle and her sister came over with their mother often in the spring. We often played upstairs in our bedroom, usually under the bed where we could pretend all sorts of stories and scenes. One day, Gabrielle asked if she could see my penis, telling me that she would show me her vagina if I did. I knew about vaginas as I had often seen Béatrice's when my mother changed her diaper or when we were all in the bathtub together. Regardless, we took off our clothes and studied each other closely while under the bed. Gabrielle didn't have a brother so didn't really know anything about penises. She wanted to touch it and have me touch her. I hadn't touched Béatrice's vagina so the idea sounded good. However, that interest soon turned into disgust on my part. Gabrielle hadn't cleaned up well after going to the bathroom and I got shit on my fingers. Curiosity was settled for both of us and what was discovered wasn't all that interesting at all as far as I was concerned.

~

My father's job must have collapsed under him as we left the house on Sunnyside and moved into a dingy little place above a diner, a small restaurant where my mother got a job as a waitress. My father went to work for Diamond Taxi. Life somehow was good in spite of the rat infested restaurant and apartments above it. When my parents were both home they would often have my father's taxi work buddies over for spaghetti feasts. There was a lot of laughter from my father and his friends and plenty of smiles on my mother's face. When she was at work in the restaurant, we were often in the restaurant as well.

I would take care of Béatrice and Kevin while my mother flirted with the customers which earned her good tips. She loved the attention and admiration of the men with whom she flirted.

~

I started grade one in a school that I remember had an asphalt playground surrounded by a wire fence. The school was an old, red-bricked structure that was crammed full of kids who were constantly pushing and shoving. The teachers tried to keep order in the school yard by having us line up in our class groups before the end of recesses, making us stand still before we would then troop back into the school once the bell rang. This school wasn't a happy place for me as I was constantly being shoved and knocked down. As soon as we were let outside for recess I would head away from the kids and tuck myself next to the frost-wire fence that surrounded the school playground. I didn't dare go near any of the playground equipment or groups. I tried hard to disappear, not to be seen. Yet, I wasn't successful as the class bullies would still find me and knock me down. It didn't help that I was the smallest kid in the classroom.

~

The art of disappearing while in plain view had begun for me as a child hiding from my father's anger. School was teaching me that danger lurked everywhere and that I was the focus of that danger. The idea of retreating into silence and as close to the edges of the fence as I could reinforced my belief that the danger would pass by and leave me alone if I was invisible.

~

We again moved, this time into a nice place that we had to ourselves, a small white house, a house that was part of a long row of townhouses not too far from Saint Patrick's School.

The school was nicer than Hopewell School which I had thought was beautiful in comparison to the school I had just left. St. Pat's was more modern and more important for me, it was a Catholic school. Being Catholic was getting to be something that I knew was vital, something that would allow me to fit in with others. I had often heard from Mémère about going to Heaven, a place reserved for Catholics. According to her, Protestants were destined to go to Hell, even if they were good people. I could hardly wait to be like my young uncles, Roland and Réjean, and get to go to confession and communion, to be a good Catholic and ensure my place in Heaven.

It didn't seem to matter that I already knew how to read. I had Catechism lessons and writing lessons that brought me into a better relationship with my classmates. As we learned together and practiced together, we became serious little saints for the most part. The fear of going to Hell was enough to motivate even the worst of us to learn our Catechism lessons.

When it came to writing, I felt a rush of excitement, almost joy. I was learning how to be a writer. One day I would write my own stories, my own books. I was happy in school and that happiness was enough to convince Kevin that school was going to be a good place to go for him as well. Kindergarten was filled with friends, toys and games for him and he loved it.

Before Easter, the students in my class and the other grade one classes were marched down the street to St. Pat's Cathedral. We were lined up in a double row. All of the grade one students were lined up according to the class they were in. The nuns who were our teachers walked along with us making sure that we kept a pious silence, not hesitating to pinch an ear or give a tap on the head of any offenders. It was a Wednesday and we were going to practice the proper rituals in the church, rituals we had been learning in the classroom during our Catechism lessons.

On Saturday we would be formally giving our first confessions in preparation for our First Communion the following day. As I walked along with my head slightly bowed, I was smiling with an excitement that I kept buried so that I wouldn't be reprimanded by the teacher. I pretended I was a saint, that somehow these holy sacraments would change the world around me and make it a kinder place, a happier place.

About a month later, one of my classmates died, an Italian girl named Carmela. Again, I walked with my classmates down the sidewalk to see her in her coffin in the funeral home where we would say prayers for her soul. I was confused. How could this have happened? Why didn't God keep her alive and make her well? Somehow I had thought that by receiving the sacraments, she would have been healed and we all would be protected. I learned from our teacher that Carmela was now in Purgatory, safe from suffering and pain. Again I was confused, almost angry, why Purgatory and not Heaven? Carmela was a good girl. She missed a lot of school because of her battle with Cancer, but that shouldn't have been a good reason to keep her out of Heaven.

~

I don't know why we moved again before the school year was over, but we ended up moving in again with my French grandparents who had recently moved into a bigger apartment above a flooring store on Wellington Street. Though there was still a month left of school, my parents decided that there wasn't any need to have me enrol in a different school to finish the school. Kevin was happy as it meant that we could play together a lot more. For me, I felt sadness at having to leave my classmates at St. Pat's. They were my first friends. At Hopewell School, my friends had been the books which the teacher had let me use while she taught the other students.

At the school where I had begun grade one, I had no friends, just people who tormented me as they tripped me, hit me, laughed at me, and called me names. St. Pat's was different. As a group we had come together because of going through the initiation rituals of Catholicism.

However, moving back in with my French grandparents was moving back into familiar territory where there was no quiet spaces. I had discovered quiet corners in our townhouse near St. Pat's School, corners that would somehow ease my anxieties and fears about life in general. I would retreat into these quiet corners to escape the growing bitterness that was becoming part of my mother's response to our poverty and the unpredictable moods of my father. At my grandparent's place, it was a more chaotic territory that was so busy and filled with people that one was easily lost in the shuffle. Yet in spite of becoming invisible in the crowd, there were no places to which I could retreat, no quiet places. It was as if in the larger group, the sense of being an individual was blurred and almost lost. For a child like myself, an introvert that needed space and quietness the chaos left me sitting anxiously on the sidelines until others decided otherwise.

~

Life on Wellington Street was busy and confusing. The Catholicism of the extended family dictated patterns that began to make sense only to have those patterns disrupted for no apparent reason. Mémère and Pépère would invoke the rule of meatless Friday's and going to confession Saturday's and communion on Sunday's for their children. I was old enough to take part in the confessions and communion and that was exciting. Meatless Fridays became days when we would eat fish and chips. On Saturdays I would go with my aunts, uncles and Mémère to say confession. Then on Sunday's we would all head off to church.

Mom was exempt from these rituals as she wasn't Catholic, something that worried me. Learning that only Catholics could go to heaven, I began to pray that she would stop being stubborn and become a Catholic. Though Dad was a Catholic, he rarely went to mass and no one said anything to him about it.

One part of the weekly routines which was enacted each week, a routine that included my mother, was the Saturday evening party involving playing cards and games, singing and dancing, and eating. I soon learned how to play thirty-one, a card game that almost all could play, including Kevin and I. Since I was almost seven, I was included in the cast of performers for the entertainment part of the evening. My contribution was to sing which I loved doing. Kevin and I would get to dance with our young aunts as well. Then, just before midnight, all games and entertainment stopped so that all could have a final snack. Come midnight there would be no food eaten until after communion the next morning.

One Sunday morning I woke up very hungry. I hadn't eaten late the evening before nor much for Saturday evening supper as well because I wasn't feeling well. My mother took pity on me and gave me a small bowl of Puffed Wheat to eat while everyone was busy getting ready for church. I was already dressed and soon joined my aunts and uncles and grandparents as they headed out the door and then down to a nearby church for Sunday morning services. All was well with the exception of a slight sense of unease that I assumed was a continuation of the day's before flu. I joined the line for communion behind Roland and Réjean and was followed by Mémère and Pépère. I took communion not thinking about the fact that I had eaten just an hour earlier. As I walked back towards our pew, I got sick and threw up all of my breakfast cereal. Besides the pain of vomiting, I was horrified that I had committed a sin, the sin of eating before receiving the Eucharist.

Now everyone in the church would see that I had sinned, that I had sinned twice as in throwing up the host I had received, I had desecrated the body of Christ within me. I wished that I could just crawl away and disappear, become invisible. But, I knew that I was never invisible in God's eyes. The God I knew punished more than my father could ever punish by condemning me to Hell where I would burn forever.

~

The state of horror that I had submersed myself wasn't reflected in the attitudes and opinions of my family. I was just a little kid and little kids got sick. But for myself, it was a different story. For myself, it became something of dire importance between God and myself. I saw myself through his eyes as a sinner and sinners had to be punished. I resolved to become a living saint so that perhaps God could forgive me. It seemed my only hope at that time. I resolved to never again break a Church rule or disobey a priest or a nun who were the living eyes and ears of a God that could grant me Heaven if I would only be good. With that resolve, I became vulnerable in a way that I would learn to my peril. But that, is a story to be told in the next chapter in the second part of this book.

Part Two

"The wound inflicted by sexual abuse cuts deeper than a physical wound. The wound caused by abuse is invisible and often rendered almost inaccessible through an unholy alliance whereby victims are convinced that they must protect the abuser by their silence. Wounds such as these damage children to the very core of their being and their fundamental self-identity. For the victims of sexual abuse, the pain and suffering is not, and my never be, over."

*[**Catholic Diocese of Calgary**, Alberta, Canada]*

Chapter Five

As the story continues, the issue of memory has been something that has bothered me, sometimes tortured me. Quite a few memories have continued since various events in my life happened. Sometimes those memories were placed in the background and ignored as I kept busy with day-to-day life. However, with midlife and the growing uneasiness that I was feeling as though I was living and perpetrating a lie, the memories returned from the background to add to the uneasiness and contribute to a growing depression. I knew that these memories were authentic. However, when other memories began to emerge, I wasn't so sure of their accuracy. At the time, I dismissed those memories as more due to my mood than to factual history. Over time, and with listening to the stories and memories of others, I had to readjust my thinking to accept that these memories emerging from a denied, past were real. I then searched the field of psychology to find a scientific answer about forgotten memories of children re-emerging in adult life. There is a study called, *Adult Memories of Childhood Trauma: A Naturalistic Clinical Study*, by Herman and Harvey, 1997 that describes the issues of memory with which I had been wrestling. Bottom line, these memories are more likely to be of real events than manufactured. With that said, I continue on.

The next part of my history has been a struggle to write in spite of all the work that has been done to heal. Even to admit as being what had happened to me as a child, still elicits some sense of personal failure and shame. For forty years I had blocked out any hint of awareness that I had been sexually abused as a child. Of the abuses that were remembered, physical abuses at the hands of my father, I had repressed by for the most part though I hadn't completely forgotten.

So, when images from childhood began to emerge as I dug deep to heal during analysis, images that involved priests penises and sensations, I responded with disbelief and doubt. It all had to be my imagination. Yet as the images began to become clearer as I worked through psychoanalysis and psychotherapy. As I learned more and more about how such sexual abuse works on the psyche and how it influences behaviour and self-identity, I came to accept the facts that my memories presented to me. I realised that my way of being in the world contained too many signs of having been sexually abused for me to continue denying the truth of what the memory images were telling me.

Sexual abuse began, as best I can remember, when I was in grade two in a Catholic School in the Overbrook area of Ottawa during the 1956-1957 school year. Two years later, in the fall of 1958, another priest in Alberta also found that I was ripe for his special attention. Were my parents aware? Why didn't I report? Was I guilty of complicity in having these adults engage in sexual molestation? I can't answer these questions though I do have some thoughts why I don't have answers. When a child, and sometimes even an adult, suffers trauma, there is a survival response of burying the traumatic event. They simply disappear into black holes where they work below the level of consciousness influencing responses to life and relationships. And, given my previous magical thinking with regards to religion and the Catholic faith and fear of going to Hell, I had learned to stay silent and to obey without question.

~

I began grade two while we lived on Wellington Street, while living above the flooring store with my grandparents. During the summer, Mom had delivered another baby, a boy she called, Gilles.

It wasn't long after school had started that Mom and Dad decided to again have their own place for their growing family, so we moved to a different end of the city in another old townhouse that had suffered neglect. It was the best Dad could do at the time. This section of the city was called Overbrook and I was again put into a new school, again a Catholic school which was important as it was while in grade two that Catholic children prepared for the sacrament of Confirmation, the final sacrament that would mean I would be a full-fledged Catholic ready to fight and die for Christ if necessary. The school was a depressing place with a dark and heavy atmosphere that was accentuated by the nuns who seemed hell bent on making learning something to be endured rather than uplifting. It was rare for a day to pass without one of the students in my classroom getting called to Mother Superior's office where they would get a strap across the hands or butt. I was the rare exception in the class being the only boy to avoid getting into trouble with the nun who was my teacher.

For Catechism lessons like most of the other courses, learning was by rote memorisation. No reasons or explanations were given. A student either memorised what was presented as fact or was punished. I sat in the classroom listening to the priest talk about the path we would be following as young soldiers of Christ. The narrow path that we were to follow was described as though one was always walking up a steep hill. The path was strewn with broken glass and stones. If one stumbled off the edge of the path, it was a long, long fall to the bottom, a bottom that opened up into one of the pits of Hell. We had to follow the priest up the hill on this path, doing what was asked and required of us. To fail to do so would have the path open up and swallow us into yet another pit of Hell.

If we obeyed all of the rules of the church and the wise guidance of the priest who was our personal shepherd then we wouldn't suffer too much other than cuts on our feet. There was no simple way to get to Heaven. This description caught my attention and I had no trouble visualising the scenes presented. I knew that I was at extreme risk of falling into one of those pits of Hell. In response, I worked even harder at becoming quieter and more obedient, I worked harder at trying to please the nuns who somehow could never be pleased.

I was afraid of the priest who taught us our Catechism lessons. I saw that the nuns were also afraid of him which made me even more frightened. One day, late in September, the priest asked for me to meet him in his school office. I approached the door to his office in fear. Was I going to be tossed off the path? Was he going to deny me the sacrament of Confirmation? Was I going to go to Hell in spite of my efforts at being saintly? I stood at the door to his office shaking. I knocked timidly at his door which then opened to let me in.

"Robert," began the pale, dark-haired priest. "You are the best student in my class."

The priest's words caught me totally by surprise. "You aren't going to deny me the sacrament of Confirmation?" I blurted out in relief.

"No," replied the priest. "I want to give you a few extra lessons so that you will be able lead the class into the church. You will be carrying the banner for the new Soldiers of Christ. Robert, do you want to carry this banner?"

I was awed by the idea of being the leader of this new army of Christ and quickly agreed.

"Good, we'll begin our extra lessons today, right away. You will come twice a week for these extra lessons while the others are having their reading lessons.

Your teacher tells me that you are far above the class when it comes to reading, so that class seems to be the best time. I don't want to interfere with your learning. How does that sound to you?"

"Good, Father. Thank you, Father, thank you."

"Robert, to be a soldier of Christ means that one will be put into many difficult and sinful situations. In these places of sin and darkness, it is the heart and mind that keeps the soul pure. It doesn't matter what happens to the body, as long as the soul stays pure. You remember the story of how Christian saints were thrown to the lions and still refused to deny Christ in spite of being eaten alive?"

"Yes, Father."

"Well, it is like that. To be a leader in the Army of Christ, one must learn to separate oneself, one's body, from the sin that is buried deep within and with the sins being committed by the unfaithful that are just waiting to tear us apart and feed us to the Devil, Satan."

This dark-haired priest tested me every time I went to his office. He would take on the role of an unbeliever that sought to tempt me through sexual exploitation. It began with the priest taking off my pants and touching my penis to see if I could refrain from getting stimulated. Every time my penis would respond, he would have me go down onto my knees and say a prayer of forgiveness. When I learned to dissociate from his touch, he commanded me to touch his penis while he held mine in order to determine if I would be able to not be stimulated. His penis was different, uncircumcised. It was pale white and surrounded by long, stringy pubic hair.

This new test of faith then lead to my kissing his penis and sucking it at his command while saying prayers in my head to keep the demon of sexual stimulation at bay.

I fought the devil who would have me gag when the priest's semen filled my mouth while he was calling on the Lord Jesus Christ to keep him from the grips of Satan, the Prince of Darkness. I heard his prayers and his pleas and knew that I had to be strong for him as well as for my own soul. The special lessons to become the standard bearer for the new Soldiers of Christ came to an end the week before our class was to celebrate the sacrament of Confirmation.

Instead of treating me better for all my efforts at becoming a saint, the nuns looked at me with revulsion as though I was a disease. They knew what had been going on behind the closed door of the priest's office. It wasn't something new. Every year a different boy, sometimes more than one boy would become his project, his victim. It seemed even my classmates created a bigger space around me leaving me even more isolated. I convinced myself that it was because I was almost a saint and that they were jealous.

~

As an adult, I know that this was a serious crime against a child, an innocent child by a pedophile in the frocks of a priest. At the time, I didn't see of feel myself as a victim. I believed, truly believed in that priest and what he was telling me at the time, and I didn't resist him. In time that innocence would be shattered and I would begin to pay the price for being sexually molested. The lesson of dissociation wasn't a new one for me at that point. I had learned very early how to disappear into myself to escape the chaos of life at home with my mother and father. What was new, was the association of sexual activity with dissociation, with the disappearing into my mind. Dissociation is a problem that has not quite managed to be solved yet in my life.

In spite of my belief that I hadn't been doing anything wrong, the increasing hostility from my teachers and classmates made me balk at going to school. I began to have stomach aches and headaches that couldn't be explained.

And, I began to hide. Whether it was at school as I disappeared in silence into a book, keeping myself as small as I could on the sidelines in the classroom or at the edge of the fence in the school yard, the idea of being invisible as a way of staying safe became a habit. At home, when there was any tension at all, even if that tension was only within me, I would again turn to hiding, usually in closets, sometimes within the empty boxes kept in the closets in case of needing to pack at a moment's notice to move again.

~

Another move to another house was made in November, 1956. The move was into a one and a half storey house that was old but nice. This new place on MacArthur Road was still in the Overbrook area, still within walking distance of the school I was already attending. With the move, I began to feel an urge to explore the larger world outside of our home. Each time I would go out the door, Kevin would come with me on these journeys of discovery. It didn't take long before we could easily make our way around the neighbourhood. Close by to our home was the Ottawa Boys' Club which was one of the places we would often find ourselves on a Saturday afternoon.

With Christmas coming and money continuing to be an issue, Kevin and I were encouraged to pick up discarded cigarette boxes and take out the silver foil paper which would then be used at home to make garlands of silver rings for the Christmas tree. As we wandered further afield in search of this silver foil treasure, Kevin and I would also collect some of the packages, especially the packages from Sportsman cigarettes because of the images of fishing flies. We wanted to collect all the different pictures to complete a collection, our special treasure. But we learned that it was the silver paper from Players and Export cigarette packages that made the best foil rings for the garland and so we left off collecting Sportsman cigarette packages.

Two evenings before Christmas, Kevin and I went with Dad to find a Christmas tree. Dad didn't have much money so the tree we ended up with was very scraggly and lopsided, a Charlie Brown kind of tree. Dad managed to convince the tree salesman to give us a handful of broken branches to take along with us as part of the sale. Once we got the tree home, we helped as best we could while Dad drilled holes into the trunk of the tree and then stuck in the extra branches. Then he would secure the branches with thin wire to existing branches so that they wouldn't fall out. When the tree was deemed ready, it was left on the back porch. Then my father took me aside and told me that this year I could help set up the Christmas tree once Kevin and Béatrice were asleep on Christmas Eve.

"You've made us proud of you when you carried the banner during your Confirmation. You aren't a child anymore, Benjy," explained my father. "You've shown us that you can take care of your brother and sister when Mom needs help. Why, you're almost a grown up, almost a man!"

Not only was I going to be able to help set up the tree, I would also be helping wrap the few Christmas presents that would be placed under the tree and then staying up to have the late Christmas Eve tourtière with a few of my younger aunts and uncles who were going to stop over for a Christmas Eve treat of this French-Canadian meat pie.

On Christmas Eve, as I helped, I saw the magic of the sad tree turning into a treasure of colour and light. The silver garland that was wrapped around the tree evoked a sense of pride within me. The last part was the draping of tinsel over the tree which masked all of the remaining imperfections of the tree. It didn't matter anymore that beneath the glitter of silver and gold and coloured lights that the tree was wounded and broken, held together with glue and wire. What appeared before my eyes was something from heaven.

However, once it was time to wrap the presents, the magic fell apart. Before the few presents could be wrapped they had to be checked to see if all the pieces were there, to see that everything worked. The child puzzles for Béatrice had to be checked to see if all the pieces were there. All of the presents were used toys and articles that came from Welfare Services. As my father explained what needed to be done, I could see the pain in his eyes, and the anger behind that pain at not being able to be a better provider. For the first time in my life, I fully understood the fact that we were poor, very poor.

~

That Christmas of 1956 when I was seven years old, was a turning point in my life. For the first time in my life, my father didn't seem so powerful, so heroic. I saw this in his eyes and that scared me. It was somehow a point when I stopped being a child. I was expected to take a more adult-like role in our family. With the family growing and the real need for helping with the two younger kids, my role as a caretaking helper was voiced clearly. Curiously, the thrusting of this role upon me was met with both pride and satisfaction on my part. Here was something that I could do that would make me worthy of my father's love and respect. As an adult, I now see and understand better, my behaviour patterns in adult life. It seems though years as decades had passed, the behaviour patterns continued to be repeated.

~

For the rest of the winter, the depression that began each day in school would follow me home and too often I would crawl into some dark closet once I got home, hoping no one would find me. My mother became angrier with me for disappearing just when she needed me to play with Béatrice, to watch over Gilles, or to do some other small task.

I was having nightmares as well and would wake up screaming and explaining how thin, pale snakes were crawling into my mouth wanting to eat me up from the inside.

I would often come hope with bruises and sometimes a bloody nose. The kids at school had begun to torment me on a daily basis. It seemed the harder I tried to be nice, the meaner they got. When one day I returned with my jacket torn, my father demanded to know why I had ruined the jacket when we didn't have enough money to get a new one for me. I cried as I spilled out the story of being punched, pushed, shoved, tripped and called a little cocksucker by the kids in my class and from some of the older boys in other grades.

My father didn't have anything to say though his face got dark and threatening making me think that I was going to get it worse, more painful than anything the boys at school could ever do to me. But, he didn't hit me or say anything else. He told my mother to repair the damaged jacket and then took me to the Boys' Club and signed me up for boxing lessons.

"Benjy, you're going to learn how to defend yourself against those boys," explained my father. "You can't just turn the cheek. I don't care what those god-damned priests tell you. Do you understand?"

"But I don't want to hit people, Dad."

"Think of it as stopping them from hitting you. If they can't hit you, they can't hurt you. And, it'll make them think that you can hurt them if you wanted to. You don't actually have to hit them to make them afraid of hitting you. Okay?"

"Okay," I agreed.

And for the next few weeks I went to the Boys' Club and learned how to hold up my hands to protect my face and how to throw a punch. Every time I went for lessons, Kevin would stand outside of the practice area and watch me, proud of me for being a boxer.

One Saturday afternoon, while I was in the boxing ring with another boy, in early 1957, John Diefenbaker, came into the Boys Club followed by a number of photographers and newspaper people. While I was getting a bloody nose, Kevin got his photo taken with the future Prime Minister of Canada. Kevin and the Diefenbaker were featured on the front page of the Ottawa Citizen newspaper the next day. Rather than being happy for Kevin, I was jealous. I was the one who had taken a beating in the ring, and I didn't rate being noticed at all. I just didn't seem fair.

Easter was approaching and we were getting excited about treats and the big meals that always came with special holidays. Easter was also when we got together with the extended Laflamme family. However, for me, the excitement was tempered by the role our class was to play in a parade down the aisles of the church. I was to, again, lead our class in the procession. Again, I was called to the priest's school office for special lessons. When I saw his penis, I saw the snake of my dream and I began to cry. When the priest finally calmed me down and found out about the dream, he spoke gently and convinced me that the dream would disappear if I again prayed with him to deal with the deadly temptations of the body. The priest prayed in Latin as he had me hold his penis while he held mine. Making the sign of the cross on my penis, he bent down and then kissed the blessed penis. Guiding my mouth to his penis, he began another prayer while making the sign of the cross on the top of my head. Again, a flood of semen began to choke me. He held my head in his hands while looking up to heaven and asked for forgiveness for me, for the sins that gave me nightmares. Then, with a kind look into my eyes, he wet the tip of his fingers on the semen that was on my lips and cheeks with which he then blessed me. He promised that the nightmares would now end if I would pray every day for forgiveness for my daily sins of thoughts, words, and deeds.

The nightmares continues and it became obvious to my parents that something was seriously wrong. However, it wasn't until one morning when I saw both my parents in bed, asleep that I felt pulled to uncover my father and look at his penis which was so different from the priest's. My father woke up startled by being uncovered, and flew into a rage, grabbing me and throwing me across the room. He spat out words of my being a fucking cocksucker, a priest's go-to boy. I saw the disgust in his face and his real hatred for me. In spite of the pain, I picked myself up and ran out of the room, went into the closet in the kids' room and crawled into a cardboard box putting empty clothes hangers above me, hoping that they would hide me so that my father couldn't find me and punish me more before throwing me out of the family.

~

It wasn't very long after this scene that we moved again to a distant part of the city. Kevin and I were put into a public school called Woodroffe School. Our being placed in public school was my father's response to what he knew about Catholic schools. Our new home was a rundown little cottage on Woodroffe Avenue, close to the Ottawa River. Near the river was a set of railway tracks that separated an undeveloped area that held only a few old houses such as the house we lived in. Across the road from our house was a house where there was a huge garden area, and a girl who lived with her father. The girl soon found herself hired on occasion to be our babysitter.

My father seemed to be always angry with me at the time, an anger that I realise was really directed at the church. As an adult I know that his life in a Catholic school had its own crosses that he continued to carry with him.

Mémère had, for more than a year, been telling everyone how I was the one chosen in the Laflamme family, chosen by God to be a priest, that I was to be the religious offering for the family that would finally allow us all to have a more blessed and fruitful life. I could sense the bristles rise on my father's neck each time she would speak this way. My father had never asked me what had happened at the Catholic school in Overbrook, but it was evident that he had a good idea. I wasn't the first nor would I be the last little boy to come to the notice of a pedophile in the church. And, I began to wonder just what my father's experience was in a Catholic school.

From the viewpoint of an adult in the years just before old age, I can begin to understand that there are no easy answers or explanations for why the adults in my life seemed so oblivious to the fact of my being sexually molested by a priest. I know that I never had told anyone what had happened. At that time, I thought that this is what was supposed to happen if I was going to be a priest that my grandmother hoped for. I was disgusted with myself for my responses to being sexually molested, believing that the dreams were Devil sent to try and sway me away from following through with the vision of becoming a priest. I knew I just wasn't good enough as a person, and so I hid as much as I could hoping that somehow all the nightmares would just go away.

~

With only two months left in the school year, the change to Woodroffe School allowed me to find the courage to come out of the shadows and risk connecting with classmates. At this public school no one knew about priests, Catechism or about me, a boy who was destined to go to Hell. To them, I was just a new kid who joined in games of marbles, Popsicle stick toss, or who just hung out on the sidelines smiling at everyone.

During these last two months of the school year, there wasn't enough time for me to make friends, but that wasn't important to me. What was more important was that I stopped hiding in the shadows as much now that the fear of being called to the priest's office has retreated. No one was calling me a little cocksucker, or pervert. I wasn't being punched, taunted, tripped or harassed like I was in the last school.

At our new house which was really an old, dilapidated, summer cottage, there was a large yard with lots of space for Kevin and I to run around in, with trees to climb and forts to build using old fallen branches. Béatrice was old enough so that she could be outside with us and was usually watching what Kevin and I would do. Kevin was the daredevil and would try things where I would hesitate.

When summer came and Kevin and I didn't have to go to school anymore, we would often go across the road to the house with the big yard, where we would pick strawberries or raspberries. We would sometimes wander down to the edge of the river and drag branches in the water. Partway through the summer, my father brought home some building materials and some paint. He had arranged to do improvements on the cottage in lieu of rent for the summer. The house needed to be insulated if we were to live in it for the winter. Tentest insulating panels were being used so as to make the cottage warmer in cold weather. Dad worked to fix up the cottage using materials supplied by the owner. While he did the necessary repairs and alterations on the cottage, he also built a fort for Kevin and me. He strung an electrical cord with a trouble light attached to the fort so that we could use the fort in the evenings as well. In spite of living in real poverty, that summer was a magical time when we, Kevin, Béatrice and ,I could simply be kids.

One day, Dad was taking Kevin and I to the edge of the river as our mother was complaining that she was worried about us drowning.

It was time for us to learn how to swim. Unlike most parts of the shoreline, where we played was a sheltered bay with a set of log booms creating a swimming area. I was excited that I was going to learn how to swim. Kevin and I walked into the water with Dad and wondered what we were going to do, how we were going to learn. While thinking about this, Dad simply picked me up and threw me out as far as he could with a shouted encouragement to swim back to him. I panicked. Rather than swimming to get back to shore, I tried desperately to crawl to the top of the water while going under again and again. Dad easily plucked me out of the water and put me back on the shore where I continued to cry. Kevin begged Dad to throw him in as he wanted to show Dad that he could do it, that he could swim. Dad threw him in and Kevin dog paddled his way back to shore. It was the first time I heard Dad say something positive about Kevin as he congratulated him while in the same breath ridiculing me as being a pansy.

It seemed that the good times of summer ended that day. The work on the house stopped as well leaving it unfinished. Both Kevin and I began to always be in trouble for one reason or another, usually because we just weren't old enough to do more to help our mother. When our father returned home from work on those days when we hadn't moved fast enough or simply because she was in a mood, our mother would report on us and we would be spanked with his belt over our bare buttocks. Both Kevin and I learned that it was best never to cry, to just take it. Crying made it worse, as Dad would get angrier. He only respected toughness, not weakness.

I was now eight years old going into grade three at Woodroffe School. Kevin was in grade one. With a return to school there was a sense of escaping the dragon's den. During school hours life was a lot easier. With a return to school, our being poor became more noticeable to our classmates.

We didn't return with new school bags or new clothes like the other kids. It was just enough to have students keep a distance from us so that making friends was difficult. We were still strangers in the school and community. Kevin was occasionally getting into trouble with his classmates and I would have to rescue him. Sometimes I wasn't able to get to the skirmishes soon enough and he would end up getting into more trouble with the teachers. When that happened there was a beating waiting for both of us at home; Kevin for getting into trouble and me for not keeping him out of trouble.

~

At home, there was no listening, no questions to find out why Kevin was getting into trouble. In both Kevin's and my point of view, the exclusion and the subtle and sometimes not so subtle bullying justified a response. What was important was the image or the face that we brought to the outer world. By getting into trouble, we inadvertently had tarnished the family name. At least that was what we were told. However, looking back knowing the larger picture, it was our father punishing us for what he didn't know about himself, his shadow that was being reflected in our actions. His unspoken belief that we had a hard time learning was that appearances was everything.

~

One Saturday morning in late September Mom sent me to the store for some sugar and some powdered milk. I was given a five dollar bill, a lot of money at that time, to pay for these few supplies. The store was across the tracks but not too far of a walk. On my way back from the store, I was daydreaming and I stumbled as I crossed the tracks, spilling the grocery bag and the change that was in it. I cut my knee on the ground as I fell and scraped my hands. The bag of sugar ripped open and some of the sugar fell out.

The paper grocery bag was ripped and I knew that I was in big trouble for losing some of the sugar. I knew that with money scarce, even a small loss was going to add to our hardship. Putting as much sugar as I could back into the sugar bag, I began to look for the money. I panicked. I couldn't see clearly with tears in my eyes. Finally I grabbed the powdered milk box and the torn sugar bag and rushed home.

When my mother saw the torn sugar bag and the blood on the edges, she lost her temper and struck out at me repeatedly, furious that I had done this. When she tired of knocking me around, she grabbed me by the ear and took me to my father who was still in bed, sleeping. She woke him and told him what I had done, about the lost money and the spilt sugar. It didn't matter that my knee was cut and my hands still stained with blood or that my head was ringing from the blows she had given me in her anger, it was now time for me to face my father. I was stripped of my pants and told to lie on the bed while he took his belt from his pants. He struck again and again while I bore it without voicing the tears that were escaping. It only made him even angrier. He then turned the belt so that the buckle would make contact with my buttocks drawing blood. Seeing the blood, he stopped.

His anger still not quenched he forced me to put my pants back on and he dragged me to the train tracks where I had had the accident. We found most of the money that had been spilled out, but there was still some change missing. Not able to find the last of the change, about thirty-five cents, Dad accused me of spending it on treats for myself. In spite of my protests, he struck me with the back of his hand sending me flying. When I landed, it was on my bruised buttocks shooting pain all through my body. He picked me up from the ground, gritted his teeth and told me to get my ass home as fast as possible or else there would be worse, a lot worse, waiting for me.

That evening after supper, a meal which I wasn't allowed to eat because of the lost money and spilt sugar, I ran away from home.

I ran across the road and hid in the garden, in the raspberry patch. It didn't take long for the girl who was our baby sitter when Mom needed to go for a checkup during her pregnancy, to hear me in the garden. She listened to my tale of woe. When she told her father, he was upset and very angry. In spite of that, he said that I had to be taken back to my home, that he couldn't interfere with how another father disciplined his children. As he saw it, I must have deserved punishment for some reason as all boys frequently misbehaved and needed to be punished.

When Dad came to pick me up, he told the man how I had stolen money for candy, money that was needed to feed the family. He said he was ashamed to have to admit that his son was a thief and a liar. And when we got back to the house, Dad only hit me once with the back of his hand across the face with enough force to knock me down while he promised that if I ever embarrassed him again by running away, he would break my legs so that I would never run anywhere again.

~

Absolute fear entered into my life at that point. I didn't doubt for a second that he would break my legs or even worse if I embarrassed him again. I didn't doubt that he would do the same if somehow I didn't measure up in every way possible. I lost my confidence to make any decisions and knew that the best I could do was to obey without question just like I had to obey the church without question.

Today as an adult, this giving up authority over myself still is quite active. Without thinking about it, if there is any possible conflict of ideas, I go silent and agree so that the peace can be maintained.

I know that this is irrational as most conflicting ideas are trivial and would never put me at any risk. Yet, the complex that grew out of the repeated beatings and threats and seeing others in my family become victims of anger was buried deep. I react instantaneously and could only think afterwards. That is the problem with complexes, they are automatic when triggers are touched, beyond our conscious control. However, in becoming aware of the existence and power of my complexes, I can catch myself as soon as I become aware of my anxieties, fears, anger, etc. Seeing the affect coursing through me, I can then recognise the source and release the grip of the complex. Awareness makes a difference.

Part of my response at that point in my life was to limit the world of importance and focus for myself. School and schoolmates were placed in the background. I still maintained my learning efforts as poor marks would be considered as an embarrassment which would then be translated into punishment. Even printing skills and writing skills, or penmanship was to be rigorously and carefully done as my father believed that penmanship was indicative of one's character. I obeyed teachers, I excelled in my studies and that was all. Friendships, playing, and organised activities were not on the agenda. After the basics of school, the rest of my world was our family and being in a state of constant hyper-awareness so as to not screw up. But of course, adults are not always predictable. Sometimes it was impossible not to get into trouble because of an irrational mood swing, or because factors outside of the family at home triggered anger in one or both of my parents. Like me, they had issues with their own complexes that arose out of their early lives in dysfunctional families.

Not all of my life in the cottage on Woodroffe Avenue was about living in a nightmare. I had a brother who saw me as his hero and there were hours when we could play, when our parents were thankfully in good moods.

When he was in a good mood, my father was a good man, a happy guy that made the world a happier and better place. When he was in a good mood, my mother would begin to glow and for a while not turn her resentment towards life against her children.

The only school story that I can recall is a positive and funny story, that of learning how to write rather than print. When the teacher began to teach us writing skills, I believed that I was learning French. Since I had been in Catholic schools learning English and had only learned printing skills, I assumed that writing was French because Dad frequently wrote and it was always in French.

Growing up with two languages sometimes made it difficult to separate the languages. Because Mom only spoke English, the language spoken in the house was English. However, because we were so often with Dad's parents and siblings where French was used almost exclusively during my earlier years, I learned many of my words in French only. One good example comes to mind. When it came to Sundays, usually the clan would go for a ride in the countryside around Ottawa. All of the farm animals and scenes of the countryside were learned in the French language.

Another story that bares telling is one of Halloween, 1957.

~

It was Halloween and Kevin and I were looking forward to going out trick or treating as it would give us a lot of candy and treats which we rarely saw. We rushed home from school in order to start as early as possible. We didn't have costumes but did the best we could wearing some old clothes that belonged to our parents as costumes. For masks we used paper cut out as eye-masks with plain white string as ties to hold them on our heads. Dad wasn't home from his work yet, when Mom sent us out with pillow cases to hold our loot.

She gave us strict instructions to come home after doing the first two streets along Woodroffe Avenue and not to eat any of the treats we got. When we got back she told us we could go back out again and that we could eat some of the treats from our second expedition. The treats from the first expedition were to be used as our family's treats for those who would come to our house. Kevin and I didn't question our mother. We knew that if we didn't do just as she told us to do it, we would be in serious trouble when Dad got home. We wanted treats. We rushed through those first two streets collecting a surprising amount of candy and treats including apples, popcorn, and small chocolate bars. As soon as the treats were dumped into a holder, Mom turned on our porch light to let trick-or-treaters know that there were treats at this house. Before we could go out for our own treats, Mom had us take Béatrice to a few of the local places along our street.

With that duty done, we were sent out again with just one instruction – don't eat any apples as there might be pins or razor blades in them.

~

I can still see the two of us laughing as we walked down the neighbouring streets, collecting candy and treats until we could hardly hold up our pillow cases filled with loot. We ate freely from the treats with the exception of fruit, chocolate bars which we knew Mom wanted for her own sweet tooth, and licorice which was Dad's favourite. There was no sense of seeing ourselves as being deprived of these set aside treats as what was left over was more than enough for all of our fantasies. Suckers were the biggest treats that we would make last and last. The Halloween toffee candy wrapped in orange and black paper were a popular treat given in many of the houses we visited.

The images of good times are important to be voiced and honoured as well as dark images when one is healing from the trauma suffered in growing up. Very few lives are all lived in total suffering. I was reminded of this two years ago while I was in Thailand with my wife. As we walked down the rough streets we passed a work site that was busy preparing an area for underground water lines. The work site was primitive with the handful of men working with spades and pickaxes in deep holes. On the edges of the holes, beside concrete sewer structures that would be eventually lowered into the holes, we saw that a few women and children were very obviously living in the concrete structures. One little boy about four years old stood near the roadway which we were walking down playing with a stick. I stopped, smiled at him and nodded a smile towards his mother and asked if I could take his photo. The mother smiled brightly and nodded her permission. With the photo taken, I gave the boy a treat for himself and a bit of money for his mother. Life was good all-around in spite of conditions that might say otherwise, at least for that moment.

Though my story here is mostly about the dark times, there were other times when laughter was real and life was as perfect as we could imagine it. For me, the writing about the dark times is my way of acknowledging the wounding so that healing will follow. Burying and denying the wounding only continues to empower the ghosts and shadows to continue to dominate our lives as victims.

~

Less than a week after Halloween, we woke up to my mother's screams. She was awaked by Gilles's screams from his cradle, a rat had crawled into the cradle and bit him. The house was freezing cold with only a small space heater that used coal for a source of heat. She begged Dad to find us a different place to live, one that didn't have rats and wasn't so cold.

A few days later we were again woken in the middle of the night. We were moving and had to be gone before daylight. Dad hadn't paid the rent for September and October or November and the landlord would be coming to confiscate everything we owned in payment. A handful of Dad's relatives were there to help us put everything possible into the cars that they came in. We would go to Mémère's until Dad found us another place to live.

~

Displacement was becoming the norm for us as a family. We didn't know where we were going, where we would go to school or even when. All we knew as children was that life circumstances demanded that we constantly flee. We didn't place any blame on our father for being unable to hold onto a job or to prioritize his money so that rent could be paid on time, something that would have allowed us to become a lot more stable and set down a few roots into community and school. The only roots that existed for us were the roots of family and extended family.

By the first of December we found a nice two-storey home on Rosedale Avenue which meant that I would be returning to Hopewell School. Rather than being put into the grade three classroom, I was put into a split grade three-four classroom because of my academic abilities. That meant that I would finish grade three in January and then grade four in June if all went well. In spite of the academic pressure from my father to be at the top, it wasn't all that difficult for me. I was already reading books years ahead of my age-grade level. What stood out for me for the school year at Hopewell was taking part in a Shop class where I got to make things out of wood, and clay, simple things such as an ashtray and a match striker. The other things that I remember about school was taking part in speed-skating during physical education classes.

I had to take cod-liver oil pills to prevent getting polio, and assigned lines for not handing in homework even though I had been absent (a very frequent event) when the assignment was given. I learned how to hold and write with two pens at once and make the task a lot quicker.

My father must have found a good job as we got to stay in the house on Rosedale until May when we would again find ourselves back on the road like gypsies. For Kevin and me, December 1957 was a likely one of the best winters of our life. With a lot of December snow fall, the two of us would pester our neighbours to let us shovel the snow from their sidewalks and driveways. We didn't earn a lot of money, but more than we expected which allowed us to buy Christmas gifts for the first time with the money we earned. For me, the most magical part of that December was the rushing home from school in order to turn on the radio and listen to a broadcast of Santa, his elves and the reindeer. I was transported into that magical world and saw it as real as the one where I lived, perhaps even more real as it had the intrigues, the shadows and the constant victory of good over bad. For me the daily broadcasts were all about hope, about how it could all be good.

~

Mom was happy on Rosedale Avenue. She was often singing along to songs on the radio and would often be baking pies and cakes, cooking favourite dishes such as scalloped potatoes with crisp bacon floating on top. One particular treat that I enjoyed was her fudge. I remember her always telling me that we had to use Carnation evaporated milk to make good fudge. Sometimes she would put crushed walnuts in the fudge making the treat taste even better if that was possible. I began to think that we were like the television program, Leave it to Beaver (of course I would be Beaver as we were both eight years old.) with Mom wearing the same hair style as Beaver's Mom, June.

Television became a big part of our life with the favourite shows including Lassie, Ozzie and Harriet, Father Knows Best, and I Love Lucy.

On our walks to school, with snow piled deep, we would often stop and play. One scene that comes to mind has Kevin and I climbing up a large bank of snow that took us to a rather gentle-sloped roof of a garden shed. We would take turns jumping off the roof into a pile of deep snow, over and over again. Of course that meant we would frequently be late for class, and that meant more lines to write, something I felt was worth the joy of playing in the snow with my brother.

~

My third brother, Gordon was born in February, 1958. Gilles was still in diapers which made things more difficult in the house for our mother. Béatrice was months away from being four, so she couldn't really be of any help with our mother. Georgie was less than two years old. During this time, our French family relations were around often enough to help out. But, when Kevin and I were home from school, we ended up doing more than one would think an eight-year old and a seven year old could do. Kevin would play with Georgie and I would have Bea tag along with me as I helped with sweeping floors and doing dishes and fetching things for Mom. As the eldest of the five kids, I had a level of responsibility that became critical in a large family. A child grows up quickly when the environment requires that to happen.

~

In late spring 1958, I am helping Mom put away groceries. I didn't know where all of them went, but I had to make sure the table was cleared off and everything was put away while she took care of the baby, Gordie. For some unknown reason, I ended up putting the package of toilet paper in the small oven.

Later, when Mom was warming the oven in preparation for some baking, she went back to check on the baby and the paper began to smoulder and the kitchen filled with smoke. Dad rushed in and put his fist through a window in order to get air into the room and allow the smoke to escape. He quickly saw that the smoke was coming from the stove oven. Turning off the stove oven, he then opened the oven door and removed the smouldering paper. Both Mom and Dad looked at me and I knew I was in trouble, big trouble. The look was all about hatred and anger. Knowing that the blow was coming had me cover my head with my arms. The blow knocked me against the table and was followed by my mother kicking me while screaming that my father was bleeding and how it was all my fault. Dad had several bad cuts from putting his fist through the window.

~

There is no question that my ignorance had put our home in peril. What if my father hadn't been alert and hadn't broke the window to allow the smoke to escape and then remove the paper from the oven? I was old enough and should have known better, but the lack of common sense and being more focused on getting the task done so that I wouldn't get into trouble was the real problem. I didn't ask where the paper was to go because I was afraid to get a slap and I was in a hurry to go and play with Kevin.

Before the end of the school year, my father got a new job, and we moved to an old row house on Waverly Street near Bank Street when my father worked for Rankin Hardware. Kevin and I transferred to Glashan School as Hopewell was too far for us to travel. I was placed in the grade four classroom and Kevin continued on in grade one with both of us passing our grades at the end of the school year.

~

Living on Waverly was marked with memories of rainy Sundays, watching Mighty Mouse on television after school.

One particular memory emerges from my interaction with some of my new classmates. I was the youngest and the smallest and naturally found myself to be a target for the class bullies. In order to avoid the kicks and punches, I tried pleasing them when they demanded that I shoplift at a small convenience store on Bank Street and give them the loot. They would create a distraction for the storekeeper and I would steal bags of chips and chocolate bars for them. They became my friends as a result and I stayed safe. However, I knew it was wrong to steal.

One day, I kept a bag of stolen chips and took them home to share with Kev and Bea. However, by the time I got home, the guilt was gnawing away at me and I confessed to my mother what I had done. I didn't tell her about the boys at school. She gave the kids the chips and told me that Dad would deal with me when he got home. Strangely, I didn't get a beating. His idea for a punishment was for me to go back to the store and tell the storekeeper what I had done and to pay for the chips. The store keeper was more sad than angry when I gave him the money and told him what I had done. He actually thanked me for being honest but asked that I didn't come into his store anymore. When I got back to the house, I decided I had to punish myself even more, so I denied myself the right to watch Mighty Mouse for the rest of the school year.

Early summer scenes which involved taking weekend rides into the Quebec countryside with cousins and other relatives in the back of the Rankin Hardware truck soon followed. Dad would drive down the winding and hilly roads to a lake in the Gatineau Hills, just one of several vehicles filled with family making the journey. Roland, Réjean, and Héloise; my father's three youngest siblings, rode in the back of the half-ton with Kevin and me and a few other cousins. Héloise, as the oldest, led us as we sang songs in both English and French.

A final scene from that early summer was the trip I got to go on with Dad and Pépère to go fishing in a very small river, the Little Mississippi, where I caught the largest Bass and earned praise from both my father and grandfather. It seemed like it just couldn't be any better than this.

~

If there is anything to learn, for me, about this last period, it was that with the engaging in shoplifting, I had somehow become more normal. In spite of all the trouble I seemed to get into, I was too much the innocent saintly kid than a normal kid, I was particularly confused by my father's response to shoplifting. After the punishment I had received for losing a bit of money, and having that called stealing from my family, and how running away was dishonouring the family name; I was sure that I was going to face the harshest of punishments ever. But somehow, it was almost brushed off and with humour on his part.

As an older teenager and then as an adult, I learned that my father was no stranger to theft, to issuing non-sufficient fund cheques. As long as the theft wasn't from the family, it was not something to worry about in terms of morality. Too often our family moved to avoid creditors or legal action because of my father's inability to view debts owed as debts that needed to be paid. With the new job at Rankins Hardware, and access to the delivery truck, that job was short lived because he saw an opportunity to use that job and the truck for his own personal gain and perceived needs. Using the truck for pleasure instead of for business resulted in my father once again being out of work.

As an adult, I have worked hard at doing the opposite, making sure that I followed all the rules, gave back all that was owed and even a bit more if it would keep poverty at bay, if it would ensure that my family name in small-town prairie Canada was a name to be trusted.

Chapter Six

At some point just after my ninth birthday, my father had another dream. He had heard how some of his buddies from Korea had taken up their land grants in northern Alberta and were now doing well. He didn't have the money to get to Alberta and claim his free quarter of land, yet that wasn't seen as a barrier. He talked one of my new uncles, Art who had married my Dad's sister Denise, into partnering up with him to go to the Peace River country where my father would claim his quarter of land. Four adults and five kids, including the new baby, piled into a car and made the journey to the Peace River country. As a veteran of the Korean conflict, he was entitled to a quarter-section of land and $3,000 to assist in developing the land.

~

It was late morning and I was lying in the back on top of the shelf that was behind the rear backed by the rear window; I was warm in the sunshine that came through the window as the car continued down the highway heading west. The car was crowded with little kids sitting on laps and voices talking, singing and laughing so my laying by the rear window helped make some room in the car. Dad was busy explaining that he would have a few years of grace after claiming his land to clear a set amount of acres of the land. He would also have to erect a house in order to keep his land during that period of grace. The talk in the car was always of Dad and Uncle Art working together and then claiming or buying more land once they built the original quarter into a big and prosperous farm and ranch. Dad talked about horses and about hunting and rodeos; he talked of a huge ranch house in which everyone would have their own bedroom. The images of luxury and well-being filled the car with hope and sunshine that matched the sun pouring in through the back window.

It was late afternoon when we came at last to the land that Dad was entitled to claim as his. We piled out of the car on a sunny and warm early summer day, exuberant and filled with laughter.. Freed from the confines of the car, we poured down into the ditch that bordered the treed land. Mom pointed out the wild strawberries growing in the grass alongside the road. Showing us what to look for sent Kevin, Béatrice and I into a frenzy of picking while Dad and Uncle Art went exploring the quarter of land. Mom and Aunt Denise stayed with us while we kept hunting for the wild strawberries. Mom made sure we picked enough for Gilles and for the adults as she wanted Dad to enjoy them as well after his scouting out the land with Uncle Art.

With Mom's warning still ringing in my brain, I was careful to fill up the container she had given me unlike Kevin who had Béatrice sitting beside him with both of them stuffing every strawberry they could find into their mouths. I didn't dare eat one until Mom would tell me that I had picked enough for her, Aunt Denise, Uncle Art, Gilles and Dad. I knew that if I ate one, the stains would give me away and then they would assume that I had been selfish and eaten most of the strawberries with no consideration of others. I felt guilty even for thinking of eating one. Aunt Denise came over to pick near me and soon was teasing me about not eating any. As I turned to look at Mom, she gave me a dark look as though to tell me not to even dare thinking about eating any strawberries until she gave me permission.

~

It's amazing to me to see this childhood response still active and strong within me almost sixty years later. I still don't eat berries while picking them. Without thinking, I pick until done and then wait to see what is left after others have had their fill before then hesitatingly tasting the harvest. No one tells me not to eat them. If anything, I get good-naturedly teased about denying myself berries while picking.

Each of us build in these internal censors, those judgmental inner voices that harshly tell us what to do and what not to do. And, without questioning these inner voices, we respond as we did when we were children at the time when the inner voices were a repetition and internalisation of outer voices, usually parental voices.

As I look back on this scene with myself laying in the hot sunshine that poured through the rear window of the car, I can see my current response to laying in sunshine as being another late life return to those valued moments of my youth, those places and habits that nourished. Not everything that comes out of our past is negative. This is an important thing for each of us to remember. Sometimes we lose too much if we deny the past. Our woundings do come from the experiences of the past, but also coming from that same past are the behaviours that helped us to begin healing those wounds, that show us how to more than survive.

~

Finally Dad and Uncle Art returned, not looking too happy. We listened to their complaints of mosquitoes and black flies. The land itself was not what they were expecting – so many trees, ponds, and outcroppings of rock. Dad had hoped that there would have been a few open fields, natural meadows and pastures already waiting for us. The work of transforming this wilderness into a ranch seemed to be something that hadn't really been considered. They were city boys with no real knowledge of how this would happen.

As we drove away, all talk of a bright shiny future with horses and a big farm home was noticeably absent. Now what? With the Northwest Territories so close, the decision to go to Yellowknife and to the gold mines there was made. Perhaps there was a better way to finally becoming rich, perhaps this was really the journey they were supposed to take to a future of wealth, the road we needed to follow.

With a new dream ignited, we took the Mackenzie highway to Hay River on the southern shore of Great Slave Lake.

Money was becoming more and more of an issue as we were now on the road more days than had originally planned for. Along the way to Hay River we got a flat tire with the next town, a small town, still several miles away. Stuck on the highway with no way to get the tire repaired and no spare tire that could be used to replace the flat tire, the decision was made to drive to the next town. From the back window, I could see the cuts in the asphalt made by the rim once the last of the rubber tire had broken off. Just before the town, Dad had Uncle Art stop so that most of us could get out of the car so that there would be less weight on the rim. His idea was to hopefully save the rim so that it could be used again with a replacement tire. When we finally got to the next town which was even smaller than we had expected, we were able to get a replacement tire and rim.

We arrived at the ferry dock in Hay River in darkness just before dawn with the dock surrounded by mist. Mom was crying and there was a lot of arguing. Aunt Denise had begun to think that there wasn't going to be jobs in the gold mine. She was worried that if we took the ferry across the lake to Yellowknife, she would be stuck there as there wouldn't be enough money to get back home to Ottawa. The debate was carried on in anger and only concluded when Mom persuaded Dad that we would come back another time when we had enough money to set up once we got to Yellowknife. We didn't board the ferry, but turned around and headed straight south where Dad knew there were jobs in the Lethbridge area, vegetable harvesting jobs. We didn't have enough money to make the drive to Ottawa, a drive of almost five days. The trip to Lethbridge would only take two days and with just two weeks of work there would be enough money for us to go back home, back to Ottawa.

~

The dream was a bust for both Dad and Uncle Art. Yet the dream that their fortune would be made in the west wasn't done for. Ottawa had too much history of poverty and too many burnt bridges. Like most relationships with people, when there is too much history, change becomes almost impossible. The idea of someplace where one could escape history and thrive was what drove my father and his siblings. And, I have to admit, this same belief had been instilled in me, for when I was old enough, I left the east and headed for the promised land of hope that was western Canada.

~

As we pulled into Lethbridge, Dad found us a motel from which he and Uncle Art would scout out for work. We didn't stay there very long once Dad found that the work was closer to a small town called Coaldale. Dad and Uncle Art went working for a farmer near Coaldale. Kevin and I joined in picking green beans that were placed in gunny sacks which were weighed at the end of the day. Kevin and I didn't end up picking that much, but the beans we picked did count in the weight and there was ten cents a pound to be paid to Dad for our efforts. We both felt like little men, grownups helping bring in the money that would let us finally have a home and be rich. For the next few weeks, our small contributions were added to their wages and soon there was enough for Dad to rent a house in Coaldale which seemed a promising place for work.

~

Before the end of the summer 1958, we moved into a decent house in the south-east part of that town, well away from the highway. With no work left for Kevin and I, we got to play with some of the neighbourhood kids that we met. Then, it was time to start school. I went into grade five, Kevin went into grade two.

We were registered in Saint Joseph's School which wasn't very far from where we lived. Near the school was the church, Saint Ambrose's. The house was a fairly modern bungalow with a large front yard with large poplar trees. As I started school, I found myself with a friend, a boy a year older than I who was in my class, a boy who lived on a farm not too far from town.

~

Going to school, I made a new friend. In the early fall I did get to go to his home. He lived on a farm and he was poor. I can still see his house as it appears in my memory. The kitchen had a wood stove and the house was made of rough lumber. I remember eating a piece of toast at his house, the toast that had a thick layer of lard spread on it. After that snack we walked through fields of sugar beets passing "Indians" working with hoes. As we passed a few little granary sheds, I saw a few children and an Indian woman sitting in the doorway of one of the granaries. Apparently the Indians were migrant workers who worked for a little money hoeing the sugar beet fields. My friend pulled one of the smaller sugar beets and peeled it enough so that we could chew on the white insides. I was surprised at how sweet it was.

My friend and I would often steal a sugar beet for a treat during the fall and sometimes a cob of corn which we would eat raw while hiding in the rows of corn. Somehow we had access to a few golf clubs that had wooden heads and bamboo shafts. We would take these and pretend we were golfing on the small course that was on the edge of the town. Irrigation ditches that cut through the golf course were empty at this time year and my friend told me that we had to be careful of rattlesnakes in the ditches. I had seen a rattlesnake that a different classmate had in a big jar. It was still alive in the jar.

The last thing I wanted was to meet a real rattlesnake in the tumbleweeds that were scattered in the dried out bed of the irrigation ditches. Life was a big adventure in Coaldale.

Laughter and smiles were found in our house. It was as though everyone finally could breathe a sigh of relief and cherishing hope that we had left all the bad stuff in Ottawa. After we had settled in, we began to have a guest visit our home, a relatively young man who was the local priest. Needless to say Mom and Aunt Denise were thrilled to have him visit. I remember Mom telling me that he would come for hours several times a week because of her cooking. Though Mom forgot quite a few events of our family's adventures, she never forgot about this handsome young, red-haired priest from Saint Ambrose Church, Father Flanagan.

~

During the last ten years, the images from the past became clearer. Many of the scenes of my childhood and youth are captured and are easily played back as I am watching a movie. I had just turned nine years old and the images, sounds and even smells of the time we lived in Coaldale have remained vivid. Perhaps it was the constant promise of a better life that created a sharp sense of presence at that time, perhaps it simply was the fact that the world had radically changed from life in Ottawa to this rural life in southern Alberta that served to embed the memories so deep. I find myself having to limit what I write so that you don't get buried under an avalanche of words. What follows is too vital to get lost in telling too long of a story.

~

Now this priest began to pay special attention to me and told Mom and the other adults in the house that I would make an excellent altar boy. While at the house he would teach me a few of the Latin responses that altar boys would be required to say in a service. Since learning was easy for me, I was quick in picking up these sentences.

After this initial interest in me by the priest, the stories of how our family had accepted years earlier that I would become a priest, Father Flanagan responded by saying that I was a natural for the priesthood. I was required to be beside him every time he came to our house and told to not embarrass the family as it would mean the end of the priest's favour for our family. When this priest suggested that I get special Latin and altar-boy lessons from him at the church, there was no refusing on my part though I was reluctant.

~

By the time we had moved to Coaldale, I had repressed the events surrounding the Catechism lessons and the pedophile priest in Overbrook. Yet in spite of forgetting, there was a distinct discomfort or unease that surfaced, that had me want to refuse becoming an altar boy for Father Flanagan. However, the idea of eventually becoming a priest, the idea seeded within me by my grandmother, was still in my head, an intellectual idea that was more about obeying family need rather than being a passion to become a priest. I assumed that at some point a few more years into the future, I would have to go to a seminary and do the appropriate studies in order to become that family priest. Yet, that shadow crept close when Father Flanagan visited our home sat beside me. When he looked at me, that shadow began to gnaw at me. In spite of my inner reluctance, I responded with my typical unconditional obedience. It was unthinkable for me to rebel against any decisions that my father made on my behalf, perhaps even more unthinkable to rebel against what God wanted from me.

~

But I went as was expected of me, trusting that the adults knew best. That my father and mother thought he was almost a saint and that they looked up to this priest told me that they must be right. If Dad saw the priest a good guy, and Dad was my hero, who was I to think otherwise?

In the church, I remember a darkness, a mood of defeat and resignation that I felt in spite of the white walls. The darkness I felt was reflected in the eyes of the other altar boys, especially as I was called to a back room to be with the priest, alone. It was as though a dark cloud floated in the church, a cloud that stole children's smiles and left small dark holes in their eyes. I didn't realise it then, but the other altar boys knew what was going to happen in that back room. In their eyes was both sadness and strangely, anger – anger that I was potentially going to become the priest's favourite, sadness because they knew I was going to be hurt like they had been hurt.

~

I can't remember much of what happened inside that room. The dominant scene is a swirling mass of heavy and cloying fog. I do know that I dreaded approaching this room. It was as if the world was turning dark, and in the darkness, the pale pink penis and its curly bed of red hair was the only image that has emerged. Perhaps in time, the rest of the scene will unfold. Perhaps with any luck it won't and it has been banished forever. The certainty of being sexually abused in that room is absolute. The smells, the feel, the shadows, the darkness that hovers over the scenes behind the altar are still active though not brought to consciousness, or should I say into the light of the video camera that had captured all the non-threatening scenes before and after. As soon as I stepped out of the church, the images from those days in Coaldale jump into vivid consciousness.

The priest continued to come to our home and wanted me to sit beside him all the time. If anything his laughter and joy at being in our house was greater than before. He would tell all about how smart I was, what a natural I was for the priesthood. My parents glowed as though somehow this was a statement about them as parents than it was about me. If anything, the priest became like a god in our home sitting in the rocking chair and his constant presence and chatter.

I wondered why such a good person would do what he did to me. Was there something about me that caused him to sin? I began to believe that not only was I a sinner damned to go to hell, I was going to be responsible for his sins upon me, that he was the victim of the darkness that was within me, the darkness of my soul that haunted me. The darkness swallowed all the sunshine that might have existed, that must have existed for everyone else to be so happy in Coaldale.

~

And then, the movie stops playing as though life had ceased. It is at this time in my childhood that I began to develop what I can best describe as "black holes" in my memory. Sometime during the early winter, before the New Year, our family left Coaldale, Alberta. Why had we left Coaldale? Since my parents have both died and both Aunt Denise and Uncle Art have also passed away, there is no one to ask about the events that had us leave Coaldale and arrive in Pte. Gatineau, Quebec. Only one "blip" on the inner screen appears from the remainder of our stay in Coaldale, a scene in which Aunt Denise was having her teeth removed so that she could wear dentures.

Part Three

On memory loss and repression:

"Repression causes what is called a systemic amnesia, where only specific memories or groups of ideas are withdrawn from consideration. In such cases a certain attitude or tendency can be detected on the part of the conscious mind, a deliberate intention to avoid even the bare possibility of recollection, for the very good reason that it would be painful or disagreeable."

C.G. Jung

On Rebellious youth:

"Once it has been established that God is the One making the rules, parents must establish in the child's mind that they are God's instruments and will do anything and everything necessary to carry out God's plan for their families. A rebellious child must be taught that God's plan is for the parents to lead and the child to follow. There can be no weakness on this point. The strong-willed child can spot indecisiveness a mile away and will jump at the opportunity to fill the leadership vacuum and take control. The principle of submitting to authority is crucial for the strong-willed child. If submission is not learned in childhood, the future will be characterized by conflicts with all authority, including employers, police, law courts, and military leaders. Romans 13:1-5 is clear that the authorities over us are established by God, and we are to submit to them."

Got Questions Ministries.

Chapter Seven

Memory loss, or as Carl Jung calls it, repression, is a normal strategy that each of us uses in order to escape the parts of our lives that haunt us, that render us unequal to the task of moving forward in life. Jung also goes on to talk about how and when these repressed images tend to re-emerge into our consciousness. The move to get mental health help often creates a safe place where the barriers begin to lower allowing the repressed contents to spill out. When I examine my own experience as a therapist, I have seen this in others who found safety in my office and in my presence. When I examine my own experiences as a client in another therapist's office and then in two Jungian analysts' offices, I begin to accept that the black holes of memory have served me well until it was time to do the work to become a whole person again.

I had been the obedient boy, believing in the authority of adults, priests, teachers, parents, police and all the other adults in my world as a child. I took all the abuse and believed that I deserved what had happened. But that changed in Coaldale. I buried everything away so far that it couldn't touch me anymore and was left with a simmering anger that would leak out. I became resentful and even disrespectful. Since I couldn't blame God or my parents, I blamed others. At home I obeyed but not with the same will to be a good boy while obeying. At school, I took aim at my teacher who would bully me only to have me bully her back.

~

I began to remember in Pointe Gatineau, with a winter scene in which we are living in a white house that has a veranda. It is a Wednesday, a day that had become our day for spaghetti. The image shows us watching television, a program called The Honeymooners. Somehow, Christmas has come and gone without my mental presence.

It was at this point in time that I learned about having nephritis. Mom always was complaining about how everything tasted flat, "tasted like shit." These were the words she would often use because she had to cook with as little salt as possible because of my disease. Anytime anyone complained about the food she prepared, she would always use me and my nephritis as the reason for the food "tasting like shit."

It wasn't until later in the winter with the first melt of snow beginning to happen that my memory returns to what I can consider to be full memory which allows me to see the modern school, a Catholic School, which we are attending. I was in Grade Five just as I had been at the start of the school year in Coaldale. I was the youngest in the classroom because I had done grades three and four in Ottawa the year before. My teacher's name was Mrs. Law, a large lady who wasn't a very happy woman. Scenes in the classroom are filled with Math lessons, Catechism lessons, and English lessons with Mrs. Law teaching all of them. I loved the English lessons as they demanded more of me, especially the weekly memorisation of poetry for recitation at the front of the classroom. Here everyone got to see me as I confidently recited poetry with relative ease in comparison to the other students. However, when it came to Catechism lessons, it was a different story.

The walk to school through the snow was pleasant. Usually, Kevin and I would follow the streets meeting other students along the way. Kevin was quick to make friends and soon wanted to walk with them without having me to look after him. He was confident and impulsive. Since it was almost impossible to get lost along the way, I would fall behind when he met his friends so that he could feel more independent. Yet, I often would catch up when they began to dawdle and get distracted. Every time Kevin was late or in trouble meant that I was in trouble at home for not keeping him in line.

At school, Catechism classes from the Baltimore Catechism booklet were boring for me. Mrs. Law was required to teach these lessons, and it was easy for me to see that she wasn't teaching with confidence. When it was time for Catechism lessons I became sullen, resentful and angry, reactions that were unusual for me in Catechism classes let alone any other subject. At school, as at home, I was always anxious to please, afraid that if I didn't do well, afraid that if I made the teacher mad at me there would be harsh punishment waiting for me at home. But now, it didn't matter. In Catechism classes it was as if a different boy emerged from within me. I challenged the teacher asking questions that I was sure she couldn't answer then I would watch her squirm and either invent answers or simply ignore the questions as though they weren't asked.

Mrs. Law saw what I was doing and began to reprimand me in front of the class for not being obedient and paying attention to what the book said. She told me that my arrogance and pride was a sin and that if I continued to think I knew everything, God would punish me worse than she could ever do. Her threats of Hell had no effect on changing my behaviour. If anything, I became even worse. I began to challenge her with the meaning of Latin expressions and phrases that were part of church services which were conducted only in Latin with the exception of the priest's message from the pulpit. As soon as I found out that she didn't know the English translations, I had more than enough ammunition to humiliate her in the classroom in front of the other students. Father Flanagan had taught me the Latin of mass, the priest's part, the altar-boy's part, and the parishioner's' part. Because I needed to know what the words meant rather than just memorized meaningless responses, Father Flanagan taught me what I needed to know. And it was this knowledge that I took to the classroom as a weapon so as to defeat Mrs. Law.

~

Now, as an adult, I can understand that I was trying to punish Mrs. Law through Catechism lessons because of the harm done to me by Father Flanagan. Mrs. Law was a good teacher that I respected in my other classes and it was only in Catechism classes that the dark side of me made an appearance. I was brutal in my assault and did reduce her to tears, something that got me reprimanded in the principal's office with the strap over my hands, a punishment that didn't cause me to flinch. I had long learned to put up with pain and the pain inflicted by the principal only made for swollen hands. What made it worse for Mrs. Law and the principal was the fact that I was also the youngest and smallest in the class, smallest among the boys. They realised that I needed to have the arrogance dealt with or that I would become a serious problem student for the remainder of my schooling years.

~

On the way to school in late winter, just as the snow began to melt making the world a soggy mess, with Kevin and I wearing rubber boots, we would trek to walk alongside a small creek that was running freely. That creek had been the source of barbotte fish, a catfish that was a treat for us to eat, especially on Fridays. More than once both of us ended up at school with wet feet as the water from the puddles would slip over the tops of our boots. It felt great to be alive with both of us curious about everything we discovered on way to school and back home again at the end of the day.

One day, as we were crossing the small bridge over the creek, somehow my Catechism book fell into the creek. I knew that I had to rescue the book as we couldn't afford to replace a lost school book. I got soaking wet as I had to wade into the creek to get the book. When I arrived at school soaking wet and explained what had happened, I was sent by Mrs. Law to the office.

She didn't want to deal with me, especially as it was the Catechism book rather than any of the other books which had fallen into the creek. In the office, I was again given the strap. The principal said I had deliberately dropped the book into the creek; and, he told that every time I did anything to my Catechism book, or asked any inappropriate questions, or made fun of the teacher, or embarrassed her, I would be given a failing mark in Catechism. What wasn't told to me was that if I failed Catechism class, I would fail the school year in spite of my other marks.

~

I failed Catechism class at the end of the school year. All of my other marks were in the eighties or higher. Strangely, I didn't get punished by my father for this failure of school year. Somehow, my rebellion resulted in a bit more respect from him. Perhaps he saw that I was starting to become less of a sissy, less a little girlish boy, and more of a man. As I look back from today, I recognise the first emergence of what I could best call a shadow personality. I hadn't been a good student, I had consciously resisted – or at least the personality that was activated by a complex being triggered resisted – in spite of knowing there would be consequences. I also learned that life isn't fair, that those who had the power got to make all the rules. And, I also learned that though they might have power, such as Mrs. Law who had the power of the teacher, it didn't protect them from those who knew more than them. I learned that ultimately, it was knowledge that was the source of true power. All I had to learn was how to use this kind of power without putting myself in jeopardy.

Chapter Eight

Before I can go on with the story there is something that needs saying here, something important about the process of this writing and the context within which I am writing. I began to write this story almost twenty years ago while living in Lanigan, Saskatchewan following the suicide of one of my brothers, Gilles. My father had died eight years earlier, an event that had precipitated the beginning of what I then thought was a midlife crisis. My brother's suicide plunged me into a deep depression and I used writing as part of my self-prescribed healing process. What emerged was a twenty-five paged manuscript which I had thought had exposed all of those things that had wounded me as a child. However, with the document done followed by an intensive course of psychoanalysis, it became evident that I had hardly begun the work, that there was so much more to write. Following the death of my mother, I began to be overwhelmed with so much more, so many more memories began to bubble up. I again submersed myself into writing what appeared and the twenty-five paged document became over a hundred pages of remembered scenes.

Today, as I have this last document beside me for a reference point, I have been using meditation and what I will call a form of alchemy as a way to bring clarity and then release from the scenes that have marked me, formed me, and in the process have come so close too often to destroying me. The scene that will be unveiled in the coming paragraphs first came to my awareness on Christmas Day, 2011, just over a month following my mother's death. I was walking home from the Metro store in Changzhou, China where my wife and I were teaching English at a university. We were in our fourth year of teaching at this university. We had just left the store's parking lot with our backpacks filled with our groceries for the week when I just had to stop and sit down.

The scenes which had arrived had shaken me to the core of my being. My wife immediately became concerned, worried that I might have been having a heart attack. When I finally was able to talk, I told her what I had just seen. Strangely, she wasn't surprised and told me to be ready for a lot more to be bubbling up from the past.

The practice of meditation has given me a safe place to meet these scenes over and over again so that I can let them go over and over again with the power of the images to wound me becoming lessened through this "touch and release" of dark stuff from the past. My alchemical work involves laying in the sun long enough in silence, almost like meditation, so that the intense heat stirs up the stuff within that has been percolating below the level of conscious awareness, below the threshold of remembering. As the heat cooks my body, it is as if the effect of my memories are being reduced to ash in the process so that I become freed from shame, shock and fear. I am becoming transformed in the process, ceasing to be a perpetual victim of the past.

Fear! It seemed that life was filled to the brim with fear for me as a child. I feared my father who bounced from positive exuberance to a dark and dangerous anger that found its expression in physical beatings and verbal humiliations. I had come to fear priests, especially those priests who had seen me as special, sometimes even as a prodigy that would blossom with their attention, blossom into another Soldier of Christ in the womb of the Church. I feared bigger children in school who somehow seemed to be drawn towards me, seeing my vulnerability and unconsciously discerning that it was safe to physically punish me as I wouldn't and perhaps couldn't fight back. And, I feared my mother.

Research has repeatedly shown that any child that has been abused has an increased risk for re-victimization. The psychological and behavioural patterns which an abused child has adopted to survive, sets the child apart from his or her peers which then makes the child an easier target.

My mother used the expression that I was an old soul in a child's body. She saw that old soul as the centre of who I was and lost sight of the fact that I was just a child. It was confusing, but at the same time, it made me feel so grown up, so responsible and important. It was difficult to remember that I was just a child and not her equal or her caretaker. In our relationship as mother and child, the child had been banished. Childhood was denied in the rush to have me be a small adult.

~

During the summer of 1959, we moved to Hull, Quebec. Dad had found a job as a city policeman in Hull and that meant we would be economically secure in comparison to the past. We lived only a short distance from Lac des Fées, which soon became Kevin's and my favourite place to be when we were freed from doing things for Mom at home. When it came time to go to school, we had a relatively short walk to Our Lady of Annunciation School another Catholic School on Rue Bisson. I was returning to grade five, Kevin was going into grade three and Béatrice was starting in Kindergarten.

Our house on Rue Dumas was one of the wartime houses of one and a half storeys, a house that was more of a box than we were used to living in. As you entered the front door, the living room was on the left side. One had to pass through the edge of the living room in order to get to the separate kitchen and dining room. The kitchen was to the rear of the house with only the bathroom separating it from the outside wall leading to the back yard. Up the stairs, there were two bedrooms and one bathroom. Gordon, Béatrice, Gilles, Kevin and I shared one bedroom which was above the kitchen and dining room. A bathroom separated our bedroom from the master bedroom which was over the living room, where Mom and Dad slept.

Our house was near the corner making the walk to a nearby IGA for groceries an easy task for me.

Usually I was sent to the store to get small things such as a quart of milk or some eggs or other such items. Whenever I bought things in the store, I was supposed to make sure that I got the grocery stamps which my mother would then paste in her little booklets. The booklets would then be redeemed for items that we wouldn't otherwise been able to get. Since Dad was working at a good job, there was money, more money that we were used to having. But the habit of saving stamps still was viewed with a lot of importance. Sometimes I would forget the stamps as I had bought something that would only have a few stamps given. When that happened, it was as if I had stolen from the family and a beating from my father using his belt would follow.

Close to the end of the summer of 1959, I ended up in hospital with another attack of nephritis. I thought I had a bad case of Poison Ivy from all the time I spent in the bushes around Lac Des Fées. It was only when in the hospital and one of the other patients told me that they heard I was scheduled for a kidney operation that I realised that I was in real trouble. Yet somehow, the day before the scheduled operation whatever it was that was going to require surgery simply disappeared. It was as if my body simply decided it wasn't sick anymore.

~

Following the hospitalization in Hull, Quebec that year, I stopped having issues with my kidneys which had often resulted in bloating, especially on my face. It wasn't until three years later that there was confirmation that there was no more nephritis in my system. But at the time, I suddenly came to realise that I was mortal, that I could die just like a boy with Leukemia had died while in the hospital just a few rooms down the hall from me.

~

As I was getting older, now ten years old, I began to be more responsible with helping Mom with chores.

I would do things such as doing the dishes and cleaning out the bathroom and, of course, taking care of the kids when she wasn't feeling well. Mom was pregnant again and she was often lying down, unwell. I was supposed to keep the kids in the back yard and keep them quiet. I learned how to change diapers and was given the chore of washing the diapers out in the toilet before putting the rinsed out diapers into a pail that was filled with water and Javex so that they were ready for the washing machine. Sometimes as I was rinsing out the cloth diapers in the toilet while flushing the toilet to take away the shit that was clinging, the diapers would plug the toilet. There was a timing that had to be just right in order to avoid this mishap. I wasn't always successful and the stink and mess would soon have Mom screaming at me, then hitting me, and they forcing me to clean up the mess that had been made. I didn't complain as I had made the mess. I only hoped that she wouldn't tell Dad as I didn't want to be on the receiving end of his belt.

Often, once the diapers had been rinsed out and made ready for the washing, after Mom had put the diapers into the ringer washer, she would have me push the diapers through the wringer of the washing machine. I learned by watching her do this, seeing how at times she would have to reverse the wringer when a diaper wound up on the wringer rather than passing through the wringer into the tub waiting on the other side. I wasn't always able to avoid having the diapers finally get into the tub as they would get stuck on the wringer, which meant I was in trouble because I couldn't fix the problem on my own.

~

As an adult, I see these scenes from the past from a different light. My mother was suffering and had just miscarried. Though she had five children already, she hadn't been able to escape her own woundings as a child and youth.

She spent too much time crying at her helplessness, at being an out-of-shape mother to children at a time when she needed caring herself. There was no escape and my father, like her, was too self-focused to see her need or even understand it. Everyone suffered in silence keeping everything locked up tight inside. The slipping into the role of caretaker and pacifier seemed a natural response on my part, a role that I took on willingly as a small, ten year old boy. Perhaps in the role of tiny adult I could atone for my own sins and faults which both my mother and father were so quick to point out and hold up as a good part of the reason we suffered so much as a family.

~

The expectations on me to help became even greater. And with the expectations, more failures on my part to meet all of these expectations resulted in more punishment. I would break a dish while washing dishes, I wouldn't keep the kids quiet enough, and I would ask too many questions. In spite of the punishments, I didn't think of running away anymore. Mom needed me too much; my brothers and sister needed me too much.

As the fall turned to winter, Mom got better; in a better mood as well as better health. Dad's work paid well enough to allow him to buy all of us Christmas presents. Our home became Christmas central for the Laflamme clan.

Kevin and I got some short skis for Christmas, the ones that went on ordinary boots like the felt boots that we wore in winter. We would take the skis to Lac des Fées and climb the short hill and slide down. After quite a few falls, none of them bad as the hill wasn't that steep, we became quite good at doing snowplows down the hill. After a number of visits to the hill, we thought we would try taking the rope tow to the top of the hill and skiing the whole way down. We managed to go up a couple of times successfully but then Kevin caused a panic on the hill as he forgot to let go.

They stopped the tow in time and then had to get him down from the rope as he dangled too near the gears for comfort. Of course Dad found out. That was the end of our skiing. He broke the skis and I got a beating for risking Kevin's life, for not taking good care of him.

We got to host the special "Jour de l'An," the New Year's celebrations with Pépère giving "la benediction paternelle," the New Year's blessing to all in the house. Listening and watching Pépère made me proud to be French Canadian and I thought that perhaps one day I would be the one giving the family blessing to the gathering of the Laflamme clan.

As the spring of 1960 approached, Kevin and I would often get into trouble because we were constantly getting our felt boots wet even though we wore rubber over boots that were supposed to keep the inner boots dry. The problem was our habit of wading through the thick slush and the melting snow in the fields near the lake. When the spring run-off began to flow, we would build slush dams in order to see how high the water would get. Of course we would test the depths and get our felt boots wet. We both got spankings from Dad for this.

Then, the beatings stopped and all we got were slaps, pulled and pinched ears with the threats of worse from Dad when he came home. But, Dad had disappeared from home. I never knew my mother could swear so much or that she could be so vicious. None of the kids were safe from her anger. I found myself taking on more of the household tasks, some basic, washing clothes and hanging them out to dry, and always being on the lookout for trouble. If Mom was upstairs I had the kids stay downstairs or in the yard if it was warm enough out. If she was in the living room on the sofa, I had them play quietly in the kid's bedroom.

I was getting to be quite good in the kitchen heating up corn soup from a can mixed with powdered milk, heating up the powdered milk and putting in broken up bits of bread with a sprinkling of white sugar for a warm breakfast, or filling bowls with puffed wheat for our breakfast. With Dad gone, it was only us kids at the table for most of these meals. Sometimes Mom would give me enough money to buy French fries from the chip truck that would pass our house every so often and that would be our supper. I loved putting these fries on a slice of bread coated with margarine. The margarine was in a bag that needed to be kneaded in order to allow the yellow dye to make the margarine look like butter. Kevin and I had a lot of fun working the bags of margarine to make our butter for our bread. Of course I didn't do all of the cooking, just when Mom was in a mood and had no energy. Some days she would be okay and we'd be okay. But the number of bad days increased the longer Dad was gone.

~

My mother was quite depressed because my father was gone again, depressed because she had lost another baby, depressed because she was getting fat and because she believed that her husband was likely with other women. My father had gone to Alberta, again. For some reason he wasn't working as a policeman anymore in Hull even though it hadn't been a year since he had started being a policeman. I had thought he loved his work, as he was always talking about it, showing off his gun and his handcuffs to us.

~

With Dad gone, Mom would retreat to lay on the sofa during her depressed moments which often lasted several hours. Sometimes I wondered how she could take care of Gilles and Gordon while the rest of us were at school. And at times she didn't as I would find Gordon crying in his crib, his diaper overflowing with shit which had smeared onto the blankets and sides of the crib. Gilles would be silent, just waiting. I cleaned Gordon up as best I could while waiting for the water to boil for Mom's tea.

That was my job, bringing her tea. Kevin did his best to get Gilles and Béatrice playing some game, taking them outside if it was nice while I cleaned up and found out if we were going to have a real supper or heated bread and milk or corn soup.

While navigating around all these things, Mom would often call for me for some reason or other. She often would have me run to the IGA or to do some small task that I wouldn't have thought of on my own. Sometimes she just wanted me there so that I could listen to her. She would tell me of her aches, of her pain, of her loneliness. She would cry as she apologized for my having to do so much around the house and with the kids, cry because she felt so helpless. She would tell me that I was her little man and that she could count on me to never leave her.

~

I was overwhelmed with all of this emotion, all of this disclosure; I knew I was just a kid, that I wasn't a man. But, Mom needed me to be a man, to fill in for our missing father. But sometimes that filling in was a journey into darkness. Many of my memories are triggered by images that come while I am on the edges of sleep, images that wouldn't dare show up when the mind is alert and on guard during the day hours.

~

Mom needed me to go to the store to get her some sanitary napkins. I didn't know what she meant so she wrote it on a piece of paper. She was specific in instructing me to make sure that I got the package that had the small belt that would hold the napkin in place, also telling me the purpose of the napkins. I remember feeling embarrassed as I handed the note to the clerk at the store as if I was doing something I wasn't supposed to be doing, doing something a woman should do for herself.

But Mom wasn't well, so I suffered the indignity of standing there waiting for the product to be brought to the counter. Remembering Mom's instructions, I asked if it included the belt to hold the sanitary napkins in place. The clerk was surprised at the question coming from a small boy.

Taking the package home, I forgot about it until later when Mom again needed my help. She began by showing me how the belt connected to the pads, telling me that if I needed to help her, then I would know what to do. I had to practice until she was satisfied that I would be able to do this task if needed when she was suffering from another migraine during one of her menstrual periods.

~

This remembered scene crossed the line from unacceptable parenting behaviour to incest. I was a young boy being initiated into the mysteries of womanhood that would only be appropriate for a girl almost ready for her own initiation into her pending womanhood. The shift from knowledge into an intimate zone was one that would forever change the mother-son relationship. Yet, this was only the first incidence of remembered incest. The next image was another one of those images that flittered in and out of my mind as I tried to fall asleep an image that I hoped was unreal and would disappear like any false dream image.

~

The kids are upstairs asleep and Mom is talking to me in the living room. I am sitting on an old rocking chair, Dad's favourite chair and Mom is weeping while complaining of how her life was so unfair, so unkind. She cries more as she tells me again that she didn't know what she would do without me, again telling me that I was her little man. She had me come and sit beside her on the sofa where she lay with her head on a pillow which was resting on the arm of the sofa.

She looked pale and wan and seemed to moan as she talked. She caressed my hair as she apologized for being such a terrible mother. She needed me to be strong, to be her man. And then her dress was over her hips and I saw that she wasn't wearing any panties. I quickly turned my eyes away, angry with myself for looking. What was wrong with me? I knew that she was suffering and that she wasn't thinking well. I had seen her pubic are before, when she was teaching me about sanitary napkins, but this was different.

I could feel a tension within me. 'What was going on? Why did she lift her dress? Was she not aware that I could see her sex if I glanced?' I tried not to look but she saw me looking and pulled me closer to her. I could feel her breathing with my head on her stomach. She shifted and my face was between her thighs. She guided my face to her vagina and I found myself struggling for breath as my nose entered into the damp opening. "Oh Laurent," she moaned, "I need you." And then all that remains is darkness, another dark hole that sucked memory from me.

Chapter Nine

The next phase of my life as a child was marked by constant moving from place to place; it was as if we had become gypsies unable to put down roots. We got back together as a family in Standard, Alberta in May 1960, stayed in a farmhouse for that summer, returned to Ottawa, then to Gatineau, Quebec until just after Christmas, then to Guelph, Ontario until April 1961 when we moved to Bassano, Alberta until we moved into Calgary at the end of June. We stayed in Calgary until near the end of October before heading south to Fort Worth, Texas for a while before again relocating to another American city, Salinas, California where we stayed until the middle of January, 1962. We returned to Canada in order to avoid deportation for being illegal aliens. The whole group travelled north to New Westminster, British Columbia for a month before then taking a train to Aylmer, Quebec at the expense of the provincial government that didn't want us on the welfare roll. We stayed in Aylmer where we stayed until the end of the school year. Then it was back to Alberta and a small town called New Dayton for the two summer months before relocating to Bow Island, Alberta where the wandering came to a halt for two years.

~

We moved into a farm yard near the town of Standard, Alberta in early May, 1960. Dad had found a job working for a rancher up in the prairie hills. Kevin, Béatrice and I returned to school in order to finish the year in the small Standard Public School. Kevin, Béatrice and I would ride a school bus to get to the school, a short ride as the farm house wasn't that far from the town. The school was different from anything I had ever experienced to that point in time. Each day, we had to sing a song called the Maple Leaf Forever, while facing the Union Jack flag. I thought I was in a foreign country.

The farm house was big and comfortable, especially the kitchen. We now had a car that Dad would use to get to work. He was working for a rancher and his wife who became great friends of Mom and Dad. The house was in a well-kept farm yard. I can remember going to get potatoes and carrots from a small building that had bins filled with sand that covered the potatoes and carrots, preventing them from getting frozen in the winter or getting too soft in the spring. It became my job to get them when Mom wanted them for cooking.

Sometimes I would walk home from school as it was faster. In the mornings we were the last people picked up on the bus route; in the afternoon we were the last people off the bus. So in poor weather I would take the bus with Kevin and Béatrice. But in good weather Kevin and I would walk to the farmyard on the lookout for any stray pop bottle or beer bottle so that we could trade them in for some kind of treat. Of course, most of that was just wishful thinking most of the time. The bottle money always seemed to be needed by Mom for some needed item or groceries.

The rancher that Dad worked for had his ranch in the hills between Standard and Bassano, Alberta. The call of the open hills and his love of horses made living in the cities of eastern Canada a living hell for him. Dad was a gypsy, or as the French Canadians would call it, a "voyageur." The rancher and his wife would often come to our home for a meal that Mom would cook, meals that featured eggs, hash brown potatoes, chicken or pork; and upon special occasions, her famous spaghetti using hot peppers. On one of the visits we heard about a terrible windstorm that, according to Dad, had been so strong that it would pushed his car backwards if the car's speed wasn't high enough. The story resulted in a lot of laughter. With the stories told, it was time for playing games including Monopoly and various card games. Dad's boss drank a lot of beer, but Dad managed to avoid drinking alcohol.

The truth is, I never saw him drink though I can't say the same for Mom. She had no trouble sharing a bottle of wine with the rancher's wife, sometimes more than one bottle. Mom was happy, dancing around the kitchen and dining room with whoever was closest at hand.

Just before the end of the summer, we again moved because of some argument between my father and his boss, something to do with my father's excessive interest in his boss's wife. It was a hasty retreat to Gatineau, Quebec, to a house on Archambault Street. I don't recall which school I attended that fall. We lived at this large house until just after the New Year of 1961.

Very early in the fall, I went walking with two friends whom I assume must have been classmates, school friends who were girls. We were walking down country roads eating green apples we had taken off a tree that were so tangy that they made one's mouth water with the first bite into the apple. The walk took us past a golf course where Kevin would often sneak off to in hopes of finding some golf balls which he would then sell to the golfers. My friends and I were heading to a farm where we were to get a ride on horses. For one glorious warm fall afternoon we rode down the country road, the three of us, using English saddles, a saddle that seemed rather strange after the time spent in Alberta.

A few weeks later while the weather was still a bit warm. I was in the back yard with Kevin, Réjean and Roland. Dad had somehow obtained a motorcycle, a Norton motorcycle, which he told us was the kind he used to ride while he was in the army in Korea. It was a military motorcycle. At the prodding of the others, I got on the bike, got it started and promptly drove it into the fence. I didn't get hurt, nor did the bike need fixing. However, the fence suffered a bit of damage. Dad laughed and told us to fix the fence. There was no beating as I had been expecting.

Then it was time for Béatrice's First Communion. After she received her First Communion, we all went to Grandpa Schiller's house for a celebratory meal. Photos were taken of Béatrice in her beautiful white dress at the Schiller home. Strangely, the arrival of five children into that home didn't change the atmosphere of the house which was quiet and well-ordered. There were older children already in the house – Robert Jr., Neil and Patela who was a year younger than I was. Yet, in spite of their presence, it was as if the house was a museum in its quietness. It was so quiet I could hear the grandfather clock that stood tall against the wall in the dining room, and the cuckoo clock that had two wooden people dance in and out of the face of the clock. By the fireplace a stuffed collie became the prime prop for Béatrice's photos.

The last scene that emerges in Gatineau was of Christmas morning. After the gifts were all opened, gifts even for Roland and Réjean who happened to be at our house, I was the only one without a gift. Kevin, Béatrice and Gilles had their gifts and were playing with them until Kevin noticed that there wasn't a gift for me. After a long pause, a long silent pause, Dad laughed and told me to go to the basement where my Christmas gift was waiting. I let out my breath and ran down the stairs with the other kids following me. There in the basement was a brand new red bicycle. I couldn't believe my eyes. A Bike, a new bike, my bike! I can still see myself riding around in circles in the basement for the rest of our stay in Gatineau.

Barely into 1961 and we were on the move again. This time it was a bigger move involving not only our family but with Uncle Art and Aunt Denise joining us, as well as Mémère and Pépère with Roland and Réjean. We rented two townhouses that were in the same complex with Aunt Denise and Uncle Art staying in Mémère's house.

Mom was again pregnant with the new baby due to come in June. Kevin, Béatrice and I returned to school, an old school that had the desks bolted to the floor in long rows with the chairs and benches scarred with what was likely many decades of use. It was a public school where I attended grade six, Kevin in grade four, and Béatrice in grade one. Roland and Réjean, also were going to school though not to the small elementary school that we were attending.

While we were in school, Dad, Pépère and Uncle Art, with some help from Réjean and Roland, got busy building a large trailer. The plan was to make it big enough to take all of our stuff to Calgary, Alberta where Dad and Uncle Art were going to start a restaurant business together. They were supposed to take over as owners of a restaurant in Calgary on July 1st. In late April they bought a Volkswagen van so that the whole clan would fit into the van along with our stuff put into the trailer being towed. The idea was to take off as soon as they could, to make the drive and get settled before starting up in the restaurant business.

In mentioning the move to her parents, Mom heard about Granny Schiller's dream that had Dad standing beside the vehicle wearing a certain jacket and with police lights flashing. Nothing else was said about the dream but it was enough for Dad to change his plans. Apparently he had just had that specific jacket mentioned in the dream recently dry cleaned with the intentions of wearing it on the trip. Dad took the jacket and cut it up into strips and told Uncle Art and Pépère to make the drive without him. We would meet up in Calgary as our family would be travelling by train.

~

We got to Bassano, Alberta at the beginning of May after spending a few weeks in a motel in the Bowness area of Calgary. The move to Bassano was made because of the availability of a rental house there and the need to get us kids back in school.

Bassano became our home base for the next two months. It was a big enough house that would hold everyone one the others arrived with the van. We had a house on a beautiful boulevard that was filled with old trees in the median that separated the two halves of the road. The house had a large, airy sunroom with the light pouring into the dining room and living room. When our stuff was finally claimed from the train storage, my new bike was nowhere to be seen. I sort of expected it. Though my parents made protestations that the CPR must have lost the bike, I knew that it had been sold along with most of our other things in order to pay for the train tickets, a cost that hadn't originally been planned for by Dad and Uncle Art.

~

Dad and Uncle Art spent a lot of time in Calgary getting the restaurant they had "bought" ready for business. We expected that come July 1st the restaurant would be open. We also expected Mémère and Pépère to arrive with Roland and Réjean when their schooling was finished. Since Mom was expecting a new baby, I was again busy with taking care of the younger kids. Kevin was a good help as well as he got Gilles busy with various activities and sometimes mischief. Béatrice was still a bit too young to be much help though she did like to play with Gordon when he woke up from naps if he wasn't too cranky. Aunt Denise's task was to humour Mom and keep up her spirits about the great opportunity that was ahead of them. Finally life was going to be fair and we would have nice homes and a secure future.

Mom gave birth to Suzanne in mid-June in Bassano. It wasn't long before she was back in the house and we were playing cards, a game called five hundred was the latest game of choice, a game Mom and Dad had learned from their friend the rancher and his wife back in Standard, Alberta. Somehow whatever it was that had cost Dad his job, had been forgiven so that they resumed being friends, at least for the time we lived in Bassano.

Dad had called his old boss for a bit of work while he was waiting for the restaurant to change hands, and his old boss had agreed. When he worked, Dad was a good worker and help was needed on the ranch.

One day, soon after Suzanne was born, Dad travelled with Uncle Art to Calgary in search of a house. They returned with the news that we had a new home to move into at the end of the month, a house in the Forest Lawn part of the city. Since very little was left of our stuff and most of that still in boxes, moving was an easy and quick task.

~

At the beginning of July, Dad and Uncle Art opened their restaurant, the Pardner's Café, located in the Inglewood district of Calgary, which was not far from the Calgary Zoo. They decided to have the restaurant open twenty-four hours a day in order to capture as much business as they could, especially with summer holidays with the Stampede grounds not too far from the restaurant and the Calgary Zoo even closer. Since I was almost twelve years old, I got to take Kevin, Gilles and Béatrice with me to the Zoo on occasional afternoons when we would otherwise be in the way. Mom stayed in the new house with the baby and Mémère who had finally arrived with her family that was now down to four. Aunt Denise would take her shifts at the restaurant with Roland and Réjean helping out during the rush hours. The restaurant had a good business because of its location on 9th Avenue S.E. near the corner of 12th Street S.E., near the Zoo on St. George's Island.

~

We had just moved into a relatively new home in Forest Lawn, a house with a garage that went under the house. Mom gave birth to Suzanne and was glad to have some adult help from Mémère and Aunt Denise, especially as Gordon wasn't old enough to go to the zoo with us.

During the summer, I found myself helping out a lot at the restaurant, as well as at home. At the restaurant, I got to peel potatoes and then cut them into fries using a chipper, and help out with the dishes. Sometimes I even got to try making meringue for the lemon pies that were a popular desert at the restaurant. I remember getting to eat liver and onions and occasionally kidney stew. Neither of these became a favourite meal, but they weren't all that bad to eat.

As the summer came closer to an end I found myself helping out more and more at the restaurant, sometimes helping with the late shift, usually when Uncle Art was in charge with Roland and Réjean completing the late night crew. As the weeks went on with not much time for sleep, fraying tempers needed the adults to take some time off. Usually Dad and Uncle Art would take opposite shifts, with Uncle Art drawing many of the midnight to dawn shifts. Often Roland and I would help out but it was soon going to come to an end once we were back in school. Roland and I would make the long nights as much of a party as we could, especially when there were no customers. We would play songs on the juke box over and over again singing at the tops of our voices. But when it got late into the night we would often fall asleep in one of the booths. I was glad that we were working with Uncle Art as I knew that it wouldn't have been allowed with Dad.

~

I was old enough to realise that different adults had different perceptions of what was right and wrong. I was also old enough to do real work and have that work recognised though without getting paid for that work. The recognition was more important to me at that time than money was. I was given money from time to time from the till with the thanks. For the first time I began to have confidence in myself, to have self-respect.

~

It was time for school to start. I went to a junior high school in Forest Lawn to start grade seven while Kevin, Béatrice, and Gilles attended the elementary school that was near the house. Réjean and Roland went to the Forest Lawn High School which was near the house. Since I entered the school at the same time as all the other grade seven students, with no history for the most part, I was able to make a small circle of friends. It helped that the kids thought our family was relatively well off since we owned a restaurant. I would hang out with a group of boys who would gather under a fire escape to talk about anything and everything. Like young boys on the verge of puberty everywhere, there was a lot of talk about women and sex, especially when one of the boys would have snuck a wrinkled Playboy magazine out to prove just how much he really knew. For the most part, no one really had any ideas. As for me, I would simply remain quiet, the quiet and mysterious boy.

Of course we liked the girls in our class though we were often too scared to even say 'Hi' to them. I was surprised one afternoon when one of my classmates, a girl called Theresa, invited me to her place for her twelfth birthday party. When I asked Mom and Dad if I could go, I was pleased and surprised when they said yes. The day of the party arrived and I went to the party wearing a tie and carrying my small present. Needless to say, I was the only one wearing a tie. When some of the boys started to laugh about my tie, Theresa told me they were just jealous of me. She was beautiful and she liked being near me. The party was a time of magic as we played games and ate cake and watched as she opened her presents. My present wasn't big or expensive, just a simple small bottle of cheap perfume. But that didn't matter as she opened the bottle to smell it and then put a little on her neck like I always saw Mom do. She smiled at me and sat next to me as we played the last game of the party, a game of spin the bottle.

When it was her turn, I saw her cheat as she stopped the bottle as it pointed at me. I couldn't believe it. She wanted to kiss me. And so, I experienced my first real kiss, not the kiss of a mother or an aunt or of Mémère. A girl wanted to kiss me and I fell in love with her.

With summer over, the restaurant was not very busy. The tourist season had given everyone high expectations and money had been spent as if the income from the restaurant would hold up with the end of tourist season. Nothing had been set aside. However, with money coming in much more slowly, the arguments about the restaurant and bills grew in intensity. It didn't help that Aunt Lola, another one of Dad's sisters, had also arrived with her young family. It wasn't long before Aunt Lola and Uncle Fern were settled into hastily constructed bunk beds in the basement of our house in Forest Lawn. It seemed that the whole basement was filled with these rough beds with very little in the way of room dividers to mark the space for one family or another. Of course all the kids were in the basement with the three upstairs bedrooms for Mom and Dad, Uncle Art and Aunt Denise, and Mémère and Pépère. The arguments grew more and more intense making the atmosphere that fall very toxic. Even the kids were fighting, constantly bickering and crying.

At night, in the basement, the fact that there was little space due to the fact that the garage took up a good part of the basement made the lack of privacy an issue. There were no walls, just hastily put up sheets to divide the small space into bedrooms filled with beds that creaked when one just breathed.

One image that emerges from this mayhem, this time of anger and confrontation, was that of Roland and Réjean fighting in the driveway in front of the garage doors. The fists flew with intent to do real harm; I saw them trying to bash each other's head into the pavement.

While this was going on I heard a scream and saw Mémère racing out of their injuries if that made any sense. The boys stopped their fighting and soon found themselves fending off the blows from their mother as she hit them over and over again with a broom. Roland was a lot like my Dad, an extrovert who loved being at the centre of attention; and Réjean was a lot like Pépère, quiet and small and on the sidelines almost unseen. And already, I felt that Réjean was the most like me simply because like me he was small and quiet and tried to stay hidden on the sidelines.

~

Amid all the chaos, life was getting darker and darker for me. Nights were turning into times of dread, of nightmares that disturbed any hope of sleep. It was as if I was drowning in the darkness, if I was being sucked into evil. Becoming aware of what was happening under the cover of darkness in the basement crowded with people made my nightmares even worse. I became part of that darkness, crossing the line from protector to abuser of my brother who had always looked up to me as a hero. I became aware of just how much I had hurt my brother just a few years ago when talking to him after many years of no contact. He wondered why I had sexually abused him, a question I couldn't really answer as so much had still been locked away within the dark holes that hid so much of my past.

~

Sometime in October, in spite of the poor business at the restaurant, Dad bought a truck and a cabin trailer, something I had not really seen before except on TV. The mood around the house began to change; there was an excitement in the air.

Uncle Art and Aunt Denise were still trying to make a go of the restaurant, but it was as if everyone else had already given up on it and were now the house to add to setting off again on another gypsy adventure. There were still arguments, but they didn't get to the same level of heat and bitterness. Then, one morning in mid-November, we packed up and left.

Chapter Ten

The four months spent in Calgary was a point in my life that saw a shift within me. I had somehow broken through the thin membrane of my family and discovered a separateness to myself that could exist without the family. I had found a girlfriend who showed me that I existed outside of the family and that I was worth liking-loving. I had experienced another adult's approach to me through my Uncle Art that was softer and less judgmental. And, I had experienced a deeper kinship with my two young uncles, Réjean and Roland that demanded nothing of me other than being with them as an equal. My relationship with my own siblings was more as a guardian and caretaker than it was of being a brother. This was new territory for me, having older brothers who simply accepted me as I was.

~

I was caught by surprise. A big argument between Dad and Uncle Art over the unpaid bills at the restaurant, as well as unpaid rent had Dad decide it was time to leave Calgary. I had the feeling that he had been planning this for a while as he had just bought a small travel trailer. One morning we woke up, and like every other morning, Uncle Art went to work at the restaurant. Almost as soon as he was out the door, Dad had us gather essential clothing to put into the trailer as we were leaving. I didn't have time to goodbye to Theresa, or to get her address so that we could write back and forth to each other. I didn't get to say goodbye to my new friends at school. I was angry, a silent angry. As with the times in the past, we left the house as if we were being chased. I began to suspect that we were indeed being chased as I knew that bills hadn't been paid at the restaurant for quite some time and that the half-ton truck and trailer weren't paid for either.

We were escaping, not racing towards a new dream. I didn't know where we were going and assumed that like always in the past that we were heading back to Ottawa.

The family made a small caravan with Pépère driving his car and Dad driving the truck pulling the trailer. Uncle Fern and Aunt Lola rode with Mémère, Pépère and Réjean. Roland rode with Mom and Dad in the cab of the truck. All of the kids, except Suzanne and Aunt Lola's baby, rode in the trailer. I was to take care of all the kids in the trailer. For some reason, we didn't take the main highway out of the city, going east back towards Ottawa, or west heading for Vancouver. We headed south on Highway 2. Before too many hours, we got to Fort McLeod where we stopped for a late breakfast at a gas station café.

The ride as far as Fort MacLeod hadn't been all that bad as the kids had soon fallen asleep. I had huddled beside the window watching as the miles slipped by. While we were stopped at the café, Mom had me give the kids some cereal for breakfast rather than take them all into the café. She told me that we would all eat supper at a restaurant later that day, and that I should just give the kids some peanut butter on bread when they got hungry in the afternoon. I didn't protest. I knew that it was useless to protest and that it would only result in some sort of physical punishment and more humiliation. And, at that time, I just didn't care anymore. What was the point? I had lost everything that I had come to value while we were in Calgary.

~

I felt the first conscious experience of loss. I had invested in my school, in my friendships that were still being made, in my opening up of my heart to a young girl; I was being forced to leave all of this, to lose all of this. It was at this time that I became aware of being powerless and at the mercy of my father's whims, and I was angry for all that I was losing and for being powerless.

And, in that realisation of my powerlessness, I sank into a depression.

I thought we had finally found a home and I had risked making friends at school, had opened myself to hope. I was twelve years old, old enough to be aware of what was going on, yet not old enough to assert much control of my own life. Had I any way of living on my own to continue going to school in Calgary, I would have walked away from the family. And the realisation that I was helpless left me retreating to an inner place where I could hide and protect myself from the pain of losing hope.

~

The novelty of riding in the trailer had worn off and the kids were cranky. As the miles continued to be covered, I began to hate being stuck with the kids, and I am sure the kids felt it. Soon there was shit all over the place. One of the smallest ones in the trailer had crapped and it was falling out of the diaper and I hadn't responded soon enough to deal with it as I had been sulking in a corner by the window. When the trailer finally stopped so that Dad could get gas for the truck, I got in trouble when the trailer door was opened and Mom was met by a barrage of crying and the smell of shit. We stayed long enough at the gas station for me to clean up the trailer as best I could, using rags and paper towels and hot water from the gas station. In case that wasn't enough of a punishment, I got a few extra slaps and threats to make sure that I didn't screw up again.

As promised, we got to join the adults eating in the restaurant. I can remember the noise of the restaurant, the juke box blaring as we sat along the long straight counter. We had only travelled 300 miles but that journey had taken a lot of hours as it was now dark out though it wasn't late. After eating, we stopped at a motel for the night as it was too cold to sleep in the trailer.

The next day we continued our journey to the south heading to Wyoming hoping to make it to Denver, Colorado. The weather turned bad as we found ourselves in a snowstorm which slowed us down quite a bit. Once we ran into mountains, Dad had to stop and put winter chains on the truck tires in order to pull the trailer up the mountain roads. At one point, Dad had to get Réjean, Roland and Uncle Fern to push the trailer so that the truck could make it past one slippery part that had a layer of snow covering the road. Eventually, the caravan made it to Casper, Wyoming where we stopped in order to allow some time out of the vehicles for tempers to cool down and the tension of winter driving in the mountains to ease. And so, we checked into another motel.

The drive to Denver the next day was difficult and long so it was decided that rather than continue going straight south, we would head east and then south again, going to Wichita, Kansas. Everything then became a blur for me. Sometimes Mom would come into the trailer with the baby and I would get to go in the truck to ride and with Dad. When this happened I would stare out the front window. Eventually we made it to Wichita with the decision to rest there for the night before heading on to Texas.

~

My father found a cheap motel in Fort Worth, Texas where he decided we were to stay for a while so that the adults could check out the job situation. He booked two long-stay suites with kitchens as we couldn't all fit into one suite. The trailer and truck were sold and replaced by an older car. The money left over was used to finance our stay in Fort Worth. The idea that the truck and trailer hadn't been paid for didn't matter since there was no intention in returning to Calgary where creditors were owed too much. My father never looked behind at the mess he left behind. There was just the chasing of his dreams of fame and fortune.

How long we stayed in Fort Worth ended up being a mystery to me. Though I was old enough to remember everything, it wasn't long before all memories stopped only to restart in late December as we were driving through New Mexico on our way to California. I can only attribute this complete blacking out of most of our time in Fort Worth as the result of suffering from a concussion. Before the blackout, I have vivid memories which included a large family meal with Uncle Fern and his family, Pépère and his family and all of our family, an American Thanksgiving meal. When the memories return, Uncle Fern and his family were no longer with us.

~

We were sitting at a table having a meal. Uncle Fern was our family joker, the small man who loved to play pranks and tricks and get everyone laughing. One of his usual tricks was to sneak up behind one of the kids and stick a wet finger into one's ear and turn his finger as if drilling into the head while he laughed. The meal was a festive affair which reminded me of Thanksgiving as we had a turkey on the table which Dad had carved up. Uncle Fern snuck up behind me, stuck his wet finger in my ear and made a buzzing sound as though drilling into my brains. Everyone laughed including me. Then, a few moments later when everyone's attention returned to the meal and the conversation, and feeling a bit brave, I decided to do the same thing back to him. I got up from my chair and while he was talking to Dad and Aunt Lola, I stuck my finger in his ear and made a buzzing sound expecting laughter as a result.

Before I could finish the trick Dad was beside me. With a mighty heave he sent me flying across the room. "You disrespectful little bastard! What the fuck do you have for brains? That isn't the way you treat your uncle." Silence. All conversations had stopped. Then I felt the breath coming back into my body, I stumbled up and ran as best I could while wishing I was invisible, wishing I was dead.

Fear. I tried staying out of the way as much as possible especially as tempers once again began to flare up. The safest thing to do was to stay in the shadows unless Mom needed me to do things for her, usually about taking care of my brothers and sisters. I took them to play in the small, duty playground near the motel or else watched them as they sat in front of a small television in one of the motel rooms while the adults were in the other motel room.

One day during a hot afternoon, I had decided to take a shower after everyone else had taken their showers and the bathroom was free. I always waited until everyone was done before I took my turn. Somehow it got to be expected by others that they always came first. It was a belief that had become deeply embedded within me. I had barely got into the shower when Mémère decided she needed to go to the bathroom. She mentioned it to Dad while also mentioning that I was in the shower. Rather than telling me to hurry up and get out so Mémère could use the toilet, Dad stormed in, hauled me out of the shower and in a fit of anger threw me across the room. Of course I had no clothes on and the room was crowded with most of the adults and some of the kids. I sat dazed for a bit before I realised that I was naked and that everyone was looking at me. All I could think about as I covered my genitals with my hands was of being ashamed. Somehow I had done everything wrong and everyone could see my shame, my nakedness. But, before I could get far, my father caught me. I saw pure fury in his face and eyes, and then all went dark.

~

I don't know when we left Fort Worth. No memories are found until a place called Deming, New Mexico. As a boy just beginning puberty, one who was self-conscious almost to the extreme, to be violently exposed had me retreat even more into my shell like some turtle.

It wasn't that nudity was considered so shameful, but rather more about being exposed as defective being, not worthy of regard or respect, worthy only of abuse.

It was in a small café where I find myself coming back into awareness. Perhaps it was the taste of hot chili which we were eating at the café that brought me back into my body and awareness; perhaps it was just a matter of time for the effects of a concussion began to wear off. Even with that return to awareness, there are only a few brief snapshots of memory to be accessed as though I was coming into awareness and retreating back into unconsciousness. The drive through New Mexico and its mountains and the desert of Arizona, before reaching San Diego, California only have one other brief moment of awareness, a moment where we had stopped in the desert while in Arizona to see an armadillo.

~

We arrived in San Diego on a bright, sunny and hot day. Dad got two rooms at a motel for Pépère's family and our family. The four adults decided to go into Tijuana, Mexico while the rest of us were left at the motel. The adults told us that we would be going to the beach the next day as a treat, so that we could swim in the Pacific Ocean in January. We got to drive along the ocean all the way to Los Angeles with stops along the way to check out the beaches. The adults were happy and there were no more arguments.

We arrived in Los Angeles late in the evening and Dad again booked us into a motel. Because it wasn't late, Roland and Réjean decided we could go check out the neighbourhood. They had seen orange trees not too far from the motel and decided that we could pick a few to take back to the motel.

We found the orange trees and saw that there was a fence that we had to get over to get the oranges as well as some grapefruit that were also growing in the small fruit orchard in the yard.

I was boosted over the wall so that I could open the gate and let them into the garden. No sooner had I landed in the yard when there was a loud racket. A pair of geese began to protest with a barrage of angry honking and charging at me. I quickly ran out of the gate before we could pick any of the fruit. The three of us had a good laugh as we walked a bit further where we found more fruit trees that provided us with more than enough oranges and grapefruits for the family that evening.

We only stayed there in Los Angeles the one night. We knew that we were near Disneyland, so Dad decided to drive by the Disneyland site as close as we could so that we could say we were there at Disneyland, before he drove on to our planned destination, Salinas, California.

~

My memories continued to be spotty though not so bad in Salinas. We stayed in Salinas for some time as my grandparents, my father and my two young uncles went to work harvesting vegetables – carrots, cauliflower, and other crops. My mother stayed at the motel which was in a desert-like setting.

~

There were other families staying there as well, other families of migrant field workers. Like us, the children of these families weren't in school. Our meals were mostly pinto beans and whatever vegetables that were brought back to the motel from the fields. If we wanted to watch television, we had to put a quarter into a meter connected to the television. Usually, it was only for football games such as the Cotton Bowl, the Orange Bowl and the Super Bowl that saw my parents spend money on the television.

Kevin and I began to hang out with some of the other boys in the motel park. Most of the kids there were Mexicans and couldn't speak any English.

However, there were enough English-speaking kids there to play with for us. The younger kids didn't have any trouble with playing with the numerous younger Mexican kids, but for Kevin and me, it wasn't really a matter of choice. The English-speaking kids didn't want us to hang out with the Mexican kids who in turn didn't trust us because we were Gringos. In the end, it wasn't long before Kevin and I were on the outside of the English-speaking kids because we were foreigners, not Americans.

~

It wasn't long before tension again filled the air. In the second week of January, we left in a hurry trying to stay ahead of immigration authorities. I have to admit that I was glad that we were again on the road, again staying just a few steps ahead of whatever it was that was chasing my father. I had been in a fight, and lost, with the American kids at the motel. I was a stranger in their country and didn't belong – I didn't want to belong. I just wanted to be somewhere else.

This was the first time in my life to that point that I had been out of school so long, more than two months of the school year had been spent in motels from Montana to California, never long enough to find even a thin tendril of roots, not even a remote chance of being able to deceive myself that there as a chance for any of these places to become a home so that life could return to some sort of normalcy, even if a very dysfunctional normalcy.

~

It was near the middle of January, 1962 when we left Salinas, again on the run. We travelled north, my father hoping that we would escape notice of any immigration authorities along the way and arrived in Vancouver not many days later. The first stop was to a welfare office as we had run out of money.

A house in New Westminster was made available for us with the requirement that Dad would put us back in school while the paperwork was done to have us sent back to eastern Canada by train. Roland and Réjean also had to go back to school. Roland was put into grade nine and I returned to grade seven, both of us going to the same junior high school. Réjean went to a different school as did Kevin, Béatrice, and Gilles who had begun the year in Grade one in Calgary. Gordon and Suzanne were too young for school.

Finally, back in school, I returned to life; I came back to wanting to be present. I revelled in the opportunity to be again with books and to learn how to play a few tunes from the Sound of Music on a recorder in my music class. Then, caught by surprise as no one had told us about the coming train ride back to the east, that school disappeared from my life as we found ourselves being herded into a sleeping car on a Canadian National train. I didn't know why we were leaving or where we were going. I was in shock. It was only while we travelled through the mountains and then the snow-covered prairies that I heard we were going to Aylmer, Quebec, a town I had never been to before, a town just a little west of Hull, Quebec.

~

Today, as I read what I wrote and take some time to try and piece together the frenetic movement of my family and how it was aiding in the formation my disconnected way of being with others, I find it hard to hold it all together as being real, as actually happening as I remembered it. Each of us needs to be in relationship to others in order to discover one's own reality. Without the opportunity to do this self-identity work in a rooted outer world container, one turns inward in search of self-identity, and in the process, one typically tilts out of balance.

I see now part of the reason why I am so slow to connect with others and why I sit on the sidelines as though life belongs to others because I am an outsider just passing through town. My present way of being didn't change very much even though I now understand how I adapted and why I adapted to life. However, I have learn to be easier on myself, gentler with myself when I catch myself again sitting, disengaged, on the sidelines.

~

In Aylmer life started to settle back down and I returned to school. Again, because of the conflict in educational systems between provinces, I found myself back in grade six in a split classroom. My math teacher noticed at some point that I knew as much if not more than the grade seven students did in Math, but it didn't matter as far as the system was concerned. Grade seven in other provinces was considered like grade six in Quebec by the school system. I didn't protest as I knew it wouldn't do me any good. If anything, making a fuss would only make it harder and perhaps even backfire. So, I buried myself in school work after having basically missed almost four months of schooling that year.

We lived in a walk-up flat on the second floor of a two-story building. The stairwell was on the outside of the building and it led to a semi-covered porch from which we entered the apartment. We were beside the parking lot of a nightclub of sorts, a place of live music and noisy people enjoying their evenings with booze and entertainment. It was February and it was very cold with snow and ice making the walk up and down the stairs to our flat a risky activity. Our apartment was heated by a coal oil heater which required frequent trips to a nearby store where coal oil was bought and put into a tin fuel tank with a handle for carrying. It was my job to get the fuel from the store and carry it up the stairs to our apartment and then fill the tank of the oil stove.

The oil can was heavy when filled, heavy for a small boy which was what I was. I always struggled as I carried the filled tank up the slippery steps to the apartment. It seemed that we always ran out of fuel after school when it was dark outside and it was hard to see properly in the poor light. One evening, the steps were slipperier than usual and by the time I struggled to the top of the stairs I was totally worn out. I was unprepared for the ice patch by the apartment door and I fell. As I fell on the ice, the coal oil tank tipped over. Down the side of the building went the heating oil for our stove. I panicked as I worried that with the side of the house now covered in coal oil, the place could catch fire easily. My fears were echoed by Mom and Dad. Not only had I put the lives of the family at risk, as well as the family who lived on the ground floor, I had wasted oil and money. Again I see and hear the fury in my father, and again I disappeared into darkness.

When my memories return, it was already spring and Dad was gone. I had no idea when he left. I learned that he had returned to western Canada, back to Alberta where he was taking a course in order to be an Alberta Municipal cop, sort of like a provincial police force officer. Somehow, I had made a few friends somewhere along the way, in Aylmer in spite of my being unaware of the passage of time since the heating fuel accident. I have an image of about four of us, two boys and two girls, sitting outside the back door of the nightclub, singing the songs being played in the building. It was obvious that I was having a good time, with these memories. I must have told them of my previous intention of being a priest for the guy in the group asked if I was still going to be a priest. I can still hear my response to his question, "No, I like girls too much, so I could never be a good priest." The girls laughed and then we sang along to more of the songs coming from the club.

Music became a big part of my life while in Aylmer. Every chance I got I would sit outside the back of the nightclub listening to the songs. I listened to the radio in hopes of hearing those songs and others and eventually learned the words so that I could sing along to almost all of the songs. The weather was warm as spring turned into summer. I remember taking Kevin and the rest of the kids to a place along the parade route for the June 24th celebrations just before we got on a bus to leave Aylmer in order to rejoin Dad in Alberta. In Québec St. Jean Baptiste Day was bigger than July 1st in Ottawa. I was a noisier and happier celebration with the fleur de lys flags on poles, on houses, and being carried by those in the parade, as well as being held by most of the people watching the parade. The pride of being Quebeckers was strong. School has just finished, and this was our last day in Aylmer.

~

One school year in which we got to go to school for six of the ten months of a school year, a period of time in which we lived in Calgary, Fort Worth, Salinas, New Westminster, Aylmer, and our final stop for the year in New Dayton, Alberta – the impact on all of us going to school would mark us forever. And it wasn't just a negative impact on learning, it was the lack of people skills, skills needed to connect with others in a safe and healthy manner that became part of our ways of being in relation to others.

My mother took us to New Dayton, Alberta by bus where my father had rented us a place to stay until he finished his course and was given a posting. We arrived a few days before school let out in the tiny, dusty, windswept village of New Dayton. It was hot, very hot.

While we were in New Dayton, my father visited a few times on weekends.

He was filled with all sorts of dreams of how good life was going to be a soon as he got his posting. But, neither Kevin nor I believed in him or his dreams anymore. Trust had been broken too often leaving us broken a bit more each time we had to uproot ourselves. The only thing we could trust was our eyes when we woke up in the morning, eyes that would tell us where we were. Belief in the past and in the future was abandoned for a necessity to be in the present, a present that was very unpredictable and unreliable.

~

The air smelled a bit strange at the edge of the town, a fact that was due to the alkali sloughs and the sulphur smell that came from the water pump in the kitchen of the small house Dad had found for us. Alongside the house was a bunch of bleeding heart plants which I had to make sure that the smallest kids didn't try to eat as they were considered poisonous. When Gilles and Gordon were outside, I took them to play at the edge of the Caragana bushes in the tall grass, away from the Bleeding Heart plants. Gordon was getting good at hiding and not always squealing on himself when someone came near. Gilles somehow managed to hide quite well, usually close to the safe zone, staying quiet. Playing kick the can was Gordon's favourite game, but not Gilles' as he invariably got caught because of a brace he wore on one leg because of polio. When Kevin or I was "it" he was always able to make it to home base safely. We played another game called Anti-Anti-I-Over and soon had some of the local kids come over to see what all the noise was about and then joining us in the fun. No one had any ball gloves but it didn't matter. As long as we could play outside, nothing mattered.

Mom stayed in the house in spite of the heat, always complaining of the flies, the smell and about how noisy we were.

It was easy for me to tell that she was depressed and stressed out with Dad being away. Dad had come home the first weekend we were there and then stayed away until the end of July when he returned driving a car, a fifty-six Ford that was white and blue. He talked to Mom and us about the two jobs that were opening up for September and the likelihood that he could get either one of these jobs, and that the choice was basically his to make. He left us at the end of the weekend promising to be back in three weeks with more information and that we should be ready to leave for our new home.

In New Dayton, my memories began to strengthen and hold. I made friends with a boy from another large family that was also on the edge of the town, but closer to the highway and Main Street. Many afternoons the two of us, along with Kevin and one of my new friend's brothers, would walk along the edge of the highway in search of beer bottles and pop bottles. Whenever we managed to find enough, we'd head off to a dusty looking café that was run by a Chinese man. Inside of the dimly lit café with its wooden plank floor boards, we would spend a long time looking at the few choices of cheap candy that were available to us. Finally we would make a choice and then sit outside, slowly savouring the candy, trying to make it last as long as possible.

I learned how to use a slingshot in New Dayton, one that was made from a piece of Caragana bush and a thin band of inner tube. We would chase gophers that were abundant, around the edges of town, never actually hitting any in spite of all of our efforts. One day, a boy from a different family, decided to make fun of us and I got angry at him and fired off a small pebble using the home-made slingshot. I was surprised and scared when the rock actually hit the boy, but perhaps not as surprised as the boy who fell off the bike he was riding. Thankfully no one got hurt and no adult was told. For some strange reason, the boy joined in our little group after that incident as a new friend.

Near the end of July, we made a group bicycle ride to Raymond. Mom had given Kevin and me permission to go to Raymond with the other boys in order watch a movie at the cinema theatre as my birthday present. Kevin and I rode on borrowed bikes and made the long ride which took us almost two hours as it was ten miles to Raymond. One of the other boy's dad was going to pick us up after the movie with his half ton and bring us and the bikes back to town in time for supper. It became quite an adventure and in the end, in spite of the pain Kevin and I felt on our butts from the bike seats, it was well worth it. Needless to say we stopped often along the way for rests and for a bit of exploring of the prairie.

Near the end of August, Dad came in his new car to get us and what little bit of stuff we had taken with us on the bus from Aylmer. He had taken the job in Bow Island and had already rented a house in which we were to live. Now with school just about to begin, he decided it was time for us to join him. I was sad to see the end of the friendship with the boys in New Dayton, for I knew that I would never see them again.

Chapter Eleven

The move to Bow Island was a turning point in my life. I had somehow become immune to the spells that my father would create. I had lost most of my respect for him, had lost trust in him, and all that remained was fear. Perhaps it was because my father was distant from us even though we were now all back in the same house.

~

We had a nice older white house on a corner lot with a big vegetable garden area and a young family of Mormons living next door to our place. There was a set of French doors that separated the living room from the kitchen and dining area in our house. It wasn't really that big of a house, but it was big enough with three bedrooms, the biggest house we had ever lived in with just our own family. It wasn't long before we discovered the garden area which was mostly covered with weeds, and a few rutabagas which were rather interesting to eat when we peeled them. However, the novelty wore off and they became just another vegetable that soon found its way into a lot of our meals until there were none left in the garden.

While waiting for school to start, Kevin and I explored the town, especially Main Street. We often took Gilles along with us as he was getting to be too much of a handful for Mom. Gilles was an angry boy. As we walked the streets, other small kids, and some not so small, would see Gilles with his awkward gait as he motored along with his braces on his one boot and leg. He retaliated by trying to kick his tormentors, or kick anything else in his reach including dogs.

The kids who lived next door were younger than I was, so I didn't become friends with them. I am not sure about Kevin, Béatrice, Gordon or Gilles though.

The neighbour's house was a disaster area, a messy house that gave the idea that the mother had given up and just didn't care anymore. Religion was the drug of choice that made everything just fine. I remember frequently hearing from our neighbours about their church, their bible, their God and the fact that they were being saved. It was as if they wanted us to believe what they believed, to save us from our religion which was Satanic in their minds, to save us from going to hell with all the other Catholics.

~

Religion was important in Bow Island. It seemed that there were three distinct groups, Christians, Protestants and Catholics. People were blocked into their religion and the lines were hard to cross socially. Since we were Catholics, we were registered with the Catholic school, St. Michaels. On the first Sunday we were in Bow Island, Dad took most of us to the Catholic Church. After the mass was done, my father introduced me to the priest and told him about my learning Latin to be an altar boy, my ability to sing, and the fact that one day I was going to be a priest. I hadn't yet told my father about my decision to not go to a seminary and become a priest. At that moment, I knew that I couldn't say anything to contradict him, especially in a public place such as in front of the church with so many other people hanging around to see the new family and perhaps talk to the priest as well. When the priest laughed saying that he especially needed a few new voices for the church choir but that he didn't need another altar boy at that time, I felt a wave of relief was over me. A choir was a safe place in which to take part in the Church. And so, with fear abated, I smiled and said I would love join the choir.

~

I got to meet a few of the local boys late that summer when I was downtown coming out of the police station after getting a tour of the small building and then washing the floors of the main office as well as the jail cells. It was our second day in Bow Island. The boys asked if I was the cop's kid and if I wanted to hang out with them sometimes so I said yes. The next day was a Saturday, and school was to start only three days later, so they suggested we could go to a local dugout to swim. I told them I would meet them tomorrow at Dad's office and go with them. Of course I asked Dad after the boys left just to be on the safe side in case he had other plans for me. He said I could hang out with the boys but I couldn't swim in the dugouts as I would get the itch and he didn't have the money to waste on dealing with the itch.

The next day I joined them. Before we went to the dugout, they showed me the highlights of Bow Island as it was just a short way from the town to the dugout. When it came time for swimming, they took off their clothes to go skinny dipping, I quickly doffed my clothes just like them, but when it came to getting in the water with them, I stopped. I could hear Dad's voice in my head and I knew that he would know if I went into the water. Fear stopped me cold. I stood there near the dugout without clothes and finally said that I couldn't go in as I didn't know how to swim. The boys didn't laugh at me. Seeing me naked and already showing pubic hair was proof enough for them that I wasn't a coward. The boys didn't tease me even though they knew I wasn't going to go to the same school as them. Sometimes kids aren't mean.

I didn't mind having to wash the floors at the police station as it got me out of the house and out of taking care of kids. I got to meet Dad's assistant, the constable, Bruce. It turned out that Bruce lived with his parents less than a block from our place on the western side of the town. Their house was a very nice modern, brick house with big spruce trees in the front yard.

Then it was time to go to school. I remember walking with Kevin, Béatrice and Gilles down the street to the school. Gilles was kicking at my feet and Kevin's feet as he didn't want to go to the school. He knew that the kids would make fun of him and his brace and big boot. I tried calming him down telling him that it would be okay, better than at the Public School. Catholics were nicer people. We got to the school early and stood around watching the other kids meeting and greeting each other. We didn't know anyone, so we just watched. Finally, a couple of small boys came over, curious about the boot and brace that Gilles was wearing. When I told them that it was because Gilles had had Polio when he was a little boy, the boys looked at Gilles as some sort of hero and asked him to play with them. As he ran-hopped alongside the two boys, it was easy to tell that going to school was going to be okay for Gilles.

At school, I realised that being a Catholic in a Protestant town meant that I had something in common with my other classmates even though I had no shared history in the school or town. That Dad was the chief constable in town added to welcome that I received. Dad had been making a good impression on the town. It wasn't long before I made friends in my classroom, with two boys and a girl. The boys were unique individuals in the classroom. Peter Z. was a big boy who was sixteen years old in grade seven, his younger sister Shirley was also in the same classroom and was the opposite in every way. He was a very big boy and she was petite. Their parents had a restaurant next to the bowling alley on Main Street. The second boy, Toni was a tall boy who was the same age as I was.

Where I was short, less than five feet tall and slight, he was tall, more than six feet tall, and slight. Toni was a fanatic of anything to do with electronics and so we often found ourselves after school in the TV and radio repair shop, when we weren't at the restaurant owned by Peter's parents.

Shirley became my girlfriend by default. As boyfriend and girlfriend, we weren't what one thinks of as boyfriend and girlfriend. We didn't hold hands or kiss or say silly love things to each other. She was Peter's sister and he was my best friend. Being boyfriend and girlfriend for us simply meant that we were friends and that we didn't have to be more than just friends until we were older.

I enjoyed school that first autumn and worked hard to have the teacher's approval and do well. Soon I was back at the top of my class, often getting perfect scores in English and History tests. Toni had the highest marks in Math and Science and that inspired me to work harder to stick near him. I soon learned that Peter was still in grade seven for a good reason – he was a slow learner. In spite of that, Peter was a gentle giant in the class, one of the nicest kids I had ever met.

It wasn't long after I started school when I took my first English test results to show Dad at the police station. I had a 100% on the test and was sure that he was going to be proud of me. When I showed him the paper, it was if the mark was less than 0% - he was furious and yelled about how my handwriting was a disgrace, how it reminded him of a country bumpkin, not a police chief's son. With that, he put me in a jail cell, locked the door and told me that I wasn't getting out until I had re-written the test in perfect handwriting. But, before I could begin re-writing the test, I would have to wash the cell floor. I was stunned. What would have happened if I hadn't got a hundred on the test? Nothing about this seemed to make any sense to me. What was I missing? What didn't I understand? Why was it that nothing I did was ever good enough? At least I didn't get a beating. I left the cell late, when Dad was finally satisfied that I had learned my lesson.

He told me he would be checking my handwriting in all of my books to make sure that I wasn't an embarrassment to the family name.

I have to admit that I was furious, and that I was burning with shame inside. As I walked from the police station towards home, I stopped and went behind an old garage and began swearing. I made sure that I was hidden and that my voice couldn't be heard. I knew that if Dad heard me swearing I would be physically regretting it for a long time. But, in spite of my fear, I swore over and over again just beneath the volume level of a whisper. And I knew, that I would have to go to confession for dishonouring, disobeying my father because if anything, I feared God more than my father

~

It was with adolescence that I found that I had stopped believing in my father, in the world being a good place, stopped believing that the Church had anything to do with God who I still knew at some level as pure goodness. Going to confession was not so much about following the rules of the church, but of being honest with myself and with God in order to avoid damnation and an eternity in Hell. To give in to anger, to add to the darkness in the world, was something that failed to make me feel better as a person. Getting even inflicted more pain on my psyche and added to the sense of suffering I felt in being in the world. Anger seemed to rebound and punish me more than the person to whom my anger was directed. Intuitively I knew what was right though I couldn't frame that knowledge with words.

The only solution I could come up with as a thirteen year old boy was to swallow the darkness and then move forward to the next moment. I was ten years away from discovering Buddhism, but I was already well on my way to embracing so much of the Buddhist way of being in this world, especially with regards to the eightfold path, the right way of being in the world; and the four noble truths which helps one understand suffering.

Yet, this time spent in Bow Island, Alberta during the first year, was a time that for me, became a time where life would show me so much that was good. I stopped believing in my father, but I began to believe in myself and in the world in general. I began to emerge out of hiding in the shadows.

I have to add that the conditions of life changed in Bow Island. For whatever reason, the small amount of money that was able to come my way through delivering newspapers or working at odd jobs for local farmers, was not taken from me. I even found myself with free time to be with friends. Kevin also found himself with the same freedoms. This would change, but while we had this freedom and a stable home and school situation, life was showing us that it wasn't all about darkness.

~

About a week after school started, Dad had found out about a newspaper route opening and he signed me up for it. He didn't ask me if I wanted to have a paper route, but it didn't bother me that he got me the job. I was hungry for a chance to earn money, to have something of my own. The paper route wasn't big, just over twenty customers with some of them being businesses on Main Street. Not long after I got into the habit of delivering papers, there was a contest to see who could get the most new customers. Since the contest was to include the city of Medicine Hat and all the towns in the surrounding area that delivered the Medicine Hat paper, I didn't think too hard about winning the contest. What I did think of was the extra money that I would earn with more customers. And so, I stepped outside of my normal quietness and shyness to ask people if they would take the paper. At the end of the contest period it turned out that I had won a new bicycle.

I got a new bike and Dad got Kevin a used bike as it wouldn't look good on him if we weren't able to be at least a little bit like our school friends.

Dad had a good job with good pay. His police car was his own car and so they provided him with an allowance for its use as a cop car. Dad being a cop, wasn't something new for me, but it was for Gilles and Gordon who were too young to remember very much of Dad being a policeman in Hull, Quebec two years earlier.

As a cop, Dad had access to all kinds of people and soon became friends with a young farmer-rancher by the name of Daryl who was also a Catholic. On Dad's days off, we would sometimes went to Daryl's place. Daryl was married but he still farmed and ranched with his parents. Since it was early fall, farmers were busy with harvesting crops that were ready. The wheat was still standing in the fields waiting for its turn. At the moment, it was time to pull the final bales of hay off the field. Dad volunteered me to learn and help with baling.

Kevin got to deliver my newspapers for a couple of Saturdays while I went and stood behind the baler. I learned quickly, how to grab the bales and stack them into small pyramids of six bales, then pull a release rope and watch them slide neatly onto the land. Naturally there were a few mishaps along the way as I struggled to lift the top bale onto the little pyramid and delayed pulling the release rope before the next bale was making its way through the chute, ready for placing on the stacking bed. Daryl laughed and would stop and help me get it set right again. He taught me how to use my thighs to lift the bale into place instead of trying to lift them with my skinny arms. I enjoyed the baling experience and found myself helping out until the last bales were piled.

Once the bales were done, Daryl decided I needed some time with him, and so he took me with him for a truck ride through the countryside, showing me the wheat fields and other things about which he was passionate.

One late afternoon while we were driving along a country road in his half-ton truck, Daryl suddenly stopped, grabbed his rifle from its holder in the back window of the half ton, and took a quick shot before jumping back in the truck and driving off. We drove on down the road to find a place to park as if nothing had happened. Once the truck was parked, we walked back through the fields until he came to a spot and pointed to a deer lying on the ground. Daryl had just shot a deer out of season. I watched in fascination as he gutted and skinned the carcass. Since I was with him, I was given a part of the deer to take home with the promise not to tell anyone about what had happened. I worried about what Dad was going to say and if Daryl would end up going to jail. I didn't realise it yet, but Dad had police jurisdiction only within the town, so Dad wasn't going to be a problem. When Daryl dropped me off at home, he told me that the deer meat would be brought to our house on a different day, after it had hung for a while to cure.

~

The appearance of a Daryl in my life, another male, showed me another way to be a man in this world, a lesson not planned, but one that emerged simply out of our being together. His children were too young to help him and so my presence and services as offered by my father became the doorway through which I was able to connect with another adult male, one who was grounded in the earth. I experienced a different way of relating to the world through that contact, and I began to change as a result. It wasn't just me who began to change, my father seemed to settle down as well. It was as if his dreams were finally coming true. Kevin also began to change, to find his own roots which made him calmer and growing confident as a boy beginning the shift into adolescence. With the beginning of a new home in a new town everyone seemed to open up to investing in this new home and new town.

~

With Suzanne being a toddler, life for Mom was getting better. She began to have friends including the woman next door, Daryl's wife, and a few other neighbours. Béatrice was now old enough to help keep Suzanne occupied, while Mom began to enjoy her time. Gordon wasn't old enough for kindergarten yet, but he was easy to take care of. Anywhere Gilles went, it seemed that it was there that you could always find Gordon. Gilles was Gordon's hero since Gilles went to school and was a tough as nails. The fact that we began to believe that we were actually going to stay here in Bow Island let us all breathe more easily. Kevin began to make his own friends at school and so began to hang around me less and less. It was strange not having Kevin with me most of the time. But since I now had my own friends, I began to emerge out of my own shell.

Once the farm work with Daryl was done, I began to spend a lot of my free time at the restaurant that Peter's parents owned. Peter's dad's name was Pete. Often I would go into the side lot between the restaurant and the bowling alley, and help Peter put pop bottles into their right wooden boxes according to their bottling company, and then stack them making more room. On rare occasions I would help out with washing some of the dishes with Shirley. But most of the time, I would just sit with Peter and Shirley in one of the booths and listen to the songs on the jukebox, singing along as we learned the songs. Every once in a while I would end up helping Shirley with her homework, especially Math homework. I was willing to help Peter as well, but he always found something more interesting to do, and everything was more interesting than homework even if others would think otherwise.

I was earning money with my paper route and soon found myself putting some of that money into a coin collection and a stamp collection.

I would constantly bug Pete if I could go through the coins in the till in search of pennies, nickels and dimes, sometimes even quarters which I needed to fill the empty place holders in a set of little coin holder pressed-board booklets. I sent away for stamps and soon had a neat little collection of mostly useless stamps that I found interesting as they were from many different countries of the world, places that I heard about in school and learned about as I studied more in the encyclopaedia.

Having money also meant that I could sometimes treat my friends as well. Every once In a while we would stop at the local bakery on the way home from afternoon classes and buy ourselves cream puffs. Since Toni was from a poor family, I would sometimes slip him a dollar so that he could buy the treat. Of course, when it was Peter's turn, we would invariably head over to the restaurant and have ice cream cones.

The pace of life had somehow become different in Bow Island in the early fall of 1962. Because of my friend Toni's interest in science and the passion of my teacher at school, I had been looking for more and more information, more knowledge in books. I became fascinated by the stars in the night sky, stars which were never seen with such abundance when we lived in the city. My curiosity led me to learn about constellations, about galaxies and about the universe that stretched before my eyes at night. On some evenings Kevin, Toni and I would lay on the grass and stare at the stars. I pointed out the various constellations that I began to recognize from the illustrations in the books I found at school. The three of us stared into the skies, talking quietly and often not talking at all but just experiencing with awe, the heavens at night.

In October, 1962 we began to learn how to deal with the threat of a nuclear war. The Cuban Missile Crisis had everyone in Bow Island in a panic.

We had practices in school in which we had to leave the classroom and gather in the gymnasium. We heard about underground shelters and about radiation. We saw fighter jets streak across the sky and wondered if they carried the deadly atomic bombs. Fear was everywhere as we listened in panic to newscasts on the radio about a possible nuclear war. All of the cold war, Russia versus the U.S.A. tensions seemed about to blow up in our faces as these two giants took hard stances over the island of Cuba. Thankfully, at the last moment, Russia found a way to back down and the crisis passed.

Fall turned into winter and life basically stayed the same. School was great with a good teacher, Mr. Samson. At church, I was enjoying learning the songs to be sung by the junior choir. There were two choirs, the junior choir which I was in and the senior choir. My confidence in my voice and my ability to learn quickly soon had the priest become more aware of me in the crowd of other kids in the choir. I got nervous with his growing attention and then had to chide myself for being so paranoid. I knew my voice was better than most of the other kids, so maybe the priest was right, that with a few extra practices I could sing with the senior choir. He thought that with enough work, I could sing with the senior choir for the Midnight Mass at Christmas time. It wasn't hard for the priest to convince Mom and Dad about my promise as a choir singer and the honour it would be to sing with the senior choir for the Christmas Eve service. My fate was sealed.

I can't remember the special lessons, but I did get to sing more, singing with the senior choir in the late fall during regular church services. As Christmas approached, the special lessons increased in number. By the time Christmas Eve was approaching, I found that I was resisting more and more. A week before Christmas, I refused to go to my special lesson.

The priest then told me, if I didn't go to his special lessons, I couldn't sing in the choir for the Midnight Mass, neither in the junior choir nor with the senior choir. It didn't matter to me. I refused to go to his special lesson and so found myself silent and downcast, sitting with my brothers and sisters rather than with the choir, sitting mostly with shame, during Midnight Mass. Dad must have suspected something was wrong because he never made me go back to church in Bow Island after that mass. There are some things you just never talk about, some things you never challenge even if you are the chief constable in town.

~

I have to admit that I am troubled by this last bit of story involving the Catholic Church. I can remember the anticipation of singing in the senior choir for Christmas Eve as well as the intense disappointment at having to sit it out without taking part in either the junior or senior choirs. I knew that I had one of the better voices in both choirs and had received very favourable comments and promises from the priest. Why did I refuse these special lessons? Something was going on in the background, something had happened that had shut down my memories. I have to admit that I tend to trust my gut that tells me that the line between priest and boy had once again been crossed. My father's untypical response to my withdrawing from participating in church services, especially after having so strongly pushing me to be active in the church hints that he knew what was going on. I can hear faint echoes and traces of rumours concerning the priest, but that is all that remains. The rest has fallen into some black hole.

~

For the rest of the winter I focused on delivering newspapers, helping Mom more at home as she was again pregnant, and beginning to take an interest in hockey on television on Saturday evenings.

When I delivered newspapers to the hotel and some of the other cafes, people would be always talking about sports, particularly hockey. I had never paid any attention to sports before so I decided I needed to learn what they were talking about, perhaps I would even have something to say to the men who sat along the counter at the hotel restaurant. For some strange reason I began to see Montreal as my team instead of the locally popular Toronto team. But the interest was incidental until it was playoff time and it became a time of hockey fever in Bow Island. Everyone talked hockey, even my classmates and teacher.

As Mom's pregnancy advanced, I was pressed into more and more service at home. As the eldest of the kids, I was again washing clothes on occasion, washing floors and dishes and making sure the kids were not in Mom's hair. As in the past, it seemed that Mom was constantly depressed, that she had some hidden illness that stole her energy and her interest in us, her children. Even the fact that Dad was still at home and not off on another wild goose chase, was not enough to brighten her mood. Since it was winter time, it was hard to have some of the clothes dry fast enough for our use. It would have been okay if we would have had a lot of clothing, but too much travelling had reduced our clothing to bare essentials. So, I would often find myself speed drying a few clothes on the small electric heater with which our bedroom was heated for the most part while the clothes rack was filled with the rest of our laundry near the oil space heater in the dining room. A few times I singed the underwear leaving the white underclothes with an appearance of toast. When that happened I was punished as was expected, but not as harshly as in the past.

~

I didn't know it at the time, but my father was having an affair with a widow in town. People in town knew about the affair as my father's police car was parked outside her place late at night too often.

I have little doubt that my mother knew he was cheating on her as well. Likely this contributed to her depression. I had heard rumours from other kids and protested them as false. Though I was a small boy, I did threaten to beat up some of the kids who were saying these things about my father. It wasn't because I believed he was innocent of these rumours, but more out of the need to deny to the truth to myself. The widow was also pregnant and the baby due a few months before my mother's due date, a fact that betrayed that my father had taken her as a mistress before we had even moved to Bow Island.

Though I was only thirteen, I found myself again in the role of an adult, a role that I wasn't mentally or physically ready for. I was an adolescent and found myself. Like most adolescents, floundering along in a mixture of curiosity, embarrassment, and shyness. Thankfully, this period of time was one where there was less dysfunctional activity in our home than in the past. Life became almost normal with typical highs and lows.

~

In the evenings that were bath nights, most of us were now able to take care of ourselves, everyone that is with the exception of Gordon and Suzanne. Gordon was already at the stage where he didn't want to take baths anymore and so that was more of a wrestling match to make sure that he got wet enough for soap to be used. Bath time began with the youngest and worked its way up to me, the last to use the same bath water in the real bathtub. Suzanne loved her bath and I didn't mind me taking care of her. I had to make sure she didn't drown as well as make sure she was clean before she left the tub. It wasn't long before I noticed her vagina as being so smooth, unlike those of adults with which I should never have become familiar. She looked so innocent, so pure.

~

Now, as I write this I wonder at my attention to her genitals at that time. Was there more than just what I have now written? Or, was it simply natural curiosity? I had seen her vagina and Béatrice's vagina in the past and had never thought anything about it. This newfound curiosity surprised me. Somehow, I knew that there was a line that couldn't be crossed. As an adult, today, I realise that the appearance of this awareness of a moral code, when it came to sexuality at this point, was what had set my moral compass for the rest of my life. It wasn't a conscious and deliberate decision, but one that arose from my life experiences that had already been buried. Unconsciously, I chose a path out of darkness than one that would lead even deeper.

I wondered about writing this next part of the story as it is a part that is not filled with darkness and family dysfunction. And then, I realised that it was because of that fact why it is important to acknowledge this part of my life. For almost two years I lived without fear of being uprooted, I learned how to have friends and trust others. Even though my own family continued to be troubled with itself, the living presence of others outside of the family taught me to believe in other possibilities for life, and that it didn't have to be the way I had experienced it growing up. And so, the story continues with more light than darkness.

~

In early May, I was sent by Mom to have a medical check-up which seemed strange to me as I wasn't sick in any way that I could determine. The doctor confirmed that I was in good health when I went back a second time to find out the results of some tests that had been run on me. He told me that I was cured and that nephritis would never be a problem again. He told me that having made it passed my twelfth birthday, juvenile nephritis was not something to worry about anymore.

The doctor said I was lucky as most kids didn't make it to their twelfth birthday when they had nephritis. He told me I was as fit as a fiddle and to go out and play a lot of sports. I was in a state of shock. I didn't know that I was considered terminal, that I had had a deadly disease. I immediately wondered if the lack of love I had received was a protection my parents had put on as they believed they had already lost their little boy when I was four years old. I felt ashamed that I had been thinking that they just didn't love me at all, not that they had loved and lost. I was so excited I ran all the way home to tell Mom the good news.

The first thing she asked me was if the doctor said she could now cook using salt. When I told her that I was completely cured, she took that as a 'yes," and that was the end of the conversation. Nothing changed other than she would be able to cook using salt more often. Perhaps it was because she was getting closer to giving birth and she didn't have the focus or the energy to show enthusiasm and celebrate my survival. I celebrated with vengeance. I tried out for the school's track and field meet. I practiced as hard as I could so as to be competitive with the other boys who had been playing sports their whole lives. When the school meet finally came around, I won the running races and placed third in long jump and high jump. Toni won first prize in those events. I surprised myself and everyone else taking part as I almost jumped my height in the high jump. Kevin won a lot of ribbons at our school meet as well, especially the throwing events. There was no question that Kevin was a strong boy at twelve years of age. Already he was stronger than I was as I neared my fourteenth birthday.

~

Though I had learned why I had been hospitalised as a youth and why I had suffered so much facial swelling, the fact that I had fully been cured didn't change the relationship that I had with my parents.

For the most part as I experienced it and understood it, I remained an outsider who was required to be a servant, especially for my mother. With my father, it was more confusing. There were moments when he became a father and had a father's pride in me as his son. These moments were fleeting as he fell back into his normal narcissistic way of being in the world of family and community.

~

As spring began to melt snow, Dad came home one day and announced that we now had horses and that we were going to learn how to ride them like real cowboys and cowgirls. Dad had bought three horses and was working on buying a few more. Dad began teaching us how to ride the horses as he wanted us in the annual Pivot Fair Days' parade riding our horses. At time of the parade we had three horses which were ridden by Dad, Kevin and I. Dad had a beautiful, spirited Palomino stallion, Mom's horse which Kevin was to ride was a big, gentle, white Appaloosa, I had a Buckskin horse which I called Buck. Kevin got to ride Mom's horse as Mom was pregnant and couldn't ride. For some reason, Dad had bought a beautiful black saddle covered in silver studs for me to use while riding Buck. I was in the parade and I had a beautiful horse and a magnificent saddle beneath me.

Over the late spring and summer Kevin and I would bike out to the pasture where Dad boarded the horses, chase down "our" horses which would have rather stayed in the pasture, and then went out riding when we weren't busy with other things. Kevin and I began to work for farmers, different farmers, once school let out for the summer.

I would have to get up early in order to help move irrigation pipes, a task that had to be done before breakfast. We would go into the wet fields that were almost knee deep in mud, to uncouple the sections of pipe, tip the pipes in order to drain the water and then carry the empty sections to the next area of the field that needed to be irrigated.

It was hard, dirty work that was made worse by mosquitoes that believed the morning hours belonged to them.

Once haying season arrived, I got to work again with Daryl doing a much better job this time around since I knew what I was doing and I was now a year older and a bit bigger and stronger. I had finally reached a height of five feet. I was still the shortest boy in my class, but I was growing. Using the technique that Daryl had taught me the year before, I soon wore holes in the thighs of my jeans. Daryl got his mother to sew patches on the jeans, but not before my thighs were totally scratched up leaving me even itchier than when I got mosquito bites. It wasn't long before haying the first cut was done.

With working on moving irrigation pipes being an early morning job, it left a lot of time for me to do other things such as my paper route, helping at home, and spending time at Peter's place. Peter's dad was adding to the restaurant in order to expand the restaurant to include a grocery section. When it came time for the walls of the addition to go up, I was of some help because the walls were brick walls. I must have learned about laying brick from Pépère because I was able to easily lay row after row of brick with a skill that I didn't know I had. The project took some time and it wouldn't be until late fall before the addition would be ready for use. Until then, I got to spend time with Peter and Shirley in the restaurant and finally learned the secret of his dad's hard ice cream flavours.

Peter and I would, on rare occasions, spend a few hours at the bowling alley. We didn't bowl but kept busy with setting up the pins as others bowled. I did get to try bowling a few times during quiet hours but soon found out that I wasn't very good at it, or very interested in becoming good at it.

At the beginning of the summer, Dad had me join the local boys' baseball team. I wasn't good at the sport though I did try.

I was put into the field where I would run down balls that were hit low, and I was not too bad in catching the balls popped up into the air anywhere in the outfield where I would use my speed to move to the right place in time. I often was able to get the ball back in play on ground hits before the batter could get home and was considered a good centerfielder. So, I made the team and got to play a few innings in most games. I rarely got to bat as I was terrible at the plate; the coach would use pinch-hitters when it was my turn to bat. The most memorable trip out of town was the trip to Medicine Hat to play in a tournament. Of course I got to travel to Burdett, Grassy Lake, Seven Persons and a few other towns for league play, but the Medicine Hat tournament was like being in World Series for me.

~

In July, 1963 my brother, Neil was born making us a family with seven children. I was given the honour of being his godfather though I have no idea who was his godmother. Neil was born in the Bow Island Hospital. Since I was old enough now, we didn't have to have any of my father's sisters or any other adult move in to help take care of the kids. I wonder if this freedom from dependence upon his family was a big part of why we got to stay in Bow Island.

Regardless, my role as caretaker and surrogate adult in the family was confirmed. I believed in my holding onto the role as much as my parents expected me to fulfill that role. For my brothers and sisters, it was just the way it was. They really didn't know family life and my relationship to them in that family in any other way.

~

I have to say that in a way, it wasn't as difficult as I thought it would be. Béatrice and Kevin helped a lot. Béatrice wasn't helpful with things like dishes or cleaning, but she was a lot of help in the care of Suzanne who was now two years old.

Kevin was good when it came to keeping Gilles and Gordon out of trouble. Well, not really as the three of them caused enough mischief, but not bad mischief in my opinion. The important thing was to keep the space around Mom quiet enough and to make sure that she had very little to complain about. Mom's friends came often enough with cakes and bread and sometimes even soups as well as to cheer her up and check up on the newborn. Mom was treated like a queen by everyone, even Dad.

I turned fourteen that summer, the summer of 1963. That meant I was old enough to get a learner's driver's license. I took the test and passed easily. But having a learner's license was quite meaningless unless I could get a chance to practice. Dad bought a 1949 Ford half ton truck that was working though it was in rough shape. It was my job to sand the truck's body down and then paint it using a paintbrush. I painted the truck body dark green and the wooden racks that formed a box for the back, a bright yellow. I ended up following Dad's instructions while cleaning engine parts with him then putting the pieces back.

Finally the truck was ready and I was taken into a summer fallow field in order to learn how to drive the truck. I wasn't the quickest study with the clutch or the pedals, partly because I was so small and it was hard to do all of the tasks and see out the windshield. Still, I did learn to drive. However, before I could get better at driving, the truck was sold thus ending my opportunities to drive.

~

Working behind the scenes, an old story was working to bring the peace and relative prosperity to an end. My father had spent more than he had earned, and he couldn't continue to juggle all of it. The cracks began to appear and those cracks would have a ripple effect on our life in the community.

During this period of time while I was earning money and our family began to take on the appearance of stability and normality, I spent some of my earnings on a guitar and a few lessons. Music became a vital part of my life that didn't cause any negative ripples in my life at home. If anything, my playing music was welcomed. As far as I knew it, this was the best it had ever been for me and our family.

~

With money I had saved over the past year, I bought a cheap little guitar. Dad found a high school student who could give me lessons; of course I would be paying for my lessons. I was in heaven. I had a guitar and I was really going to learn how to play it. The high school student was a good teacher and soon I was able to strum basic chords in various patterns. He told me that most songs used these few patterns and that those which were more complicated could be simplified into the basic patterns. Once the basics were in place, he decided I should learn to play what he called "lead guitar," that is playing the notes of the songs, not just the chords which he called "rhythm guitar."

The first effort was called "Pipeline." After that, the lessons continued for a few more weeks and then were over. The rest was up to me.

I went back to school in the fall, this time I was in grade eight. Peter didn't return to school that fall, he stayed at home to focus on the restaurant and with helping his dad get the addition ready for the grocery part of the business; Peter hadn't passed grade seven for the third time. Shirley and Toni had passed without difficulty and were with me in grade eight. For some reason I took an instant dislike towards the new teacher, Mr. McPhail. As he wandered around the room while we were working he would stop for a while, hitch up his pants with one foot on a stool so that his genitals were on prominent display beneath his pants.

Seeing his genitals outlined brought out an anger and a fear in me that I couldn't explain. Thankfully he had no interest in me and so I began to breathe a sigh of relief. He was new to Bow Island and he had a family. He was a deeply religious man so we heard, constantly from him. The fact that he had a daughter in school, in our class made everything else about him irrelevant, for I had fallen head over heels in love with his daughter.

It was a love that never went any further than my mind. I never mentioned it to her, or to my friends or even my brother, Kevin. Everyone, including me, thought that Shirley was my girlfriend. Magic filled the silent love affair that raged through my head, a magic that was missing in whatever it was that characterised the relationship I had with little Shirley. I still spent my free time with Shirley and Peter at the restaurant, helping out as much as I could, helping as they began to turn the renovations into a new store.

Pete's Place became a restaurant and small grocery store.

I wandered around the new store amazed at how it had changed and how new it appeared. Still, the jukebox was there and I would put in the odd quarter and play three songs. I was listening more carefully to the songs and then buy song books which would include the guitar chord arrangements for those songs. Listening was important for me as it allowed me to make sense of the words and chords printed on the pages of the song magazines. Often when playing the songs I found the song books were wrong, but there was enough that was right in those magazines that would let find the right chords when I trusted my ears.

~

In the fall, my father moved the family into a smaller house near the highway, saying that the house we had been living in was too cold and too hard to heat in the winter time. He didn't want the new baby to get sick in a house that was a firetrap in his opinion.

So we moved into the older house by the highway with only a Caragana hedge to help cut down the noise of highway traffic. It was almost a duplicate house of the one we had lived in when my father was a policeman in Hull, Quebec. The difference was that this house was in much worse shape. It did have a shed between the back door and the back yard. That shed was crammed with all kinds of junk. I got the sense that we were again in financial trouble.

The arguments in the house suggested that the problems were even worse, and that money was only part of the problem. But in spite of the problems, we lived outwardly as though there were no problems and that all was well. Well, that is with the exception of the horses and the tack. My father had sold most of the horses by October telling us that it was pointless to pay for feed and for pasturing the horses when he wanted us to have better horses once spring came around.

That reasoning may have been accepted by most, but it didn't make any sense to me as all the saddles and tack were sold off as well. I began to wonder if perhaps they had never really been paid for and that they had been repossessed like so many other things had been repossessed in the past. I began to become bitter and resentful.

~

Kevin and I knew more than our brothers and sisters about the real state of affairs because Mom said she needed to borrow most of the little bit of money we had saved from our occasional summer jobs. I felt sorry for Mom and didn't complain too much to her. Still, I was bitter. I gave up sending for stamps and buying song magazines. I soon resorted to reading song books and comic books at Pete's Place. Peter's dad noticed but never said anything to me other than I liked the Beatles too much, that they were just punks and that I should focus on the good music. He also let me wash dishes on and off so that I could have a bit of spare change.

It was something he didn't have to do as he didn't need the help, or the expense. And occasionally he would let me fill and stack the empty pop bottle crates giving me free pop, ice cream and fries in payment.

The first community fall dance for teenagers was held in the hall near the restaurant. I took Shirley as my date. Toni and Peter were also a part of our group as was Kevin and his new girlfriend, a girl called Ursula. It was a group date more than a boyfriend-girlfriend kind of date. I danced and sang along with all the songs I knew. I was particularly loud with "Listen to the Rhythm of the Falling Rain," "Blue on Blue," "Blue Velvet," and "Hey Pierrea." Every hour or so Dad would come into the dance hall in his uniform, wearing his gun and wander around smiling. He stopped by our table each time and I have to admit that I was embarrassed by his constant presence.

This was a place for teenagers, not adults. Still, I wasn't about to let my embarrassment spoil the night. As soon as he left each time, I plunged right back into having a good time with my friends.

~

I was getting angrier and angrier with my father during the fall after our move, and that anger was burning inside of me, eating at me. I was at that age when the process of a son separating from his father was beginning, a natural process. Of course I didn't know what was happening to me. Aside from the natural need to separate in terms of becoming a more independent person, I was wrestling with all the lies that our lives were based upon. No one knew what our history was, what lack of boundaries had led to our constantly being forced to flee, usually one step ahead of the law.

The fact that at this time in my life I was hearing rumours about my father and his mistress, as well as a growing dissatisfaction with my father as a policeman only served to increase that distance. I knew my father couldn't be trusted and I was sure that there just had to be something going on, hidden behind the scenes, which would have us once again fleeing in the middle of the night.

~

On Halloween I had decided to hang out with Peter rather than go trick and treating with my brothers and sisters. Dad and his partner, Bruce were kept busy chasing down the older teens who were doing what they always did in small, prairie towns in terms of Halloween mischief. Peter and I decided to do our own bit of mischief. We snuck across the street and soaped up the windows of the Insurance Agency and the Liquor Board store then quickly returned to sit in the restaurant while Dad searched for the guilty parties.

It was fun watching as Dad finally caught a few of the teenagers who had been doing some mischief, and had them wash down the windows that Peter and I had soaped up. Dad's only real concern was that the windows were cleaned off as the business owners had the most influence on his job and his salary. No one suspected either Peter or myself, for we were the "good" kids.

The grocery stores and restaurants in town were a stopping place for all the young kids gathering treats, so I got to see Béatrice who was taking the younger kids around for treats when she stopped at Pete's Place. In a prairie town there really was no need for costumes so they weren't wearing any, just older clothing that was old and too big. I felt sad watching them get excited about the treats which never seemed to last. Béatrice had to hurry home with the kids so that Mom would have treats to hand out to other neighbourhood kids.

It reminded me of the past when it was Kevin and I taking the first round of treats home so that there would be treats to pass out. Gilles took Gordon out for more treats once the bags were given to Mom; treats that they hoped would be theirs. Kevin was out with his friends, already raising hell and getting away with it. Kevin had the courage to do what I only wished I could do. I wasn't much of a rebel with the exception of soaping up a few windows.

In November, President Kennedy was shot in Dallas, Texas. I couldn't believe it. I watched the news over and over again seeing the assassination over and over again. I couldn't believe that someone so good could be killed like that. Where was God? Kennedy was a good Catholic and things like this weren't supposed to happen to good Catholics. I hated God at that moment. And that admission triggered even more anger in me. How did God let kids like me get molested, raped?

How did God let my Dad beat my brothers and sisters? Why did he punish us kids so that we couldn't go to school regularly, or have a home we could call our own? Why were our parents so broken? Yes, I hated God. As far as I could understand, since God could see everything, knew everything, he killed Kennedy. And, I hated my Dad.

~

In the fall of 1963 Dad had become the town's Scout Master and so Kevin and I became Scouts. The idea of hating my father that arose in November gradually dissipated as I saw my father in the role of a Scout Master. Working with all of the boys, he eventually taught us discipline and self-confidence. One symbol of that growing confidence in ourselves was the staff we each carved from a strong, straight young hardwood tree. With the staves cleaned of bark, we set to creating a pattern that we carved into our staves, each of us with our own unique set of carvings, some quite plain, and a few quite ornate.

We learned of the value of a staff as a weapon and as an aid to hiking and as a useful item to have when camping. We were told that we would use our staves on our hikes like pilgrims did in the Holy Crusades. We began to see ourselves as pilgrim-soldiers carved in the image of the famed Knights Templar. Those early lessons have come back to me in the past few years as I find myself remembering the power of walking with a staff as a pilgrim. The journeys I now take as a pilgrim have the same focus, that of building self-confidence.

~

There was a big focus on marching manoeuvres as well as badge work that fall and through the winter. Dad pushed both Kevin and me to get as many badges as possible. We had a long way to go to try and catch up to the other boys who had been Scouts for years.

I remember one particular task that was about memory. We were given a limited amount of time to study a tray of items and then expected to recall what we had seen. This was a task that seemed tailor-made for me as I out performed everyone. I was surprised at how well Kevin did on that task as well, as he wasn't very strong in his school work, not that I could blame him for all the time we had missed school over the years. I was lucky, gifted with the ability to fill in the gaps on my own between schools.

As the snow began to melt in the early spring, Dad took us on a camping trip into the Bow River valley. I loved the camping experience. We hiked to the camp site in warm weather, carrying our hiking staves that we made in a few previous meetings. Our staves carved with neat patterns so that each of us had a distinctive staff. Once we got to the camping site, a couple of half ton trucks arrived carrying the tents and the camping gear we would need for a two-night camping experience.

Dad found a large bull snake and he soon found out who was afraid of snakes. I didn't like snakes but wasn't freaked out like a few of the town boys.

It snowed that night as the temperature dropped. The next morning we could hardly get the hot bacon, eggs and pancakes back to the tables before they cooled off and became cold. While we were eating, a number of cars and trucks began to arrive with parents who were coming to take their sons home. There was no way they were going to make their sons spend another night freezing in non-heated tents. Kevin and I were amazed as the camp quickly cleaned out of Scouts. We didn't know what they were talking about as sleeping in the tents wasn't that cold at all. Regardless, a three day and two night camping experience didn't make it past Saturday noon. That camping trip was also the end of our Scouting in Bow Island as Dad soon quit being the Scout Master.

Not long after the camping trip, Dad left for Edmonton where he was to take a course in dog handling. He somehow persuaded the town council that it would be in their best interests to be a centre for a search and rescue team, a team that would require a trained dog, something that neighbouring towns didn't have, something vital since there were always accidents near and on the river. When Dad returned from Edmonton, he brought home a big German shepherd called Silver. The dog was kept in the shed which meant that everyone at home now had to use the front door. Silver was a scary looking dog and he wasn't trained to be friendly. Dad liked to show us how he controlled Silver, making us sit very still while Silver stood on guard. Dad then told us of how he had to dress to train Silver, in thick padded outfits, and how Silver would attack him over and over again until finally Dad was able to control him with verbal commands. Needless to say, Silver terrified us.

~

With the knowledge of after-sight, I am now aware that the role of Scout Leader served to weaken my father's position in the town. His tough military approach to scouting was not well received by the parents who brought Scouts to an end that snowy weekend when my father insisted that the experience would make men out of their sons. With only a few showing up for the next Scout meeting, my father quit and disbanded the troop. Later events showed that many were also opposed to having a police dog in town. The charisma that my father had always used to get his way, was wearing off with time. People began to see that the man they had hired as police chief was not the person they thought they had hired.

Things were also fracturing at home between my parents at this time. My father continued to visit his mistress, often not even trying to hide the fact from my mother.

She had given up on so many fronts including her appearance making it harder and harder for her to find the enthusiasm to try and convince my father to stay in her bed. The arguments between my mother and father began to break down the unity between the children who imitated unconsciously the patterns experienced in the house. And, as usual when life became too messy, too complicated in the house, my father did his usual trick with a distraction.

~

I don't know why, but I was getting angrier and angrier. It didn't take much for any of my brothers and sisters to ignite that anger in me. I lost my smile and my even temper and gave them dark looks that threatened. One day, Kevin said something about my friendship with Shirley, how it was really just friends, not about boy-friend girl-friend. He taunted me with the fact that he knew how to be a real boyfriend with Ursula. In my anger, I poured hot water from the kettle onto him just as he turned away from me still laughing at me.

The water caught him on the buttocks and he screamed. When my mother raced in to see what had happened, Kevin told her that it had been an accident, that he had bumped me while I was holding the kettle. I'm not sure if she believed Kevin, but there was no other questions asked as she took care of the burns. I felt an intense shame for my actions. Kevin had protected me from punishment, punishment that I deserved.

A few days later Dad announced that he was going to invest in quarter horses. He had bought a quarter horse that he had seen run flat out along the side of the road while he drove his car in order to clock the horse's speed. According to the horse's owner, this speed would win a lot of races. The young horse had speed but had yet to be broken to take a saddle.

I watched Dad work with another man leading the horse round and round in a corral until the horse was able to respond to a bit and later to having a saddle on his back. The horse bucked like crazy with the saddle on, but eventually tamed down. It was time for a human rider and I was chosen to be the rider because of my weight. I was going to be the rider to race the horse which was going to bring us a lot of money from the upcoming rodeo season. However, I was scared of the horse after seeing his antics when the saddle was first put on his back. I expected to be thrown almost as soon as I was on the horse, thrown and getting a lot of broken bones in the process.

Dad held the horse's head firmly while I mounted. Then, with care, he let go of the horse's head while holding on to the reins. The idea was to lead both of us around the corral as had been done earlier when the horse was learning to accept the bit and then the saddle. The horse froze. He refused to move. I began to think that he was more scared than I was. Dad got mad and hit the horse several times on the rump in an attempt to get him moving, but the horse refused to budge.

Dad had an idea and opened the corral gates thinking that the idea of freedom would get the horse moving. Nothing! Dad then backed up a half ton into the corral, grabbed the reins and attempted to pull the horse using the power of the truck. The horse moved, but only in jolting jerks as the truck pulled him off balance. By this time Dad was furious and he took a plank and beat the horse over the hindquarters again and again and again. The trainer was aghast at what Dad had just done. With a disgusted tone of voice he told Dad that the horse was ruined and that it would never race now.

In a fit of fury, Dad drove away from the ranch. He had a worthless horse that yet to be paid for, worthless because of his impatience and anger. He was angry with me for some unknown reason.

I had seen what he had done to the horse and knew that he could do the same to me.

~

This was a turning point. With yet another loss, my father had begun to plan his escape. I didn't know it at the time, but his response to the latest fiasco was to embezzle money from the town. He had been taking money all along, small amounts that were hard to track, but with this latest setback with the quarter horse, our economic survival was again at risk. My father had a plan that required only a few weeks to put into place, a plan for obtaining a good amount of money from a campaign of issuing traffic tickets. As long as he left town before the money from the tickets had to be accounted for, he was safe.

~

A few days after the incident with the quarter horse, Dad told me that I had to learn how to take care of Silver, and that I had to take him for walks and keep him clean. I was too scared to move. I knew that Silver wouldn't let me anywhere near him without attacking.

Silver had clawed big gouges out of the door and its frame in the shed. We all stayed as far from the shed and that door as we could. We all feared him breaking out when Dad wasn't at home, breaking out and ripping us apart. Dad then told me he would give Silver a command to allow me to do these things with Silver. So, I took Silver for walks on the outskirts of town. I was too afraid to take him anywhere in town as I was afraid he would hurt someone and that I would be blamed for not controlling him. I didn't have to worry too much because when I went for walks, anyone near would find a different place to be in a hurry. Everyone was afraid of Silver.

Silver was actually a nice dog and I came to love him. When he was locked in the back shed, he would howl and cry, scratching at the door that kept him out of the house. Two months after we had the dog, Dad had to return the dog as the town decided that it was an expense they couldn't afford. As well, the dog's presence was making too many people feel worried about him escaping and hurting children in town. The town council was having issues with Dad, issues that were serious, issues over money. Apparently not all the money collected through fines and tickets was being turned in. They began to question Dad about the missing funds. Before the hammer came down, Dad took off, left us alone in Bow Island.

About two weeks after Dad had taken off; I came into the house one afternoon while the kids were out playing somewhere. Neil was sleeping in a crib in the living room and Mom was in her room with the door open. As I walked by the doorway to check on Neil I saw Mom holding my 22 calibre rifle. She began to point it at herself as she cried more silently than usual. I panicked, raced into the room and quickly grabbed the rifle from her hands. I yelled at her, asking if she had gone crazy. I was going crazy.

I took the rifle out to the shed at a run and swore that it was going to the dump as soon as I could get it there. I took the firing pin out of the barrel and made sure there were no bullets in the rifle chamber, Dad had taught me a lot about rifle safety and the lessons kicked in automatically. As I dismantled the rifle I noticed that there had been no bullets in the rifle and that the safety was still on. Perhaps I had been imagining all of it.

A keening wail came from Mom's room; I rushed back and was distraught at what to do as it looked as if Mom was totally losing it. She was rocking back and forth sitting on the edge of her bed, crying and moaning at the same time. I tried to hug her to have her calm down. She pulled me to her breast and talked about Dad and his whore who was pregnant again, she said we had to go on welfare because there was no money left for food. Holding me tight against her she made me promise never to leave her, not to abandon her like Dad had done. She told me that I was the only one she could count on, that I was the real man of the house. She was holding me too tight, with too much feeling and I knew that I was in trouble again. Oh God! What if the kids accidentally came into the house and saw me in Mom's arms?

~

I have wondered over and over again how it was that no one noticed abuse happening. Didn't my brothers and sisters ever see their mother molesting me? I was getting desperate and feeling more and more isolated from everything and everyone. Would my father come back and save me? I didn't believe that he was coming back. He had burnt too many bridges. I wasn't ready to be an adult. I couldn't take care of our family. I knew I was still just a kid. I wasn't old enough for a driver's license and I hadn't even started high school yet.

I had fallen into despair and didn't know how to get out, how to escape. Worse, I felt that I was responsible for taking care of the family. I believed that I had to meet their needs, to care and protect them. But, I didn't know how I could do that and it frightened me.

Being responsible, being given the responsibility of father and man did teach me, did give me strength that I would need and use when I finally became an adult with a family of my own. Life experiences are lessons that allow us to learn should we dare to stick with the experiences rather than disappearing into an inner world to hide. As a youth, I had a choice to refuse the roles foisted upon me, or I could go forward, consciously and learn.

~

Bruce became the chief constable and he was embarrassed when he had to come to the house to ask Mom where Dad was, as Dad was wanted for embezzlement and fraud. It looked as though Dad, the policeman was about to become Dad, the jailbird. Mom was devastated. Since Dad hadn't told her anything about the financial issues, nor even tell her he was leaving, she had nothing to tell Bruce. I doubt that she would have ever betrayed Dad as he was still the centre of her universe in spite of what she had said to me earlier in the bedroom.

Bruce liked me and was embarrassed to have to ask me what I knew. He told me about the issues of embezzlement and fraud and about the talk in town about Dad and the widow. He didn't know how he could help me, but he would try, maybe a summer job with one of his farming friends.

Now that Dad was unofficially labelled as a crook, most people in town avoided me like the plague. As I did my monthly paper route collections for July, a few more than usual gave up their paper delivery.

Summer was always a slow time, but now the paper route was the smallest it had been since I had taken on the route. Of course most promised to start again in the fall, so I held some hope that the paper route would be of some help with money at home. I was thankful that school was almost over for the year. Of all my school friends, only Peter, Toni and Shirley still continued to associate with me. The other kids wasted no time in jeering and making rude comments about my half-brother with one more on the way, about Dad being more of a crook than a cop. It was hard to walk down any street of the town and avoid being shamed.

School finally was out and both Kevin and I got jobs on local farms. I worked closer to town so that I could continue to live at home and help out as needed; Kevin got to stay with the farm family he worked for. Both of us gave almost every cent we earned to Mom as welfare was not enough to live on all by itself. Thank God that the town didn't cut Mom off welfare because of our earnings. I had just turned fifteen and Kevin was thirteen. We weren't kids anymore. Perhaps we hadn't been kids for a long time. In our minds, there was no hope of Dad riding in to the rescue with yet another wild dream that would take us to another town, another school, another place to call home.

I spent a lot of time cleaning out barns, moving irrigation pipes, baling hay and doing whatever work I could. I would do my paper route in the late afternoon if possible or just after supper. People began to complain about the late delivery making me worry that I would lose the paper route and the money that it brought. I sold my coin and stamp collections in hopes that it would help us get through the summer. I had no idea what I would do when it was time to go back to school and grade nine. I was too small and too young to find a permanent job in Bow Island. The weight of all of this dragged down my spirits.

Then, in the middle of August, Mom called me to her room to tell me that Dad had contacted her, but that I wasn't to tell anyone. She wanted to know how much money we could get so that we could go meet Dad in Winnipeg where he had a nice house waiting for us. She begged me to find as much money as possible. Kevin and I took every penny we had set aside for the fall; I sold my bike and rifle. Mom also had a few dollars set aside in hiding and soon we had enough to take the Greyhound bus to Winnipeg. It was like so many other times before, stealing away without saying goodbye to anyone. Only this time, it was me leading the pack as though I was the one who had to run and hide.

Chapter Twelve

This time, everything was different. There was no question that the only way that the move was to happen was with the money that both Kevin and I would contribute in order to pay for the bus fares for all of us to go from Bow Island to Winnipeg. If asked my opinion about the move, regardless of my anger, I would have agreed. I wasn't old enough to take over, full-time, the role of parent for our siblings. I knew that I needed to continue to go to school if I was to ever have a job that would pay enough to raise a family. If I refused to go to Winnipeg, I would become trapped at the bottom of a very small community which saw me as no different from my father. The sons do pay for the sins of their father.

I was fifteen and no longer a child. I had grown up in a hurry and had too long been my mother's caretaker and cleaning up after the messes of my father. I had stopped feeling as the older brother to my brothers and sisters. I had become a parent and yet at the same time there was a big gulf between myself and them that left me feeling more and more alone in spite of being crowded in the house. I got on the bus with them in Bow Island feeling hopeless. I almost didn't care anymore. I didn't want to be an adult anymore. I ached to simply be a boy in school with others: playing, learning, and simply being a normal kid who did normal things. And somehow, I knew, it just wasn't going to work out that way.

~

Dad met us at the bus station. Mom flew into his arms and the younger kids were glad to see him again as he was still a hero in their eyes. Kevin and I were not all that happy to see him even though it did mean that Dad would again take over responsibility for the family. Both of us kept our distance and had little to say, no smiles to offer. Dad led us out of the bus depot to a waiting car.

Dad's car was quite new, and he proudly drove us to a house in the north-west section of the city. The house was not too many years old and in a nice suburb of city. From the outside, it was obvious that this was the nicest looking and newest house we had ever lived in. A new car, a new home and with the kids smiling and laughing started to work a thaw in me.

As we piled into the house Dad pulled Kevin me aside and said "thank you" for us helping out in Bow Island and that he would pay us back very soon. Dad confided in us as though it just was the three of us against the world and said he had an important job for two of us to do right away so that Mom would stay happy. The basement needed cleaning out, right away. Not wanting to ruin the homecoming for Mom and to disrupt the positive mood that most of the kids were in, we agreed and entered the basement. The stench was overpowering and it almost made me puke. There was dog shit everywhere. The basement had been the dog run for the last people who had lived in the house. I now knew how come we ended up with such a nice looking house – no one else would rent it. We did the work as fast as we could and I ended up throwing up a few times making even more of a mess for myself to clean up.

Eventually it got done. I couldn't believe it; again I had found myself cleaning up my father's messes with him then getting all the credit for the cleaned up results. I dared to complain to Mom about it, about the unfairness of it. With a dark look she silenced me. "Don't you dare complain. If you breathe one word to your father and he leaves us again, you will be sorry that you were ever born," she hissed at me. "Just be thankful that there was a house here for us so that we could be a family again."

With no paper route or farm jobs to do, both Kevin and I began to wander around our neighbourhood finding our way to the Polo Park Shopping Center.

We saw the football field where the Winnipeg Blue Bombers played, and along the way, we discovered the world of outdoor wrestling. For some reason, there were wrestling entertainments in the open air. Kevin loved it a lot more than I did. For me, it was way too phony. Soon I found myself wandering streets on my own. I just walked and walked trying to make some sense of where I was. Did I dare try and learn to like the place?

About a week later I began school. I was in grade nine, in a high school. The school was big and modern. I joined the school soccer team, the junior team, and did well because I could run without getting tired. But more important than the soccer team was my "Art" class. I discovered art, or should I say that my art teacher discovered my passion for art. This was different from anything I had ever experienced in elementary school. I carved and painted with all the emotions that were seething within me. I had lost my guitar and was glad to find that perhaps this was something that wouldn't get sold the next time my parents found themselves scrambling for money.

Dad decided I needed to make friends with the boy who lived next door, a boy who played music with his parents as part of a Christian church music group. Dad had told them about my guitar playing but he forgot to tell them that the guitar was sold to help pay for our bus tickets to Winnipeg. I did get to try playing the steel guitar and experience its unique sound. I didn't like the music they played as it was all church music, all praising God and Jesus. I had come to hate church music. I soon found myself avoiding the neighbours who were always bent on saving me and having me join their church. They thought it would be good for my soul if I joined them in singing every Sunday with them in their Born-Again Christian Church. I smiled and said nothing about my loss of faith.

Yet, when I walked the streets, I would peer into various kinds of churches to see what they looked like, to search for a feeling that filled the emptiness of my loss of faith. I was still caught in the grips of concern for my soul. I just didn't trust churches anymore; and, I just didn't trust God anymore.

~

I had stopped believing in being a Catholic, a loss of faith that never was recovered in the decades of life that have slipped by since the short time in Winnipeg. My depression was based in part on the failures of my biological father, and the failures to protect and nourish me by a heavenly father. Both had repeatedly abandoned me, leaving me to clean up after their repeated failures.

~

Dad was trying hard to make it better for me. He signed me up for a community football team and I got a chance to play real tackle football by the last part of September. Though I was the smallest kid on the team, I found myself playing defence on the line. My job was to tackle the quarterback. Since I was fast and small, it was easy for me to get around the bigger and slower boys and I was quite successful. The coach tried to have me play on offense as a pass receiver hoping to use my speed to score touchdowns. But I had a serious problem, an inability to catch the ball. It didn't take too many failed attempts for the coach to put me back on the defensive line where I was a lot more useful.

Dad job was selling Bibles of all sizes, particularly the large "family" Bibles, and other Catholic books such as Lives of the Saints in order to make a living. Dad was always a great salesman, always finding ways to convince people to buy what they didn't need. Dad had boxes and boxes of books from the Catholic Book Services. Every night he would tell us how many he sold and what each book was worth.

He took out a set from one of the boxes and said that he made enough that we should have our own set. And so I began to read The Lives of the Saints.

~

The bibles and other books that sat in boxes in our house, waiting for their turn to be taken on my father's sales trips gave me a new look into the world of spirit. Though they were Catholic books, there were enough stories that talked of individual men, women and children who had somehow triumphed over their own stories of abuse and hardship in order to become saints. I was amazed at how some of those who became saints chose lives that accentuated and added to their hardships as though it was through suffering that they were able to prove the purity of their souls. The more they suffered, the greater the value of their piety, the more proof that they were indeed saints. I had resisted returning to the Church, but I found myself believing in the nature of suffering and how suffering would one day allow me to transcend the poverty and crudity of my life in the family. I began to hope that it would all be worth it in the end, hoped that I, too, would someday become a saint. That was the beginning of what I could call my "Saint Complex."

~

I still hadn't made any friends yet, but as October arrived, I was beginning to think that maybe we would be staying in Winnipeg for the whole school year. I again began to hope we would, as I liked my teachers and the school. Football continued to be an exciting adventure, but I was more interested in school. Soccer had led to an interest in running, cross-country running which I felt was the perfect sport for me. Though I enjoyed soccer and football, I wasn't very good at either sport because I didn't have the skills other than running and endurance. Running was different. I was good, the best runner in my class and grade in a school that had quite a few grade nine classrooms.

I finally began to play music with our neighbours who let me use one of their guitars for the practise sessions. Though I instinctively resisted their missionary attempts to bring me into their church, the need to play, at least sometimes, was met. I knew that if I continued to play with them, eventually I would be pulled into joining them as they played for their church.

Then we had some of the Laflamme clan come to our place for Thanksgiving. I admit that though I loved seeing these people, I was leery as it often ended up in us making a mad dash across the country.

Chapter Thirteen

I didn't know it at the time that Thanksgiving weekend arrived, but my father had made a call to Ottawa, to his mother and father, asking for them to come to Winnipeg. He needed their car and another driver for his car in order to make the move back to Ottawa. He admitted to them that if they didn't come, he would likely end up in jail. This was the first time he admitted that he had made a mistake. He never admitted to fraud in Bow Island, but with the Catholic Church Services having just asked him for the money from book sales or they would file charges against him for the money he had collected on their behalf, and there being no money to give them as it was all spent, my father had confided in his parents. He knew he had to run or he would end up in jail. My father's spirit was broken. His chasing of dreams had changed into a desperate struggle to stay out of jail.

~

We were getting ready for the cross-country race, our family's version of the "Great Escape." The money pressures were mounting as Dad had again crossed the line. All the boxes of books that he had been selling? Well, he hadn't been turning in the money. He also hadn't paid for any rent or had he made any car payments since the initial payment. He hadn't spent anything on his growing Winnipeg debts.

We left the car in the driveway and a light on in the house and snuck away with Réjean and Pépère in the middle of Thanksgiving Sunday night. If luck held out, we would be in Ottawa by the time anyone figured out that we had left Winnipeg. Between Dad, his father and his brother, we began the long drive back to Ottawa, stopping only for gas and meals along the way, driving twenty-four hours a day.

It wasn't long before we left the prairies and entered into the boreal forest near the border between Manitoba and Ontario. I couldn't fall asleep as we drove on. I could tell that Pépère was upset and angry with Dad. He didn't say much, but the looks he gave to my Dad said it all.

In the darkness, the painted lines on the highway was almost all that was visible as we drove east. Then, the vehicle slowed and I saw a pale white Moose standing on the edge of the highway. Was it real? Did I imagine it? I was the only one awake other than my grandfather who was driving. When I asked him, he agreed that he had slowed down because he saw something that could have been a moose. As I sat in the front seat beside Pépère, I wondered if the white moose was a sign of something important that was to come into my life, our life. Somehow I knew that this moose was special, that in a way I was being gifted by having the chance to see it. I didn't believe in coincidences. Everything, somehow, had meaning, was meant to be. And then, I plunged into an inner space and began to question myself and my life. Why hadn't I known that this was coming? Why did I let myself hope and dream again? I was ready to give up completely, it all seemed so pointless. All the lost friends, schools, hopes, dreams, trust, innocence – what for?

Somewhere in the middle of the next morning, we stopped at a gas station restaurant in Wabigoon for some breakfast. I wasn't hungry and sat away from everyone lost in my depression. When I finally looked up thinking of asking for some coffee, I saw a girl, my age, with long dark hair looking at me. Our eyes connected and held. I knew that she was just as lonely as I was; her eyes were sad. I thought that if the world would have been fair, we could have stopped then and there and stayed in Wabigoon, I would have become best of friends with this dark girl who appeared to need a friend as badly as I did. But, that initial spark of hope that sprang up was extinguished. We got back into Pépère's car and drove on.

~

There was no home waiting for us this time. As we drove up to a block of row houses in Lower Town, old, stained brick buildings that reached up three stories; it was as if we had found new depths of poverty. Entering into the top-floor apartment that was home for my French-Canadian grandparents, we found that our family of two adults and seven kids, one of them just a year old, were to stay in one room, the back room that was originally the back porch. The room was just big enough for one double bed. Most of us kids had to sleep on the floor while my parents slept in the bed with the two girls and the baby. No one was happy: this wasn't a family reunion. Tempers flared and my father, uncharacteristically worked hard at staying quiet while his mother ranted about how tough it was just to feed her family without having to add in the burden of nine more mouths. She was right. This was not what should have been happening. But, the other option was perhaps worse: Dad going to jail and the family totally falling apart, broken.

There was no rush to have us children go back to school. Before we could be placed in a school, we needed to have a place to live. My father knew that he had to have a job before he would find anyone who would rent him a place for us to live. Our escape from Winnipeg left us with even less than we had when we went to Winnipeg. Fitting all of us into my grandfather's car – four adults and seven children, including myself and Kevin who were close to being adults ourselves – left very little room for other things, even our clothing. Somehow, room was found for all of the remaining boxes of Bibles and other Catholic books that hadn't been sold. The idea of leaving evidence behind, especially considering the books could be sold to unsuspecting people, seemed more important that clothing.

~

With time beginning to pass by without my registering in a high school in Ottawa, I complained that I would likely fail grade nine if I wasn't able to go to classes. Mom was too depressed to do anything, and Dad was rarely around. I complained to Mémère who then began to shame both my parents into doing something about my schooling. Dad and Mom decided to get me some clothing from the St. Vincent de Pierre Society, free clothing. There wasn't a lot of choice for small teenagers, so I was given old adult clothing that was long out of style. None of the clothing fit me and that caused even more of a delay while Mom worked on altering these cast-off clothes to fit my small frame. Seeing myself in the mirror with these clothes, I almost was ready to give up the idea of going back to school entirely as I knew that I would be the laughing stock of the school.

Finally, I was back in school. It was an old, stone school that looked a lot like a castle to me. Lisgar Collegiate sat on the edges of the Rideau Canal adding to the idea that it was an old castle. It was quite large and was noisy with more than a thousand teenagers milling about. As I was registered, I was given a choice between Latin and typing. I already knew some Latin from my misadventures with church priests, but Dad told me I had to take typing as it was practical, not useless shit like Latin. As a result, I was "streamed" into the less academic program. I didn't complain. Since I was back in Ottawa, I was able to take French as one of my classes. French wasn't an option in Bow Island or in Winnipeg. However, music and art were not options for me. Rather, it was a drafting and a typing course that would finish out the limited amount of options given to a grade nine student.

Though the school was ancient in comparison with the high school I had attended in Winnipeg, I soon fell in love with the place.

If we can say that buildings have character then this building was beyond interesting with its nooks and crannies and a top floor which was off-limits to staff and students, apparently condemned for use as classrooms and offices until some bureaucrat saw fit to release funds for its restoration. The basement level was where I would hide, in the weight training room, away from classmates who would tease and harass me non-stop about the way I was dressed, about my poverty that likely could be smelled by anyone passing within a few yards of space. Poverty does have a smell that sticks to old clothing that finds its way into welfare offices, soup kitchens, and shelters for the desperate and homeless.

~

Poverty was beginning to make a stronger impact on my relationship with others, at least from my perspective as a teenager in high school. Living with poverty which had me often standing in line outside of bakeries so that I could buy old bread at a fraction of the cost, doing without so many things that had me sit on the sidelines and watch others play sports, enjoy food treats, and engage with each other with confidence. I had lost all confidence and didn't know if my father was again going to uproot the new beginnings. I couldn't depend on my parents to be there for me and provide for my needs.

Two years in Bow Island had allowed me to make friends, to see myself as part of a group, and to believe that I belonged. The loss of friends in moving to Winnipeg was met with a hope for a new place of belonging with school and teammates in football and soccer. Yet the latest dislocation from place and people had left me empty and distrustful. I was afraid to make friends, and poverty accentuated that fear. I came to believe that I was unworthy for some reason, of having friends. And, as a result, there was a return to self-isolation and dissociation from others.

~

In November, Dad found us our own place to live, an apartment in an old three-storey building in Rockcliffe Park. It was an old brick structure like Memere's and Pepere's, but it seemed to have had been better taken care of in its upkeep. We lived on the third floor while the landlord had the first two floors. No sooner had we moved in when Kevin and I got jobs working for the same company trying to sell booklets of business services. The booklets did offer good deals for those who would be using the business services for tires, meals at restaurants and dry cleaning, and so on; so we were able to bring in some needed cash. The need for money was high, especially for me as I was to continue going to Lisgar Collegiate. The school was a long way from our new place and I had to take a bus to get to school.

Dad finally got a job, selling Compact Vacuum cleaners. The money started to come in and despite the fact that Dad was selling lots of vacuums and occasionally winning trophies as salesman of the week and salesman of the month, we seemed to fall further and further behind. Perhaps it was because we had nothing left to start our new home and to build up enough clothing and to get the basics needed for a family. Everything from old beds and urine-stained mattresses had to be paid for, even if the cost was minimal. With the booklet sales period over, Kevin and I then took to the streets selling Christmas cards and gift wrap. I have to admit that I wasn't much of a salesman. Kevin soon made my few earnings seem even more pitiful than they were. Kevin had the same gift for sales as Dad. Gradually we began to have extras such as dressers, and other furniture in the house. To help make tight ends meet, I would walk down to the bakery and wait for bread which couldn't be sold at regular prices because it was going stale, to go on sale so that we would have to spend less on food. It all added up and with the pressure beginning to ease, the mood in the house began to be more positive. I guess we had been away from Ottawa long enough that Dad was eventually able to buy an old car with a small down payment.

At school, life was okay for the most part. The classes and teachers were good. As always, I liked going to school and learning. However, there still wasn't enough money for clothing that didn't reek of poverty or look like they came from a welfare box. If I needed some clothing, Mom would go to Saint Vincent de Pierre's in order to find something for me to use. One day while walking down the hallway in school, one of the students stopped upon seeing me and laughed to his friends pointing at the shirt I was wearing, a unique Hawaiian print short-sleeved shirt. He claimed to recognize the shirt as belonging to his uncle who had gone to Hawaii a few years before, a shirt he knew was put into the good will box for beggars and welfare cases. I had no choice but to wear that shirt for the rest of the day, but when I got home I gave it to Kevin who was wasn't in high school. At least he wouldn't have to hear that boy talk about his uncle's shirt.

I worked out in the basement weight room at the school, a place in which mostly big guys would hang out and brag about how strong they were. To tell the truth, I went there as much to hide as to work out. In the weight room, no one paid any attention to me as I was such a runt in comparison to them. I watched what the other boys did and tried doing some of the same things, but with a lot less weight on the bar. I was in the weight room at every opportunity, usually during lunch hours and it wasn't long before I had trained my few muscles to do some of the things they needed to do as a weight lifter. I gently added weight to the bars making sure that I didn't push the weight and hurt myself. By late spring I was bench pressing 200 pounds and could clean and jerk 150 pounds. I only had one accident on my first attempt with the clean and jerk at 150 pounds. I had successfully placed the weight over my head but then I lost my balance and toppled backwards. I managed to hold the bar and weights from crashing onto my chest or head. Then the other boys heard the racket they came to see what had happened. Rather than laugh, they looked at the weights and then at me with surprise.

They decided I needed to improve my footwork to avoid a similar accident in the future. These boys were bigger than I was, but they were not the popular athletes of the school. Wrestlers and weightlifters were a sub-culture of the school. I earned their respect because of my efforts and my growing skill.

Outside of the weight room I did make one other friend, a girl who was Italian with long dark brown hair, called Theresa. She was very thin and was always wearing a sad smile when I saw her. We were both in the same typing class. She missed more school than I did and she didn't seem to have any friends in the class. One day in the spring, I asked her to eat outside on the lawn with me, between the portable classroom where we had typing class and the main school building. She agreed, so we took our lunches out to eat in the warm spring sunshine. It wasn't long before I learned why she was missing so much school – she was dying and there was nothing anyone could do to make her healthy again. She had cancer. I couldn't believe that she could be so calm while talking about her death which would happen before another school year could begin. I looked for her every day and we were together at every opportunity, especially at lunch hours outside if possible. She always brought too much lunch; I think she saw how small the lunches I had were, and so added extras into her lunches and then claim she wasn't too hungry when we sat to eat together. I knew what she was doing, and that was okay. It made her feel good and she needed to feel good. During the first week of June, she again was absent. She never came back to school and I assume that she found some relief from the pain that haunted her eyes. I began to wonder why I had ever complained. I was healthy and alive and Theresa wasn't.

In mid-April we had to move out of the house in Rockcliffe Park. Our rent was due again and we hadn't paid the last month's rent either.

With no money, the landlord decided we had to go in the middle of the month so that he could get the place ready for new renters for May 1st. We made a pathetic scene as we used Dad's car and Pépère's car to haul our stuff to a place near Bronson Street where Mémère and Pépère now lived. One of the reasons we moved in again with Mémère and Pépère was because of the fact that Mom was about to have another baby. Justin was born in early May, 1965.

While we lived with Mémère and Pépère that May, Réjean and I hung out together whenever we could. We would both wear the same style of pale yellow jacket as proof of our being best friends. As we wandered down the streets, Réjean would teach me all about the latest models of cars. We didn't really do that much other than walk and talk as there was no money for doing more. At the end of May, we moved again, this time to Rosemount Avenue near the Kingsway, another three storey house. I was still going to Lisgar the whole time, just learning how to take different buses to get to the school. Sometimes I would walk home at the end of the day and save the bus fare money for a coke to enjoy on the way home. We got the top floor which was just two large bedrooms with a bathroom. We didn't need a kitchen as it was to be a communal affair in Mémère's kitchen on the first floor. Aunt Denise and Uncle Art lived on the middle level with their young family. Dad and Uncle Art had made up and all was well again.

When school was out, I got a job working as a parking lot attendant at the Civic Hospital, once I turned sixteen. It was an easy job giving out tickets to the customers which they would return and get time=stamped when they were ready to leave the parking lot. Occasionally I got to help unlock a car door using a bent coat hanger for those who had locked their keys in their cars. At home I gave most of the money to Mom keeping a bit of the money saving for a guitar and for small incidentals.

Life wasn't smooth while we lived on Rosemount Avenue. I got my first experience as a victim of fraud during that summer thanks to Mémère, who was addicted to bingo and went to every possible evening and afternoon to bingo. Because she went so often she was always winning things, sometimes very expensive things. Before we moved to Rosemount she told us she had won a new fridge. Of course, we believed her because of her previous winnings.

One day a man arrived at the house demanding to see me. I wondered why he would want to see me, was this some doctor who had discovered a scratch on his car? Most of the locked cars I had to help with were cars belonging to doctors. No, this man was a collection agent and he wanted money and he wanted it right now or he was going to take back the new fridge I had bought. Mom was standing beside me listening watching while this guy grilled me. Mémère was inside the house somewhere. I had to repeatedly ask the man what he was talking about. I had never bought a fridge nor had I even thought about it. He showed me a bill of sale with my name listed as the buyer. When I told him I had never been in that store, he said my wife signed the bill. I looked at the man as if he was insane. I told him I just finished grade nine, wasn't sixteen yet and that I definitely wasn't married. All he did was repeat his question, "Are you Robert Gilles Laflamme, born on July 22?" Of course I was the person he talked about. I only could repeat, "But I'm not sixteen, I can't get credit, I'm not married and I don't have a fridge." It soon became obvious to the collection agent that he had been sent on a wild goose chase. He realised that I wasn't old enough to have bought on credit. Angry and discouraged, the man said he'd be back as soon as he talked with the salespeople at the store and his supervisors at the collection agency. He never did come back.

After the man left, I heard my Dad yelling at his mother. "How in hell could you put that fridge on Benjy's name? How did you get away with it?"

She mumbled something about showing an envelope that showed she was Mrs. Gilles Laflamme and saying that her husband's name was really Robert Gilles Laflamme, that he used his second name, Gilles, for normal things. She was able to get credit for the needed fridge since Pépère's credit rating was now non-existent, using my name which had no debt history and no warnings attached to it. The thought that I was now in debt and was now a poor credit risk haunted me. I thought I would never be able to buy anything without paying for it in cash, and the likelihood of ever saving enough cash to buy a real car or a good guitar was slim as Mom was always desperate for every bit of money that I could bring home for bread, or groceries, or something needed for the baby.

I wanted to play music again, I needed music. At least once a week Uncle Pierre and Aunt Jacqueline would come down to visit. Uncle Pierre was a musician and he would bring a guitar and a fiddle along and soon everyone was singing up a storm or dancing in the living room. I usually played "spoons" as accompaniment to Uncle Pierre. I did get to try out his guitar and he was impressed enough to say that I could play in his band when I got another guitar and practiced the songs that they played. I had motivation and now a goal.

The work at the hospital parking lot allowed me to make friends with my co-workers who were all adults. The work was easy and there was always time to dream and plan of the day when I would be on my own, like these men. I liked my work, especially seeing the neat cars that the doctors drove, most of which were sports cars such as Citroen, Jaguar and BMW. A black Jaguar with wire rims was my favourite. I think it was the wood panelling and the wood steering wheel, as well as the sleek laid back look that got most of my attention.

Finally, I saved up enough money to make a down payment on a small guitar with a tiny amplifier. The salesman at the music shop was used to seeing me hang around, constantly trying out various guitars. One guitar that had caught my attention was a double guitar with one fret board being a six string guitar and the second fret board being a twelve string guitar. I knew that I wouldn't be able to buy that guitar because it was so expensive, so I focused on the no-name brands. I would often try playing a twelve string guitar simply because I liked the full sound. But when it came time to actually buy a guitar, cost was everything. I finally had a guitar again and began to dream of making money playing music with my Uncle Pierre.

Just as the 1965-1966 school year was about to start, Dad decided we needed to have our own place again. We moved to the south end of Ottawa where I enrolled in Ridgemont High. Mom got a job working at a local restaurant on Bank Street and I kept my job, part-time, working as a parking lot attendant at the hospital. Dad was up to his usual and was absent as often as he was present in the new house. One day he came home with a brand new Oldsmobile Toronado, a new kind of car that I thought looked cool. Seeing it, I began to want to have a car of my own, not something so powerful, just something that was mine and that I could use to get to work as I was tired of spending so many hours on the bus getting to work and back home again. I scoured the newspapers with Réjean's help and found an old 1957 Nash Metropolitan that was in very rough shape with part of the floor rusted out; it only cost $75. I almost had enough money and I wanted that car, so Réjean went with me to see if it actually worked. The motor started and he said he would supply the rest of the money for me to buy it, then he drove it home for me. I was proud of myself as Réjean drove up to the house. I had my own car and it was paid for in full, and I would soon get a driver's licence so that I could begin driving it.

Dad didn't have any time to teach me how to drive and left it to Réjean to teach me. But Réjean didn't have time either. He was having his own problems as his car had just broken down and he now had no way of getting to work. Dad decided I should let Réjean use my car until Réjean could get himself another car. I didn't feel as bad about it as I thought I would. Réjean did help me and he was like my older brother. I told Réjean that he could keep the car and not worry about it. When I got another car, we would work on it together and he would teach me to drive. After all, I had my guitar and had just played with Uncle Pierre for a Legion dance in Hull. I had music on my brain.

At school, I found a new passion, running. During regular P.E. classes early in the fall, the teacher had us do some running in the fields around the school. Somehow running seemed to set me free. When I ran, I forgot about the world, the unfairness, the poverty. Running was just about me and it seemed that nothing could stop me other than myself. The teacher soon had me on the school's cross-country running team. As well as cross-country running, I found myself enjoying a new course, I began to learn about accounting. I couldn't see why others found it difficult as I was always getting 100% on every test and quiz. Accounting was all about basic rules and once the rules were known, it was simply a matter of simple Math and attention to detail. It didn't hurt that I had learned the hard way, to keep my work neat and tidy. As a result of my successes in Accounting, I often would help classmates as they struggled with the concepts and that paid off in breaking the ice and beginning to have a few friends at the school.

Chapter Fourteen

Life continued to be experienced following the old patterns as my father found it necessary to move again. He had lost another job, had lost his new Toronado, and he had missed the last rent payment for the house we lived in near Ridgemont High School. I didn't respond with an expected depression with this move even though I had just been beginning to fit in at the school. I had even expected the move to happen as I was more aware of what was transpiring in my parents' world. I wasn't able to fix any of it, and I needed more time to get an education, so I did my part in making the move as easy as I could for us by putting a positive spin on it for my siblings and helping my mother with the transition. Running had helped me learn to work out my emotions and music was helping me find a place of hope for the future.

~

We moved to the west end of Ottawa, too far for me to continue travelling to Ridgemont High for classes, so I was enrolled in the closest high school called Samuel de Champlain. It was along the Ottawa River, quite close to Grandpa Schiller's place. Mom's baby sister, Pat was also a student in the school. She was in grade nine and I was in grade ten. Since we were so close to the Schiller home, Mom saw this as an opportunity for me to get to know Grandpa Schiller, the man who was the source of my name, Robert. She still had hopes that someday she would be included in her father's will. She hoped that the bond between Gramps and me would soften him and make her hopes be fulfilled. And so, I finally began to learn more about the Schiller side of the family.

Champlain High was a good school and I immediately found a home with the cross-country running team.

Though it was getting late in the season, I still got to run for the school in the city championships, likely because I was the fastest distance runner in that school of 1700 students. I had to do my training in the morning before classes, running on paths that followed the river. On the day of the city championships I was nervous as this was a big race on a very hilly course. I couldn't believe that so many of my school mates were out there cheering for me to do well. Champlain had never had a medal opportunity in the past in cross-country. Because of my speed, they began to think that this was all going to change.

New to competitive racing, I went out way too fast, running at the front of the large group with the two favourites. At the halfway mark I knew that I would be able to win as the two boys began to panic at not being able to drop me. And then I did what too many novice runners do, I decided to go for the win too soon. I took off with a sprint leaving the two other leaders behind me with the distance growing with each stride. I heard the cheering behind me which added to the adrenalin flowing within me and again picked up the pace though there was almost a half kilometre left to run. And then I got a pain in the side, just under my ribs which almost brought me to a complete stop. I had never experienced side stitches before so I was panicking, wondering if I had torn something inside of me. But, I knew I couldn't quit, that everyone was counting on my. My pride was even more important. I didn't want to be a failure, a quitter. I was tired of being a loser in life. It wasn't long before the two favourite runners began to pass me followed by others.

I finished the race in seventh place, feeling that I had lost more than I gained, that I had disgraced and disappointed my school. When I saw the coach and some of the other runners I began to apologize. The coach was laughing and clapped me on the back. I had set a new school record even though I finished seventh.

He told me that there was always next year. The other boys constantly talked about how I took off on the two favourites and made them look like they were crawling. For them, that sight was worth it all. It didn't matter that those favourites finished first and second as expected.

Music continued to be a big part of my private world at home. When Uncle Pierre told Mom and Dad about my successful debut as both a singer and a guitar player, Dad began to have his own dreams about my musical career. Dad was on a high driving around in another big new sports car and thought that I should get a "real" guitar. I should have known better, but he convinced me to trade in my inexpensive guitar and amplifier for one more suitable for a career in music. We went to a music store on Gladstone and checked out the guitars. I saw a nice Fender Stratocaster but knew that this was reaching too high. Dad didn't have that kind of money. Dad saw a Gibson Cherry and was sold on it though he had been talking to me earlier about getting a Les Pierre, a professional's guitar. While he had the salesman bring it down, I was trying out a different Gibson, a single cut-away Jazz guitar, a beautiful guitar with a beautiful sound. It wasn't as expensive as the Les Pierre or the Gibson Cherry. This was the guitar I wanted.

While I was entranced with that guitar, Dad got the salesman to bring out two large Fender amplifiers, and three multi-directional microphones and stands and had the salesman write up the bill of sale. When I looked up from the guitar to see all of these electronics I was astounded. Dad was going all out in a big way to make up for my having to take his place in Bow Island, my having to sell my first guitar. Since the stuff was to belong to me and not Dad, I had to sign the bill of sale. My cheaper guitar and amplifier were used as the down payment for the Gibson Cherry and my treasured Gibson Jazz guitars, amplifiers and sound equipment.

~

Growing up in an environment where no adult was responsible when it came to money, I lacked skills and real awareness of how to financially responsible. What I did learn was the sense that I was owed, entitled to more than I had because of the way life had been treating me. I was a victim that needed to be compensated. The world owed me. That attitude didn't make me competent to a party to buying musical instruments on credit. I abdicated the responsibility to my father and assumed that because I was such a good boy, all would work out in the end.

I didn't even admit to myself that all of this musical equipment was bought on credit, my credit. It took some time before I was aware that I was expected to make the payments and that awareness came in the mail in the form of a letter from a collection agency. Why didn't I know this? I would have to say that I didn't want to know. The idea of having my old equipment used as a down payment was a fact I overlooked. I wanted the new equipment, especially the Gibson Jazz guitar, and somehow believed that I was being given all of this equipment in payment for all the wrongs committed against me, a gift from my father for all sufferings he had inflicted on me. Being sixteen, I was legally responsible for my own debts. Being my father's son, I didn't see the debts, I just saw entitlement. Of course, there was no way that this was going to end well.

~

All I needed now, was a group of other teenagers to play with as a band. I had the equipment; they just needed to want to be famous musicians. Dad promised that he would manage our band, get us, get us dances, club performances, concerts, and eventually a recording contract. It didn't take too long before I found other young guys who wanted to form a band. Everyone had their own equipment but nothings as elaborate as what I had.

Two of the boys were older than me and in grade twelve. I only remember the name of the drummer, a boy called Charlie Brown who was in grade eleven and the same age as I was. We practiced at our house on Picton Street, playing over and over again songs by the Beatles and Rolling Stones, as well as a few other British rock groups. I was declared the vocalist for the band as well rhythm guitar. We took the name, Impalas, for the group name. When practices were done each evening, we would go for a ride in Charlie Brown's car, a little Mini Morris.

As winter came, I found myself walking the streets alone late at night, I needed alone time, some quiet time. I walked up and down the streets in the neighbourhood never really going far, just walking and thinking and enjoying the darkness and silence of the late night. One day, when I stopped in at the local drug store, I heard about a peeping tom being spotted in the area. When I asked what a peeping tom was, I began to wonder if people were thinking that I was that peeping tom. I was always walking in the evening though I didn't go up close to people's windows to peer into the houses and apartments. I was in a panic, worried that I would be grabbed off the street and thrown into some jail cell as a pervert, a jail cell filled with big guys who would see a young, small male and use him as a female. I stopped walking at night out of fear.

As promised, Dad got us a few dances to play in the community dance hall. We didn't exactly pack the dance hall, but at least we were playing and beginning to make a bit of money, though not enough. Dad decided that I needed to expand my playing and he found a country band in the Ottawa valley area which played on Sunday afternoons. I would get to play with Uncle Pierre on Saturday evenings and the occasional Teen dance on Friday's with my little band. In spite of all of this, the money still wasn't coming in fast enough for me.

I had given my father almost all of my share of the earnings, enough to make the payments, so I couldn't understand why he was so anxious about money. I began to think that perhaps it was more about our group not being good enough to become professionals in his opinion. For me, it was enough to be playing and paying my way.

Payments hadn't been made for the past two months, something that surprised me considering that I had given Dad the money I had made, enough money, for those payments. Since the guitars and equipment were in my name, I was expected to make the payments and that awareness came in the mail in the form of a letter from a collection agency. I asked Dad about returning one of the guitars and amps, as I thought that if I had less debt maybe I could more easily make the future payments. I was afraid of losing everything and again being without a guitar. Dad told me that the store wouldn't take anything back. He told me not to worry that it would all work out in the end.

I had heard this so often that I knew I had to do something else if I was to keep a guitar. I got a part-time job at a new grocery store even further to the west. I was hired as a stock boy in the fruit and vegetable department. I got paid $1.00 per hour and found that working night shifts on Friday's and Saturday's gave me more money than I was making with the band. I started work at midnight and was finished work when the store opened for business in the morning. I didn't quit playing music, but the number of bookings for out band began to disappear. Dad had found something else to keep him occupied and booking dances wasn't his priority anymore.

I don't think the lack of dances bothered our little band as we enjoyed jamming together the most. When we weren't jamming, we were driving around in Charlie's little car. Sometimes it was cold enough that we couldn't see out of the windshield without scraping the windshield from the inside.

Other times we would be scrapping freezing rain on the outside, with all the windows cranked down to chip at the ice. We laughed a lot. Charlie had a good tale to tell us about being stopped by the cops. He said the asked for his name and his driver's licence. When he said "Charlie Brown" the cop got mad at him and threatened him. Charlie told the cop to look at his driver's licence as his name was on the driver's licence – Charlie Brown. The cop didn't laugh, but he did let Charlie go.

For us, being able to play a couple of songs for one of the school assemblies was our crowning success as a band. That assembly made us feel we were finally special in the school, something hard to do in such a large school. In the weeks after our school concert, a few kids would came and talk with me. Those few kids were also oddballs in the school. Together we would hang around one of the smoker's barrels because of the three girls in our little group were into smoking, and being rebels wearing black clothes and boy's boots. Jerome, a pimply and skinny French-Canadian spent all of his time, when not in classes, hanging around me and the three tough girls who smoked and also swore with a vengeance.

As winter turned to spring, I lost my guitars and amps. I couldn't afford to make the payments and the two missed payments and penalties. They were repossessed. I was only sixteen but I was already on the same life path as the rest of the Laflamme family, a life path of poverty and having nothing to show for the money I did make. Rather than having something after all the part-time work and all of the dances and other performances, all that I had left was debt and no guitar. I resolved that I would only pay with cash and never buy on credit again. Dad, Pépère, Mémère had taught me a valuable lesson when it came to credit. When I lost my guitar, and I lost more than that.

I had to face the boys and tell them that there would be no more practicing at my place and that I had lost my guitars and amplifiers to a collection agency. I lost my confidence and my belief in myself.

All grade ten students had to take an IQ test in the spring, an annual event staged in the school cafeteria. As always, when it came to a test, I tried to do my best. In my opinion at that time it was a strange kind of exam, more like puzzles than about memorized knowledge. When the results came back, I was told by the school counselor that my score was 143. I didn't know if that was good or not and so he explained that it was very good. He then asked what I was taking for courses, for the elective courses. When I told him, he told me that I would be switching forms next year to join the form that would allow me to go to university rather than continue on in the mixed commercial and technical education stream. He told me that I had an IQ good enough to let me become a university professor or anything else I wanted to be. With those words, a new dream began to grow in my head, one that I was hesitant to ever tell anyone as I didn't want my dream to come crashing down. I just needed to be able to go to school and to find the way to pay for university.

I still had running. I didn't need money to run and I so I began to run, escaping from the house, escaping from my failure, constantly running. Spring was track season at high school. With my success in the cross-country meet the previous fall, it was assumed that I would be running middle distances, the mile and the half-mile races. I was excited to be included on the team and that the coach and other athletes already had respect for me as a runner. I trained as hard as I could. As practices progressed I had personal bests of 4:16 for the mile and 2:02 in the half-mile, and was hoping that I would qualify for the city championships that were to take place the first week of June. I had about five weeks left to prepare and train for the championships.

~

I had learned a valuable lesson about debt, one that has lasted and shaped my life as an adult. Other than taking out a mortgage and buying my first new car, I have somehow found a way to avoid borrowing money through the process of raising a family. The aversion to debt remains strong fifty years later. What also emerged at this time in my life, was the retreat into my body rather than into my mind. With running, I was able to feel without guilt. I learned to respect my body and listen to what it had to tell me. Before this, I had always disappeared into my mind.

Learning that there was an adult who respected my intelligence, my school counsellor at Samuel de Champlain High School, and learning that this intelligence could give me what money couldn't give me, I found a new hope, though it was tenuous at that time. I had the brains to have a career that would allow me to escape the cycle of poverty within which I had grown up. And so, the dream of becoming a teacher was conceived and tucked away in a safe corner.

~

Mom's plan for me to find favour with her father was being realised. Gramps was turning out to be a nicer man than I had imagined. Because I had taken Pat under my care at school, Gramps decided that his old 1953 Pontiac would become my car when I finally got my driver's licence which I had hoped to do in the summer. He brought the car over and parked it near the house making me promise not to drive it until I had the driver's licence. He had already put the car in my name as I was old enough to get my license. It was a promise I vowed to keep. However, I really didn't have to worry about keeping that promise for long as Dad took the car and traded it in for a new car, a convertible Cadillac. He drove that new car until it got repossessed. Again, I ended up with nothing but more broken promises.

However, Gramps didn't say anything to me about this, didn't blame me for the lost car.

I began to spend some of my weekend hours visiting at Gramps' house, especially when my uncle Bob was at home. When Bob came home for a weekend, he would usually answer the phone for Gramps. When the caller asked to speak to "Robert," Bob would go into a routine that always got a laugh from Gramps: "Would you like to speak to Robert Sr., Robert Jr., or Robert Junior-Junior, which is how he referred to me. Bob had recently become a drafting engineer, doing drawings for bridges and big buildings. As far as I could see, he, of all the family, had been the most successful when it came to education and career. I really didn't know any of the other Schiller's that well. Aunt Enid and Uncle Horace were friendly enough but more distant than close. Uncle Ron and Aunt Doreen were in Germany as Uncle Ron was a major in the military. Mom's other sister, Barb, lived in the States. It was a rare event to ever see these Schiller family relations.

Strangely, I never called Bob, Uncle Bob, nor did I call his younger brother, Wyatt, Uncle Wyatt. Sometimes Pat got into a mood and wouldn't let up on me until I called her Aunt Pat with Mom adding her voice to Pat's, she was after all, in spite of being younger than I was, my aunt. Granny Schiller was sick a lot with Diabetes and had effectively become blind. The Schiller clan had become a real part of my life while we lived on Picton. They were a stable contrast to the chaotic clan life of the Laflamme family.

A few days before final exams began in June, the school dismissed classes so that students could prepare for these exams. All students had to write all their compulsory exams such as English, Maths, Science and History, as those exams counted for 100% of the final mark. Exams were scheduled so that there was time off between exams. The optional courses only had exams for those who hadn't done well in the school year. I got full recommends for all of my optional classes so I had lots of preparation time for the compulsory finals.

Like most of my classmates, that study time was spent by the edge of the Ottawa River getting a tan while wearing a bathing suit. One of the girls in my class decided that I should notice her hoping that I would become her boyfriend. I guess she was intrigued with my "reputation" with the girls. Her name was Dawn and she was hard not to notice when she was wearing a bikini.

Thinking that I was really going to study with her at her home which was not far from the school, I arrived with my books ready to study. I knew that she did need some help though not a lot in order to get a good mark. We began studying French grammar together. After a short while, she went to get some chips and Coke for our study snack. When she returned she had no top on. I could see her bared breasts and found I couldn't take my eyes off of them. Her breasts were swollen below the nipple creating the impression of a small breast on top of a larger breast. They were breasts getting ready to blossom. Her overt sexual behaviour stirred me enough to engage in kissing her and kissing her breasts. But I didn't go any further. I didn't dare go any further. What if she got pregnant? I knew I was too young, I hadn't finished my education nor did I have any money to support her and a baby. I guess my fear and lack of response wasn't what she had expected. I ended up having to leave early and was never again invited to her place. I don't know if I felt relief or disappointment in being considered a reject.

So, I focused on my exams and ended up getting high marks. It was now time to get a full-time job. The grocery store where I had been working part-time had an opening for full time so I took it and found myself with the overnight shift in the produce department. I spent at least an hour on the bus to get to work and another hour returning home in the morning each day. My days off were Sunday and Monday nights. I was always tired and couldn't find a way to rest in the house because of kids.

When Mom had no more work for me in the house, I spent time by the river dozing and reading. I did the work needed at night and found time for a few hours of sleep when it got too quiet at the store. I got a raise of five cents per hour after two weeks, and though it wasn't much, it did add up at the end of each week. I was determined to buy myself a guitar, one that was acoustic so that I didn't have to have to buy an amplifier as well. If I kept my wants small, perhaps I would be more successful in buying it and keeping it. I really wanted a twelve-string guitar.

I got paid every two weeks and gave more than half of the money to Mom. The rest I used for my bus fare, the odd trip to a local café for fries and coke while listening to songs on the jukebox; and, I began to put money down on a guitar, an inexpensive twelve-stringed guitar. If I kept up the payments, I would have it in my hands paid in full before the end of the summer. There was no way that I would buy the guitar on credit. What was part of the deal was my being able to go into the store to play the guitar until guitar and a cheap protective case was finally paid for. I finally got to bring home my new guitar by the middle of August. I didn't have to worry about making payments. I didn't have to worry about losing it. When I brought the guitar home, Mom asked how I come I had a new guitar, how did I get it. When I explained about how I put some money down every two weeks, paying on lay-away, she reacted quite fiercely:

"*What? You spent money on a guitar? You saw that we didn't have enough money at home. How could you be such a selfish little bastard?*"

Her eyes had narrowed and her mouth took on that pinched look of pure hatred I had come to know too well.

"*How could you be so god-damned selfish when you see how little we have?*"

She slapped me hard. "You little shit, you pious little bastard. Why do you think you are so much better than the rest of us? You're always hiding behind a book, sulking in the background, always trying to make everyone else feel guilty. What kind of man are you – man? You are a pathetic, greedy little boy who thinks only about himself."

And she hit me again and again and I just stood there saying nothing. I began to doubt myself again and my right to have things when there was so little for my brothers and sisters. Too easily, I slipped into feeling guilty. The thought that maybe I should just take the guitar back and give her the money that I could get for it from the store owner, raced through my head. I had a few dollars in my pocket and guiltily handed it over. It meant that I would have to walk to work and back for the next week, but at least she would know that I was going to do more for her, more for my brothers and sisters.

I was walking down the street with my guitar with the intentions of taking it back to the store when I stopped. What was I doing? The guitar was my only way of holding onto hope, holding onto sanity and I knew it. I wasn't the father responsible for everything in our house. I deserved at least this much. I began to suspect that Dad wasn't well that he would plunge into darkness and then emerge flying higher than possible with dreams that infected everyone who knew him. I wasn't the Dad in this picture; I was a high school student helping as best I could. It wasn't selfish to want and have a guitar. Changing my mind, I changed direction and headed to the river to find a quiet place where I could play a few songs. I didn't know what was going to happen next, but I was determined to keep the guitar. With school starting in just a week, I knew that I would have even less money to give to Mom to help out. But, I needed to go to school. If I quit, I knew that I would never escape this poverty, this craziness.

I was afraid that I would go insane and hurt someone. I was afraid. As I sat on the grass under a tree near the water, I played the guitar and I cried.

Chapter Fifteen

My focus on poverty, in which my family had lived with for much of my childhood and youth, and the guilt that had built up for not being able to fix it even though it wasn't my problem to fix, ate at my soul. There was a part of me that knew I had to survive mentally if I was ever going to escape from the cycle of poverty. I intuitively knew that mental balance was critical and that music was a significant medium that would keep me from giving up. I saw my siblings suffering in their own ways from the cycles of hope and collapse that our parents had lived. I saw that the dollars that I brought home were used for food, sometimes for clothing, and sometimes just wasted. I saw that there was never enough money in spite of the dollars that I added. I didn't begrudge my siblings these dollars and I wished that I could have given more.

My self-driven guilt was used by my mother to squeeze out as much out of me as she could. I had stopped being one of her dependent children years earlier. She was the victim of poverty and had few options left to use in order to ease the suffering that poverty had inflicted on her and her children. I didn't understand this at that time of my life, and even if I had understood it, it wouldn't have lessened my growing sense of hopelessness and depression. Rather, that knowledge would have been too much to hold and would have potentially resulted in my acting out frequent, dark, suicidal thoughts.

I had lost connection with my brother, Kevin, since the family's return to Ottawa from the west. My going to high school, a different school, was one factor. However, my creating a life in music and the time spent in the Schiller home with my mother's brother Bob standing in as an older brother were also reasons for the growing distance. With music, I was able to escape the reality of poverty. With Bob, I escaped the role of caretaker and had a chance to breathe.

Bob was getting married to Jackie, a girl from Sault-Ste-Marie just as grade 11 was beginning. He asked me to be an usher for his wedding and so I became part of the wedding party in Sault-Ste-Marie. Bob rented a proper suit for me to wear for the wedding so that I looked more like a modern and prosperous young man. Bob and Jackie made a nice couple, and as I looked at them, I saw something I had never seen with Mom and Dad; they looked as though they liked each other. Of course, that was natural given the circumstances of just getting married, but they had been together a while and their marriage was by choice, not a shotgun wedding.

Being a part of their wedding party and the celebrations after the wedding opened a new kind of relationship between Bob and me. I stopped being a kid and was accepted as a young adult in my own right. That said, I didn't exactly stand on equal footing with him. I knew, and he made sure I didn't forget, that my family of origin was dysfunctional and that I deserved to be pitied. He would always have something derogatory to say about the Laflamme clan and he wondered if I would ever be able to raise myself out of that cess pool. Bob's words quickly cooled any close bonds that may have been developing. But in spite of his words, I began to think that he was okay, especially with the kind and bubbly Jackie as his wife.

In spite of the wedding celebrations, I was very depressed. I went to work on weekends and retreated into my music whenever I could which wasn't often as there was always something that needed my attention at home. Mom was spending more time with her own mother now that the rift between her and her father seemed to be healed. Grandma Schiller was quite sick and was often in the hospital. I was in charge of making sure that my brothers and sisters were fed, that they got to school with lunches, and that the house was kept in some sort of reasonable shape.

Kevin was always making himself scarce, not that I could blame him. For some reason, Dad was perhaps harder on him than he was on me. Béatrice was a young teen yet was treated by Mom as if she was an idiot. Gilles and Gordon were best friends as they played in the yard and with their friends from school. It helped that we had again stayed in a house going to the same school for almost a year. Suzanne and Neil were easy to take care of, but Justin just wasn't a happy toddler. Neil followed me everywhere I went in the house and the yard, always checking to see what I was doing. It was obvious that I was his hero, especially when I got out the guitar. All the kids liked when I played the guitar. It became the magic tool when I couldn't find another way to bring calm out of the chaos in the house. Because there was never enough money for me to have decent clothes, I avoided being in school photos, even the cross-country and track team photos. I was still on the cross-country team, but I wasn't really training. I was too tired and too depressed.

With going to work on the weekends and constantly taking care of kids at home, I had no energy, time or ambition to run. School was someplace I went to for a few hours each day before returning to the real world of our home. Who would take care of the kids when they got home from school? Mom usually went out as soon as I got home to visit her mother.

Just as it was time to begin the fall competitions, Dad decided we had to move again. Again we moved our meagre belongings, more than we have had for years, by car. Again, the pee-stained mattresses tied to the top of the car. I was ashamed to be seen moving our stuff this way, especially stuff that was so stained and exposed for all to see. The move took a few days. The house on Merival Road was bigger than the one we had on Picton and that was an improvement. I was told that I would be able to continue going to Champlain High School once we had things straightened around in our new home.

It took longer than I expected for things to get straightened around as Granny Schiller was now in the hospital full-time as she was dying. Mom spent almost all of her time now at the hospital with her mother which meant that I was needed at home full-time to take care of Suzanne, Neil and Justin. School would just have to wait.

Every once in a while I got the opportunity to visit Granny and listen to her tell of her dreams, her dreams of walking up a mountain. She had the same dream almost every night where she found herself walking up a mountain. She told me that when she reached the top of the mountain, she wouldn't be coming back; that the top of the mountain was where the doorway to heaven was waiting for her. As she spoke to me about her dream, I believed her. I had heard so many stories of her special abilities at foretelling the future, about communicating with ghosts, and of course how she was the one who made sure I got to a hospital in time when I had a nephritis attack when I was a child. I saw Granny the day before she died; she told me that when she went to sleep that night she would reach the top of the mountain. She told me that it was time to say goodbye. She gave me a book, to help me remember her – The Divine Comedy by Dante Alighieri.

~

I still have the book. This book is the only object from my youth that still remains in my possession. As I look back over a distance of almost five decades since her death, I am left wondering how little I knew of her and how little she knew of me and my siblings. Rare visits to the Schiller home didn't give much of an opportunity to build a relationship between my grandmother and me. Often when we did go, she was ill. Yet, for all of that absence and distance, my grandmother had a powerful influence on my belief system. I learned that the world was more than what met the eye, the world was deeper and richer. In that larger universe, good and evil were constantly at war.

Each of us had an integral to play in this war, a part that was not limited to one lifetime. She taught me that blindness is not what we think it is. If one was ready, one could see what others couldn't see. My grandmother was blind, a result of living so long with diabetes. Yet, she saw so much more than others. She also taught me about the power of dreams.

As I sit in my office today, writing this story, I can see where the seeds were planted within me that allowed me to see a different world today, one that is richer in a spiritual sense. Her gift to me prepared me to have a space made ready for Buddhism and for depth psychology. Perhaps my orientation to depth psychology came out of what she taught me about the world of dreams.

~

The funeral for Granny was sombre and gray. Mom cried a lot; Gramps kept a stiff pose throughout the whole ceremony. There were other tears for Granny, but not too much attention was given to Gramps. As the funeral ended and all returned to their homes, Gramps was going to have to spend the night alone, so Mom and Dad said I should go spend the night with him and keep him company. It wasn't a matter of even thinking about it, I was told what to do and I did it thinking I was doing what I was supposed to do, doing what was needed, doing the right thing. Gramps had just lost his wife and he was suffering.

When I got to Gramps' house, he showed me where I was going to sleep upstairs. I was looking at the books on a shelf as I wondered why Pat, or Bob, or Wyatt wasn't at the house to help their father. But then, perhaps they were grieving too much to think of that. Gramps began to talk about being a boy in school and how the boys would stick their penises in the worm holes of the fence behind the school and how the girls would play with the heads of the penises while on the other side of the fence.

As he told me this tale, he put his hand inside of my pyjamas as if to show me what the girls did. I froze. This was a nightmare, a nightmare out of my past coming back to haunt me.

Gramps continued to talk while fondling my penis. He talked about how Granny had never really loved him; he talked of how his father had forced him to marry Granny. He loved a different girl but his father didn't approve of that girl. Gramps talked to me about how hard it was for him, as Granny hated sex and avoided it as much as possible and only had sex with him as a duty, a dirty duty. He talked about his father and his grandfather who had been so strict with him and all the time he talked, he held my penis, moving his hand. He told me that he didn't love Granny, but that he didn't cheat on her either. And then the semen burst out of me all over his hand and messed my pyjamas. I was so ashamed, I began to apologize saying I was sorry, I was sorry . . . I was sorry. Gramps said it was okay, and helped me clean myself off before telling me to go to sleep and forget about it. It wasn't anything for me to be upset about.

He left me sitting there on the bed and left the bedroom. My grandfather had just molested me and I was seventeen years old, and I did nothing to stop him. I hadn't resisted or protested, I had an orgasm and I had ejaculated all over his hand. I didn't tell anyone. I was ashamed. I should have said no, could have said no. I wasn't a little boy anymore unlike when I had been molested by priests. Why? Why did I just sit there and listen to him as he spilled out his stories while molesting me? I raged inside, "What the hell was it about me that made people molest me?" I believed that Gramps was a good man and that the priests were good people. And at this point, I began to believe, really believe that I was the problem, I brought out the worst in people, brought out their demons against their will.

~

I left that house no longer a boy. I left that house as a man haunted by secrets that I knew must never be told. I left that house burdened with a darkness buried deep within me. What was left of me to bring to the outer world would be just the surface, the outer shell of who I was and who I would be for decades to come. No matter what, the darkness was shoved deep, anger was swallowed and none of it was allowed to come to the surface to hurt others. I had to protect myself and others from that darkness barricaded within.

The fact that I hadn't resisted, protested became one of the weapons I continued to turn to and abuse myself with for many years. When I finally admitted out loud to a psychiatrist to whom I had been referred by my medical doctor, the events of that night, she echoed what I had told myself for too many years, that it was my fault, that I was old enough to have said no and have the abuse stop if I had wanted it to stop. It was the first, and last time, that I had a mental health practitioner blame the victim for being abused.

~

Life on Merivale Road was different for me than it had been at any other house we had ever lived in. I got to see Dad in a different light; for a while, we even became friends. Dad was at home almost all of the time. He wasn't working anymore and we were on welfare again. It didn't seem as bad as before because he was at home. Mom was quieter, staying in the background as Dad sat in the living room. Dad was suffering his own depression. I began to suspect that Dad suffered some kind of illness that didn't allow him to be a normal person. When he had the energy we would go out together to a local café where we would have a coffee and sometimes even a piece of apple pie. I still had a part-time job so I was able to use a bit of the money for these treats. The rest of the money went to Mom who had no hope of ever having enough to feed such a large family.

Dad took to building lamps using Popsicle sticks. He made beautiful creations; one in particular, made for the local base of the RCAF, was a masterpiece. I saw that Dad was an artist underneath all of the shit that had complicated his life. I began to wonder what dreams he had lost because he had to get married so young. I knew that he loved music, could play almost any modern song on the piano by ear. I kind of began to understand why he hadn't cared for me when I was young, why he was always so angry with me. I was the reason he had lost his dreams, lost his chance for a better life. He lost his life because he had to get married. That knowledge weighed heavily on me and added to my own depression and descents into darkness.

Gramps came to our house often after Granny died. Gramps made no secret that he was thankful for my caring enough to comfort him when Granny died. Both Mom and Dad saw Gramps coming to our home and becoming a part of our life as a gift from heaven. Perhaps Mom was going to be finally be able to be included in Gramps' will, something that had been denied when she had married Dad. Gramps brought gifts of fruit and sometimes meat which Mom would then cook up as though it was Christmas. Of course, because I was the one who somehow been the catalyst that made Gramps want to come to our house, because I saw how happy and hopeful my parents were, because I saw his gifts to them which helped make sure there was more food for the kids, I couldn't say anything about what had happened. I couldn't be responsible for destroying their hopes and result in having less food on the table, It was good to see Mom and Dad smile.

Gramps would sit beside me at the supper table. I didn't flinch when he would touch me while talking to Mom and Dad. I held my breath and hoped he wouldn't stroke too much as I was afraid that I would come and embarrass him and my parents and bring it all tumbling down.

Some evenings we would play cards, Dad, Gramps, Kevin and I – Cribbage. Once, Gramps dealt me a perfect hand for Crib, a perfect twenty-nine. I preferred playing Crib with Dad, just the two of us, while he was healing whatever it was that was broken inside. In November, Dad finally got a job. Gramps continued to come on occasion and I continued to go blank, to not hear, see or feel anything. I know that I was going to school, but couldn't remember anything about going to school. I know I was there, doing what I was supposed to do there, but have no memories until Christmas time.

Christmas 1966 - I had been given a portable record player and two record albums, one by Gordon Lightfoot and the other by The Righteous Brothers. It was as if I had just woken up in the middle of a play. I spent almost the whole day up in the bedroom playing the albums over and over again singing "In the Early Morning Rain" and "You've Lost that Loving Feeling." I worked hard, trying to teach myself how to play Lightfoot's songs knowing that I had discovered a new doorway to enter, the world of folk music. But then the darkness again descended for a while.

In late winter I found myself again at Gramps' house, with him in the garage. I had noticed two pairs of old wooden skis stored in the garage and asked if anyone ever used them. Gramps let me take them home. I took them home and Kevin and I began to go skiing on them. They were old skis with bear-trap bindings. For the most part, we skied on fields as if we were cross-country skiing finding small slopes to slide down. I remember one time we were skiing near a busy road on a field beside the road that had a few gentle hills. As we skied round and round, the trail got faster because the trail was packed hard enough even though a gentle snow as beginning to fall.

We had one hill that would approach the highway which was busy with traffic below, approaching it near an overpass. As long as we stayed on the fence side of the overpass, it was safe enough.

For some reason, as we raced down the hill, almost side by side, I chose to turn to the outside of the frost wire fence. I slowed to a stop about a third of the way across with nothing but a drop off to the highway below on my right side. When I realised what I had done, I froze. I couldn't go backwards as there was no room to turn. Kevin saw my terror and talked to me, talked me into slowly going forward. I only made it across because of Kevin. Why had I deliberately turned risking a fall into traffic that was racing on the highway below? It was as if I was daring myself to make it all end.

It was almost the end of the skiing season by the time I finally went to ski at the ski hill inside the city, a small hill with tow-ropes and a chair lift. It was a sunny and warm day and I was enjoying the thrill of skiing down the hill, learning a bit how to parallel ski, something Bob had told me about. Apparently these were Bob's old skis. I was getting braver and braver though not really ready to ski all out. I needed to stay in control and when the speed picked up I would slow down using a snow plow technique. I skied for a few hours and then went to have a cup of hot chocolate. I was with other people, friends from school. In the late afternoon, the temperature began to drop.

It was still warm enough for me, so I decided to go down the hill one more time, this time I would try jumping the moguls. I had been jumping the small training mogul with good success earlier and was now ready for more. I knew that I could ski out if it got to be too much. However, as I went over the first mogul, I knew I was going too fast. The cooler late afternoon temperatures had made the base icy. I landed the small jump successfully but was slightly off balance when I found myself up in the air again. When I landed, I wasn't ready. The right ski broke, one of my ski poles bent and I ended up in a heap. I felt a pain in my foot and knew I had broken my foot.

I didn't panic. Though there was pain, it wasn't all that bad as compared to real physical pain.

I calmly took off the remaining ski and stuck it upright in the snow along with my poles and then waited for the ski patrol to come and get me. I knew that they needed to get me down the hill safely so that I wouldn't be a hazard to others. I watched the ski patrol go by and go up again on the ski lift and wondered why they didn't stop to help me. Finally, I waved at them to get their attention. They came and were surprised when I told them what had happened. They told me that since I was sitting so calmly on the slope, they had no idea that I had had an accident. They brought a sled in which to take me the rest of the way down the hill. I was embarrassed that my friends had to see me leave the hill on the rescue stretcher.

I did break the foot, an impact break. I then had to have a cast. I was told that I was going to be wearing the cast for at least six weeks. All I could think about was how that meant my track season at school was over. It also meant I couldn't go to work. My memories again stopped as I descended into darkness and hid.

~

The human mind has a peculiar way of trying to heal itself. The work of burying all the stuff that stresses the psyche takes a lot of energy, energy which obviously is not then available for being consciously aware of what is going on in the outer world. Not being a conscious participant, resulted in so many events of life at that time being lost. It was as though there was a barrier between my ego self and my larger sense of self. I was on automatic pilot going through routines, avoiding stirring anything up inside of myself. I understand as a mature adult that what was happening was a period of buffering the psyche so that it could build a safe place, a foundation for survival. There was just too much to be held in memory, too many woundings.

~

One event emerges out of the darkness at school. The school was taking us to Expo '67 for the day. I don't know where the money came from to pay for this trip, but I do remember the lines at the various pavilions. My classmates and I stopped to eat at the German pavilion after touring some of the other pavilions. The line up at the geodesic dome that was the American pavilion was so long that we decided to avoid in favour of the smaller pavilions that had almost no lineups. We saw the amusement park, but that wasn't on our agenda for the day, an agenda that had to do with both and English and a Social Studies combined assignment. I am amazed at how clear the details of that day have remained for me when there is nothing but darkness on either side of the day.

I finished grade eleven with good marks for the most part, especially in English, Social, Physics and Math. For some reason I wasn't taking French anymore. I found a job, again working for a car park company, the same company that I had worked for when I was sixteen, but at a different location. I was in the downtown area working in a high rise car park. During the slack hours I would be sent out with a wire brush to scrape rust off the metal posts. Somehow I sense Dad's present at the car park as though he was the one who got me the job there; it was as if he was also working there.

And before the summer ended, we moved out of the city onto an acreage.

Chapter Sixteen

Leaving the city to live in the country, in my last year of high school became the beginning of a new stage in my life. I say this in spite of the fact that in reality, very little had changed with the move. My parents didn't become better parents. They were still the same broken people acting out the same scripts with each other, with their children and with all the others who bumped into them along the way. The first difference was the absence of my grandfather Schiller from our home. The second difference was my discovery of naturism, the act of being nude in nature which became my retreat from the world, a time for meditative and healing quiet. It was a beginning, however small, where I denied the power of the world to hurt me to the point where I wanted to self-destruct. In a way, I was also perfecting the survival strategy of dissociation, taking my soul and spirit into a safe place in order to avoid feeling too much. The third difference was a sense of defeatism and indifference that came along with dissociation. I stopped caring – well, almost.

Unknown to me, was that this dissociation was also an unconscious strategy that would allow me to separate from the family and become an independent person.

~

The new house was an old, barn-like house that was in rough shape. It sat on an acreage that had a large garden area. One of the first tasks I was given was to use a spade to dig out a plot for Mom's future vegetable garden. There were quite a few old farm buildings that were in various states of falling down, dangerous places. Dad was in his element with all kinds of plans to transform this house into a showcase home. Part of that dream involved landscaping the yard to make pathways through the scattered trees as well as to create a fake stream with a bridge over it.

I moved a lot of dirt and built a wall of stones at the entrance to the yard so that the culvert was bordered with stones cemented into place to create an impression of sophistication.

I got my old grocery store job back, full time for the rest of the summer, still working the night shift. It was decided that I could continue to go to Champlain High School for grade twelve. So, I began to save for a car. Near our old home on Picton there was a very small used car dealer. It was really a car repair place that had only a few old cars that had been left, or given up. I found a small white Ford Falcon that was for sale for $150. I promised to bring in $20 every week to the owner if he would keep the car for me; it was like buying a car using a lay-away plan. Every week I would bring the owner the money as promised. I was also saving a bit on the side, again scrimping on lunch money and bus fare. I had estimated that by the time I returned to classes in September, I would be able to drive my little car to school from the farm.

During the summer, I took to running again in the countryside on the dirt roads and on the gravel roads. I had convinced the coach to lend me some running shoes with spikes so that I could be even more prepared for the cross-country season that lay ahead. I ran in the heat, wearing my school sweats as I didn't have my own running clothing nor did I want to spend money for some. The money was being held for the car that I needed if I was to go to school at Champlain. When I wasn't running, I was working on Dad's landscaping projects in the yard or helping Mom in the house with the kids, work that seemed to never get done.

Sometimes on hot summer afternoons, before I would have to head to town by hitchhiking, I would find a quiet space in a meadow behind the old barn at the back of our yard where I would strip off all of my clothing and read one of the poetry books that used to belong to Granny Schiller.

Those moments of poetry and being naked under the warmth and light of the sun were what I felt I needed in order to heal from the torment of the past year. Nudity and sunshine and warmth – these were my weapons to fight the darkness that was forever circling around me.

Dad was sporadic in his appearances at home. When he did come home, we would find ourselves hustling to begin a new project. One day Dad came driving up the driveway in a new car. I was surprised and a bit pleased as Dad had bought the same kind of car that I was soon to be getting, a white Ford Falcon. When the car came to a stop I was there to greet Dad and starting talking to him about what a good car the Falcon was. Dad smiled and then began to tell me the plans for the next stage of making our new home, our home.

Now that the driveway entrance had been given a stone wall around the culvert and the mini bridge project had been sort of completed, Dad decided to turn the square, flat-roofed box of the house into something more pleasing to the eye. He wanted to put a sloped roof from the top of the walls to partway down the walls to create the illusion that the house wasn't an old box. This meant that a lot of ladder work was involved. Kevin and I were conscripted to help with the project. I cut up the wood and got the supplies together while Dad had Kevin carry up the pieces for the framework. When we ran out of some supply or other Kevin was sent to the village of Carlsbad Springs to get what we needed as he had his driver's license, as well as a car.

One day while Kevin was gone, Dad ordered me to carry up some needed pieces to him. I was terrified of heights but I gathered up the needed 2x2's and began carrying them up the ladder to where he was on the other ladder. I guess the sight of me trembling while carrying up the bits of lumber was just too much for Dad. He began calling me all kinds of dirty names telling me that I was a sissy fag. In disgust he threw one of the sticks at me and clipped me enough that I fell off the ladder just as I was about at the top.

Seeing me stunned and laying on the ground just seemed to increase his anger. Kevin was driving up the driveway bringing whatever he had been sent for as Dad screamed out,

"What kind of fucking man are you, you little shit? Your younger brother is more of a man that you are. You don't even have your fucking driver's license. What fucking kind of Laflamme are you?"

I took off, running. I had had enough and left to go to the city early. I had more than an hour extra to kill before I had to go to work, so I went to look at my car. I swore that soon I would drive up to the house and then Dad would see that I really was a man. When I got to the car lot, the car was gone. In shock and disbelief, I asked the owner where the car went. "Oh, your Dad picked it up. He's a good man your Dad. He told me that you would be here soon to pay off the last bit of money. He said he wanted to surprise you with the car early since you've been good at making the payments. Did you bring the last payment?"

Silence; that was all I could give in response; a stunned silence. I turned away, in disbelief. I held off the tears until I got to the river's edge. I never did make it to work that day. I decided to go home early and got back to the house just after Suzanne, Neil and Justin, the little ones, had gone to bed. Dad was long gone. Kevin was gone wherever it was that he spent his free time. Béatrice, Gilles and Gordon were watching TV with Mom. I went into the kitchen, hungry for something to eat but there were no leftovers. I was going to cook up some macaroni and cheese for myself, but the pots were all dirty, and the dishes were still sitting on the counter and in the sink. The place was a pigsty. I got angry, grabbed the pot I would have used and threw it.

Mom came into the kitchen looking at me strangely. She didn't have anything to say about my throwing the pot, all she said was that Dad needed the car for his new job and that he would pay me back soon.,

She told me that I could find another car. Looking at the mess kitchen, Mom said, "Béatrice doesn't clean up like you always used to do." Then she left the kitchen to return to watching TV. That was that. Dad needed my car; his need made it okay for him to steal my car. And, I was supposed to understand that and believe it and accept it, because that is what a good son does, that and cleaning up messes.

I did clean the kitchen and found even more pots and pans in the oven of the stove. By the time I had finished and had cooked up my macaroni and cheese, everyone else had gone to bed. The house was quiet. I sat in the darkness of the living room. I had recently bought a few Deutschland label records of classical music and began to listen to Wagner's story of Tristan and Isolde. I sat in the dark for a lot of hours that night wondering about how I would now go to school from the farm. There wasn't any bus service. I began to lose hope, lose my will in the darkness thinking that I wouldn't be able to even finish high school, let alone find a way to go to university.

~

School had been one of my safe zones as a child and youth with the bullying and the sexual molestation by priests. Being gifted with a brain that allowed me to learn easily in spite of missing so many months of schooling over the years had kindled a secret hope that I would, one day, become a university professor. No one knew of this desperately held dream except my uncle Robert. At this point, it looked as though this dream was about ready to shatter – no graduation from high school would be possible if I wasn't able to get to school. I knew that I couldn't "wing it" on the final exams which I wouldn't be able to pass if I missed too much school.

~

When Dad returned a few days later like he always did, he embraced me as if he had forgiven me for the last scene when I made him mad.

He told me that Mémère had agreed that I could sometimes stay at her place when work made it too late for me to get back to the farm. Dad said that he would drive me to school most of the time so I wasn't to worry about it. And yes, he was talking to one of his friends about another car for me. It wasn't going to be long before I had my own car and then drive myself to school. I didn't believe him about the car, but a thin hope began to stir knowing that I could stay with Mémère and Pépère and continue going to high school.

Dad did drive me to the city most mornings, to the Alta Vista Shopping Centre from which I would catch a bus downtown and then transfer a second bus in order to get to Samuel de Champlain High School. He even paid for my bus tickets for a while. I hadn't thought he would have kept his word, but he did, at least in helping me get to school. On those days he didn't come home at night, I was up early enough to catch a ride to the city with one of the neighbours.

The yard work stopped as did the work on the outside of the house. I was told to clean up the mess, to put everything away into one of the barns, a task that I did without thinking of disobeying. However, one Saturday, while I was at work at the grocery store, Dad was at home cutting the grass when he ran over some old rusty nails. One nail caught in the spin of the blades and flew into his leg as if shot from a gun. When I got home, Mom screamed at me saying it was all my fault. She ranted that because I hadn't cleaned up the old nails on the lawn, Dad would likely have bone cancer. She screamed that Dad shouldn't have had to have cut the grass when he came home. I should have done it without having to be told to do it, that it should have been me with the nails in my leg instead of Dad. It was my fault. I should have been the one injured. Somehow I accepted her words as truth. I missed picking up some nails, nails that I didn't know were hidden in the grass.

I should've cut the grass, would have cut the grass if I was not so much in outer space.

I believed it was my fault that Dad was likely dying of cancer. There was no room for rational thought when it came to life at home.

~

Trying to make judgement calls almost fifty years after, is impossible as all that remains are the left over affects, the burned in images and memories that never tell the whole truth. Now, I can see that there was some truth spoken by my mother, but not the whole truth. I was a teenager who was distant from being mentally present in the world, partially because of what I can only say was due to survival strategies, and partly because of a personality type that is more directed to the inner world than the outer world. The sensate, the function of personality that is based on sight, sound, and all the other senses, the domain of common sense, was my weakest function, taking a back seat to intuition. It was intuition that provided me the necessary strength to survive repeated physical beatings, sexual molestation including incest, assaults on my very being as a young male. Had I been more present, I would have done a better job of cleaning up the yard and the accident could have, perhaps, been avoided.

However, the failure to have done a task properly doesn't fit with a parent wishing her child would have suffered a wounding instead of her husband. In writing out this part of the story, I have come to realise that my taking on blame and punishment and then increasing the pain by adding my own voice within to confirm what the outer world was telling me was only increasing my own level of dysfunction. I had joined the outer world as I swallowed their words wrapped within my own intense feelings of guilt. This reactive response has continued unchecked across my life and still makes its destructive presence in my life from time to time.

In today's world, when this affect appears, the only recourse I have is to take a time out for meditation; sitting meditation or walking meditation or even both. When the affect passes, I begin to come back to the present and wonder at the power of such an ancient power within me. The destructive enemies had internalized themselves inside of me just waiting for triggers to activate them.

~

School was getting interesting again. I was now taking Chemistry and we were getting to write formal essays in both English and Social Studies. I was learning about research essays and how to use footnotes. The biggest assignment was to come in the spring. For the fall, the big event was a mock U.N. assembly which was to be held at Carleton University. I was selected as one of the few students chosen from our school to be a participant at the model United Nations Assembly. I was assigned as the delegate from Poland. The topic was the Vietnam War. I poured over every document I could and was soon glad that I had been assigned as Poland as it would allow me to speak out against the war even though technically I was supposed to be in support of the American involvement in the war.

I didn't get to make much of a speech during the assembly as Poland was a bit player, but I did make a statement that did draw attention with my withdrawing Poland from the supportive orbit of the United States. I was determined to say what was on my mind. I hated the idea of an army attempting to destroy a country and its people all because of a desperate need for oil.

I began to invest a lot more time into the study of politics. As fall turned into winter, my attendance at school began to be a problem. Dad hadn't been coming home a lot of nights once he was released from the hospital. He didn't have cancer. He did have a minor heart condition though.

Mom survived from welfare check to welfare check, getting some occasional money from Gramps who never came out to the farm. I got sent to pick up that money when Gramps talked to Mom on the phone. I still wasn't free of Gramps. But, I buried it deep, didn't think about it. I thought about Canadian politics instead. I was becoming quite skilled at dissociating from the problems at home.

I was following the tale of a new Liberal politician, Pierre Elliott Trudeau who had more than a few words to say in the debates about bilingualism. I was excited about the new Canadian flag and a new Canadian anthem. I even found the Socialistic ideas of the reinvigorated NDP, following a change of name from the CCF. I followed American politics as the revolt against conscription accelerated on campuses and with many Americans fleeing to Canada to avoid the draft.

~

My interest in Canadian politics had begun, a diversion from life at home. Perhaps it was the era which called many to attend to what was happening – a new flag, a charter of rights, and the constant debate about what we wanted as a Canadian society. I soon found myself in the political center avoiding the stuffy conservatives of the right, or the socialistic NDP of the left. Politics was something new, something that felt alive for me.

Politics still remains an area of interest. However, there is a difference as in the past, I used politics as an escape from my home reality. As an adult, investment in politics is about being a good citizen doing my part to shape the world for my grandchildren. Unlike many, I believe one voice, one vote does matter.

~

Finally, in November, Dad returned home with a new job.

We had money again, Dad had us working evenings and weekends on renovating the inside of the house. We were in a race to have our house ready for Christmas. Together, we created a large arched entry from the dining room to the living room. Dad was skilled with plaster. He applied an incredible plaster design on the ceiling, a design of his own creation. Mom and I painted the walls a soft buff colour. Dad then bought new end tables, hexagon tables with red velvet panels which gave the living room a "rich" appearance. He also bought a stereo cabinet with a modern record player and radio built into it. The last part of the work was to turn a tiny space under the stairs into a room big enough for a single bed and a dresser, a place that was to be my room. The house was finished just days before Christmas.

During the time we worked on this project, I was treated with a lot of respect. There was no issue with heights with this indoor work. The tasks given to me during this interior renovation showed him that I was capable when it came to helping with wallboard and plaster, mudding and sanding, and painting. Dad even asked for some of my ideas and seemed to actually listen to them. Between tasks he would cook us up some interesting meals with bologna, tomatoes, or green peas in a spicy sauce. It seemed like Dad had more energy than he could handle. Finally, I had my own room, a place for my little record player, my record albums and my few books. I was beginning to look forward to the Christmas of 1967 and the promise of a New Year.

On Christmas Eve, Robert and Jackie came for the meal as well as Gramps. Mom cooked ham with a pineapple glaze as well as Gramps favourite dessert, pineapple upside down cake. Of course we also had tourtières to eat as well as it wouldn't be Christmas Eve in our home without these French-Canadian pork hamburger pies.

On Christmas Day, we had the usual tree, decorated with our old and a few new decorations. This tree was the nicest and the largest we had ever had. I had bought presents for all of my brothers and sisters using some of my part-time earnings. It was a good Christmas Day with tourtières, left over ham and scalloped potatoes. Mom was saving the turkey for Boxing Day when the Laflamme clan was to come for a meal.

It was Boxing Day. I had never seen so many people in our house at one time in my whole life. Every one of my father's brothers and sisters and their families were there. Included in the crowd was my Uncle Jean, Dad's older brother. This man was a stranger to me. He had never been in our home or in any of the other Laflamme homes since I was born. He was a quiet man who smiled uncomfortably during the meal. With so many people in the house, the meal was eaten using every room including the attached shed where I had helped Dad set up saw horses with a sheet of plywood for a table. With everyone was there, uncharacteristically there was no one arguing or fighting. It was a different kind of Christmas in which everyone was on their best behaviour, except for Mom who had become more than a bit tipsy with drinking too much gin.

~

This appearance of my Uncle Jean was a singular event and I never saw or heard about him again. With his momentary presence and the tensions that were present, the idea of his being Kevin's father take on a greater probability. But, with most things, there is no proof since all of the characters surrounding who was Kevin's father, all we are left with is probability. The uncharacteristic behaviour of the Laflamme family, being cautiously reserved and my mother's retreat into alcohol in an attempt to add levity to the situation that normally would have been bursting with energy does indicate that there was something beneath the surface not being said.

My uncle Jean did get known by a number of my cousins, a fact that also suggests that the tension that Boxing Day was unique to our family. Added to this the fact that Kevin had been told that he wasn't my father's son, that one of my father's siblings was his real father, there it is very likely that Uncle Jean was indeed, Kevin's father.

~

Not many days after Christmas, Dad left home again. Mom again sank into a deep depression and I was lost at how I was going to cope with her, the kids, work, school and life in general. I began to miss a lot of school as classes restarted in the New Year. I sank into my own depression as the New Year also saw a cutback the store where I worked part time. There were not going to be anymore night shifts and they had to let go of people. Now didn't have a job. I began to think that there was no point in going to school anymore. There was no way that I was going to be able to juggle life and fit in time for going to classes every day. Though the school counsellor was telling me that I had the brains for university, that I was capable of getting a Doctorate, I knew that I would never have the money to go to university. Hell, I didn't even have enough for bus fare to get to high school where there was no tuition to pay.

On the days that I did hitch-hike to the city with the intention of going to school, I sometimes just wandered around hoping to find another job, but there wasn't much that I could find. Finally I found a part-time job in a warehouse working for Grand and Toy. It was only a Saturday job, meaning that I wasn't going to be earning much money at all. I did go to classes on and off, but I didn't pay attention to much of what was said in my classes, something that was quite unusual for me. I began to miss more and more classes as the winter progressed.

The situation at home was getting worse with the kids becoming harder to manage.

The lack of money and the lack of Mom even trying to take on some responsibility in the house, left the place in an almost total chaos. My growing sense of hopelessness didn't help improve things. I did dishes, cooked meals, washed clothes and that was about it. I had no energy or will to even play my guitar, or to play monopoly, or other games with my brothers and sisters. The television became the babysitter for them.

I was desperate and decided to go to the military recruiting office in order to enlist. It seemed like the last resort for me. It was still winter as I entered the recruiting centre. I asked about enlisting, telling the officer at the desk that my father and both of my grandfathers had served in the military. He had me take a set of tests to see if I was suitable. The tests weren't very difficult and I soon found myself done the tests and handing them back to the test supervisor who took them with a look of surprise on her face, asking me if I was sure I wanted to hand them in already. She told me that there was still a lot of time left for me to finish the test. When I told her that I had completed the complete test, she immediately flipped through the pages of the test. I was then told to go into the waiting room while the test was scored.

It wasn't too long of a wait before a recruiting sergeant met with me. He told me I was too smart to be an enlisted soldier. He told me that my test results were too high for me to fit in as a Private in the army, that I wasn't good material for an enlisted soldier. He suggested I go back to school and finish grade twelve and thirteen, then apply for Royal Roads and a military scholarship so that I could become an officer. He said with my brains, I should be giving orders, not taking orders. In a way, I was glad to hear that I was seen and recognised as smart, but I was even more depressed to find out that even the army didn't want me.

As I walked the streets that cold and slushy February morning, I was stopped by a stranger. He looked at me and told me to read Thus Spoke Zarathustra. That's all he said.

"You just have to read Nietzsche's book, Thus Spoke Zarathustra."

Then, before I could say anything to him, he was gone. I began to wonder if he was even there, if I hadn't just been hallucinating. I was only a block and a half away from the library so I walked there to see if there was such a book and such an author. Of course I found out that there was such a book and that there were many more such books by Nietzsche. I had just discovered a new universe; and with that new universe, a new will to live.

Chapter Seventeen

The appearance of that stranger with his instructions for me to find and read Nietzsche's book, Zarathustra was not an imaginary event. He appeared in front of me as I walked with head down in discouragement and depression down Kent Street. I didn't know before this stranger's appearance that Nietzsche even existed. In Jungian psychology, this was a synchronistic event, one that was purposeful and meaningful to how my life was to unfold, needed to unfold. He didn't tell me his name, nor did I ask him for it. And with that instruction and information, he simply walked on. It was as though he simply disappeared now that his task was done.

For the next few months following this intervention by this stranger, I spent much of my time in the public library reading books of philosophy and psychology, an untypical behaviour for me up to that point in time. Nietzsche introduced me to many of his peers and predecessors who in turn led me to so many others who had wrestled with the nature of being human, the presence of evil, and the existence of God.

~

Nietzsche's Zarathustra was a powerful book for me. I saw Zarathustra as holding some of what had been denied about myself. I felt that I had finally found a voice that I could understand, perhaps a voice that might have been able to understand me. It didn't matter that he was dead. He talked to me, taught me to look for more. One book led to another and to other writers. I discovered Spinoza, Kierkegaard, Heidegger, Leibniz, and then stumbled onto existentialism with Sartre and other writers. I began to question myself about being a broken and dysfunctional kid. In this world, I was not broken, not a child. I wasn't my past. Whatever I was, was of my choosing.

Finding the world of philosophy and psychology gave me the spark to return to school and to write. In English class I took on the challenge of writing a formal essay on existentialism. I wrote poetry, essays, critiques, and more poetry. I even tried writing a few songs. Most of my writings were not shown to anyone. A passion had been ignited and I found that school wasn't enough. To tell the truth, poverty and the difficulty in getting to school due to poverty had me look for an excuse for my absences. To blame school for being boring, to blame myself for being a rebel, I needed to find any excuse in order to hide my poverty, my family's dysfunction.

As February headed towards March, I began to spend a lot of time at the YMCA / YWCA where other young misfits like myself were to be found in a basement playing chess, playing records, or simply hanging out. I began to learn the music of protest, the music of Bob Dylan, Joan Baez, and a host of other folk musicians. A few blocks from the "Y" there was a Lutheran Church which had opened its doors a few nights each week for young people as a "coffee house." I began to play again, playing folk music for and with others.

During the day, I began to work with a few other lost souls such as myself in planning and producing a literary journal that we ended up calling "Left Center." It contained poetry of protest, poetry dealing with themes of our awakening sexuality, the laws of Canada as they applied to "cannabis," and many other topics. My contributions were both poetry and law related articles. I had a copy of Snow's criminal code and discovered there all kinds of legal minefields that could snare young people. Why the interest in the law? First, it had to do with the regular round up of other young people like me, people I had met on Sparks Street, and some people from my school, usually because they got caught smoking marijuana or trying to sell it.

I began growing my mustache and wearing an old pair of sandals that I found in a thrift shop.

I wanted to become one of the flower children I saw on Sparks Street, youth who tried using smiles and flowers and songs to convince people that love was the answer, love was the solution, love was the healing balm that we needed in order to again find a way to smile and believe in life. When the journal was finished and printed using the Gestetner machine in the YMCA office, we took the magazine to a number of different high schools where we stood outside the doors and gave them away for free. It didn't take too long before some of the schools ordered us off the property, banned the possession of the journal, and confiscated the magazines they saw. There was no dialogue, not even an attempt to tell us why our literary journal was being banned. Because we had used the YMCA's Gestetner, (we had thanked the Y for the use of space, paper and equipment) the school board put pressure on the Y which resulted in the closure of journal after only one issue. That one issue did get placed in the National Archives which meant that in a way, each of us had been accepted as real writers, in a real world. We were published authors.

~

And so began my journeys through the world of philosophy and the nature of man, as well as my passion for writing. It began with an essay, flowed into poetry and a few editorial protests about the condition of humanity. Writing took me out of the world of being a victim of abuse. The words of dead authors and poets taught me that there was life, even in darkness.

It was a beginning that would prove to provide enough hope in my darkest moments, give me the courage and the will to keep on living in spite of the pain that came with being alive in my world. All of this began simply with the words of a passing stranger.

~

The Friday night and Saturday night coffee-house sessions had me learning new songs, traditional folk songs and new songs by Judy Collins and others. This was a new world for me, one that told me that I wasn't an aberration, that even in the past others have been like me and they sang about their broken stories, the love stories, their dream stories. I played and I sang and my confidence began to return, especially as winter turned into spring and more people came to listen to the folk music in the church basement.

As summer approached, I got invited by Robert and Jackie to go to their new apartment in Montréal for a weekend. They introduced me to a different world, one that I knew existed, but had never experienced. Jackie had prepared paté de fois gras and escargot to go with red wine for the first evening I was there. Both talked of being cultured and took me to see a play called Luv. It was my first exposure to live theatre. I also got to go to a nightclub near their place, not too far from the Playboy Club. I got to listen to Muddy Waters play his blues. It was a weekend of magic showing me that there was much more to life than what I had experienced; there was more for me strive for, more reason to escape the black hole of my life as it was.

Each time I went back to the farm which was on most nights, I would always get home late as I often had to walk the whole distance from the Alta Vista shopping centre. On those nights I would enter the dark house and find the house in disarray. It was as if the mess was left there, waiting for me to come home and clean up because that is what I had always done – clean up messes. And seeing the scattered clothing, the dirty dishes and the spills, I would begin bringing some order out of the mess proving to them that they were right, that I would clean up their messes. When done, I would go into the living room, find one of my records, and listen while waiting though I didn't know what I was waiting for. I listened in silence. I would only go to sleep when I got so tired that there was no choice but sleep.

I was afraid of sleeping, afraid of what would happen next when I had completely surrendered to the darkness of night. Sleep was an invitation for nightmares to add their twisted plots to the chaos of my life.

Waking from the nightmares I would run out of the house and head back to the city away from the poison that was sucking the life out of me, out of all of us. But I would return again and again, making sure that when Mom called out, "Is that you, Benjy?" I would go to her and give her whatever money I had before darkness again closed in and I found myself on the road back to the city hoping no one would stop and see me surrounded by my blackness.

On some nights I would knock on Mémère's door and she would let me so that I could sleep on the couch. There was never a question why or a thought of not allowing me in. They opened the door and let me go to sleep. When I stayed there, I slept with fewer nightmares. It was as though I had a chance to breathe more easily without being on edge waiting for a new terror. Rested, I would go to school.

On the odd night when I played in the coffee house, I would slip up the stairs of the church after the coffee house closed. Since it usually was much too late to go to the farm or to go to Mémère's. I would sleep on a pew. Sometimes others slept there as well. Though there was no bed, no cushion or pillow, the knowledge that I was safe in this church that refused to lock its doors or to turn out the desperate onto the late night streets, my sleep on the hard wood of the church pews was treasured.

One morning I awoke in the church after a Friday night spent playing in the coffee house to find that a girl had also spent the night in the church, one of the girls who I recognised as a flower child. She stirred as I woke. She had chosen to sleep near me. She smiled at me and said she fell in love with my guitar playing the night before.

I returned the smile, flattered that I was even noticed. We went for a breakfast of coffee and toast that late May morning. Then, she invited me to go with her to a spot beside the Parliament Buildings among the rocks and greenery. She told me that I could make love to her there. She took off her panties from under her print dress and I took off my pants. She took me to her and touched my penis. She looked at the limp penis which refused to grow and swore before she laughed. "Jesus Christ! I am trying to screw a fag." It was Saturday morning and people were above the escarpment where we lay naked. They looked over the edge and saw us. I quickly struggled back into my clothing and ran. I was a fag, I could have had sex with a willing girl but didn't. I didn't even get an erection. What kind of man was I? And the answer came back, echoing the words I so often heard from my father.

~

Sexual identity in crisis. Was I a normal male? Was I homosexual as I had heard so often? Was I any different than the priests who had introduced me to sexuality, or my grandfather who saw me as an opportunity in spite of his being more drawn to women than men? Was I a woman in a man's body? My psyche rebelled at the thought of being a homosexual, but life experiences were trying to convince me otherwise. This crisis of sexual identity was one that needed to be addressed. Until a definite answer came, the boy-man that I was, was stuck in Limbo.

~

I was still going to the YMCA where I would play chess and listen to music. One of the regulars at the Y was a young man about three years older than I was. His name was Doug and he had red hair. On the evenings I stayed at Mémère's, I would sometimes meet up with him for talk and a Coke. He never asked questions about my life, and he was okay with talking about politics or music or just things in general.

Doug lived at the Y and one night decided he would show me what kind of rooms they had at the Y, what his room looked like. In his room, he reached for me and touched my genitals. I yelled "Stop!" and turned to leave as if the room had just erupted in flames. He immediately apologized saying that he misunderstood, that he thought I was like him, gay.

At that moment, for the first time I knew that I wasn't gay. Maybe I just wasn't a sexual being of any kind. I didn't know, I just knew that I didn't want to have sex with a man. And I knew that for some reason, in spite of wanting to have sex with the beautiful girl who offered herself to me, I was not capable of making love to a woman either. I heard the honesty in Doug's voice and knew that I was safe with him, that he wouldn't press his sexual orientation onto me. I saw at that moment that if anything, we could really be friends with no strings attached.

The words of dead authors and folk music became my life raft through the dark periods that flowed in and out of my life in the spring of 1968. One day I would be playing my guitar for strangers in the sunshine on Sparks Street; the next day I would get frustrated at school knowing that it was all coming to an end and that the doors would be closing for me; the next day I would be on the farm up to my neck trying to tread water in a swamp of quicksand. Words and music were my totems to carry me to safety and to the next day.

~

This was a critical point in my life as I had finally discovered a truth about myself, a truth that seemed to fly in the face of what many were telling me. My sexual identity was confirmed, at least one aspect was confirmed; I wasn't a homosexual. I also learned that the sexual identity of others wasn't a factor that caused revulsion within me. I wasn't homosexual, but I wasn't yet sure about exactly what I was at that point.

~

One evening I went to a different coffee house at the edges of Lower Town, a place called Le Hibou. It cost money to go there so it was a rare event. If I remember correctly I only went there twice. This particular evening I went to listen to Jerry Jeff Walker perform his songs and others. I knew of J.J. Walker because of his hit song "Mr. Bojangles." Le Hibou was a very small, intimate coffee house where almost every seat was next to the tiny stage. When he began to tell the story of this song before singing it, I felt I could travel through the words of the story into the soul of old Mr. Bojangles. And when, Jerry Jeff Walker began to sing, I could feel the faint trail of tears begin. Music and words are powerful things, soul things, healing things.

My sister Heather was born in April of 1968, the last child of Mom and Dad. Again I missed too much school while she was at the hospital and during the first part of her recovery back at home. When I did get to go back, I was in trouble with the school administration. In the vice-principal's office I was confronted with more than 50 days of absences and a not so glowing set of marks from my last two report cards. I knew I was in the wrong but how do you tell someone like him about your totally fucked up life and family and how making it to as many classes as I did was not a minor, but actually a major miracle. When he then went on to question how I could have these kind of marks on my second time in grade 12 I blew up. I told him to learn how to read so that he could see that this was my first, and last time in grade 12. He stood up and told me to leave and as I was going out the door he said that from now on I had to wear proper footwear, not bare feet in sandals to school; and, he added as if an afterthought, to shave off the stupid mustache. I was a student, not a hoodlum.

The school's counselor, Mr. Metcalfe was my advocate. He had read my paper on existentialism and had told me he had given a copy to one of his friends at the University of Ottawa.

His friend had told him that my paper was better than any had been given by his first year students. I know it was said to encourage me, but if anything, it made the pain worse. I knew that if I would have had the chance, I could've become the university professor that I once claimed I would be, a claim that made my uncle Robert Schiller laugh when he heard it. Brains or no brains, I was in a fight just to pass this year. If I failed, it was the end of my school career. If I passed, it was likely the end of my education anyway. I wanted to pass, badly. I had to prove something to myself.

In Math class, I met my nightmare. It seems that my ability to do well in Algebra was not enough. The teacher told me I had missed too many of his classes. Even though the final exam was worth 100% of the mark, he was determined that I should be taught a lesson. He told me that whatever mark I made, he would grade me down to 40% so that I would be forced to go to summer school. It didn't matter that I still got the highest marks in his class. I needed to learn a lesson.

Exam time came and I passed all of my exams except Algebra. Knowing he wasn't going to let me pass, I signed my exam paper and wrote him a small poem in protest. When the report cards came out, that little poem got 40%. My fate was sealed. I didn't qualify for university anymore and I was finished at high school.

~

I was angry and blamed the system and people for my anger. I felt that I was a victim trying to convince myself that I had no responsibility for doing anything to change myself in response to the world as I experienced it. I was angry with my father for not having a regular job that would have allowed us to stay in one place and to have the money to send me to university. I was angry at the school system for the games they had played with my education as I bounced from school to school and province to province. I was intelligent and shouldn't have had to play their games.

They should have seen my intelligence and promoted me accordingly and given me the scholarships that would have allowed me to go to university. I was angry and I didn't know what to do with the anger.

This shifting of responsibility and laying blame had some basis, but it wasn't an excuse for my day-to-day decisions that resulted in failing Algebra. Giving in to victimhood had only served to put myself even more at risk. There was a real chance that I could have given up and followed in the footsteps of failure set down in front of me by my parents and grandparents.

~

I wrote my last exam on Friday and by Monday I was working full time for the Government of Canada in the Department of Public Works. In between I had spent the weekend lying on the beach at Hogs Back Falls, a popular swimming site for young people. Off at the edges among the trees, I dared to tan au naturel like some of the others I had seen. I hadn't look for this job, it came looking for me via my Uncle Horace who was a high ranking official in the government department. I believed it was Gramps' doing and not really Uncle Horace's idea as he didn't really know me all that well at all. Somehow nepotism still was in full swing in awarding jobs as I didn't have to compete for the job nor take the Civil Service exam that one typically needed to pass in order to even apply for a civil service job. I became a mail-room clerk.

There wasn't a great deal of enthusiasm in the mail room in having the boss' nephew joining the "team." And, it was obvious that I was Horace's nephew as I got to see him in his managerial office from time to time, not exactly a typical place for a junior mail clerk to be found. Because I was parachuted into a job for which there really was no need, boredom became the norm for me.

It was obvious that there were too many working in the department with not enough tasks to keep them busy. Knitting, playing cards, reading novels – all kinds of ways were being explored to combat mind-crippling boredom by many working in the building. I did manage to get out of the building every once in a while when sent to hand deliver an envelope from my Uncle to some Deputy Minister or another civil service mandarin.

I finally got my first pay check and like always, gave half to Mom. She didn't ask anymore, it was assumed that it was her right to have a portion of my paycheck. I am positive that this was also in place for Kevin as well, though I am sure that he held back more than I did so that he could function a bit better than I did. Still, I had more money than I was used to having. The first thing I did was to buy some decent clothing. Since I was working in the Federal Government, dress was important. I had to wear a shirt and tie so I made sure I bought two new ties, ones that were "fashionable" and not obviously out of the Good Will basket. I also bought two pair of pants, stove pipe pants as they were called, and a Nehru jacket. I had decided that I wanted to be more of an original like our new Prime Minister, P.E. Trudeau while cultivating an Indian look which was the result of my discovering Ravi Shankar's music. To finish off the "look," I bought a pipe and some aromatic tobaccos. I was determined to look modern, cool and as far from a welfare recipient as possible.

A month and a half into my job with Uncle Horace's department, I began to look for a different job as I didn't think I could survive much longer with the dead-end job. The pay was okay, the people were okay, but I felt useless. I knew I didn't deserve the job. I found a job, a real job, on my own. The Canadian Press wire services office just across the street from Parliament Hill was looking for a copy boy. I jumped at the chance to see if I could someday be a news reporter, a journalist. I got the job and with the job, a pay raise to $176 every two weeks.

I was richer than I believed could ever be possible. I immediately went out and bought an old Underwood typewriter. Every aspiring journalist needed to own one of these old typewriters – every movie showing writers and journalists showed this typewriter. And I began to write again; poetry in English and poetry in French. I began to write articles on philosophy and took on the challenge of reading the Tibetan Book of the Dead as I had a used copy of the book in my tiny collection.

~

Tibetan Buddhism made its first appearance into my life. My initial entrance was focused on death, on darkness. Lost in my own darkness and often wishing that it could simply end, I had some hope that the book would have some answers that would ease my guilt for committing suicide which had become a serious consideration. There was still enough Catholicism within me to fear death and my likely descent into hell. The book didn't answer any of my questions though it did add a few more. However, I wasn't ready to follow the path presented by Buddhism as life demanded too much of my time simply to survive. I didn't know it then, but the seed had been planted and I would return to following those initial questions about existence, suffering and meaning in later life.

~

About a week after I began working at C.P. wire services, I met the new, young photographer's assistant. It was Peter from Hull, my old classmate from grade five, the boy who wore lieder hosen. Peter got to travel to all kinds of major events with the head photographer, events such as the going to take photos at the Expos baseball games, the first major league baseball team in Canada.

My job was simple, too simple in my mind. I was to man the teletype machines, taking breaking news stories off the machines and taking them to the appropriate staff writer.

Sometimes I was sent to the Hill, Parliament Hill, in order to get press releases from the Parliamentary Press Gallery. I then took back to the staff writers. Using these bits and pieces of paper given out by the government, our top national journalists would crank out "news" which was sent by teletype to every major and many minor newspaper in Canada. I didn't get a chance to do any writing. I wasn't going to get a chance to do any writing for a long, long time. There were dues to pay and egos to stroke before I could move up the ladder of journalism. Perhaps if I had gone to a journalism school it would have speeded up the chances. I began to think that I needed a job that needed me. I didn't quit C.P.; I just began to think of other possibilities. I wasn't going to be out of work and poor if there was any way to avoid it.

Peter's life, by contrast, became quite adventurous. He was in Montreal when the McGill University riots broke out. He got to take photos of our new P.M., one of which went on to win the photo journalism award of the year, the photo where Trudeau pretended to be hanging himself with his tie as a joke and protest against ties and traditionalism. When Peter was in town, we would wander down Sparks Street, sometimes heading to Nate's Smoked Meat Restaurant for a smoked meat sandwich; or just watch people go by as we made up stories of their lives and our future. We went to dances together trying to pick up girls. Peter had no problems on that score as he was quite outgoing. Usually I just danced with willing partners, not daring to push for more than a dance. One evening at one of these dances, I met a shy young girl who was a year younger than I was, and shyer than I was if that was possible. I had met Céline Houle, my first real girlfriend.

Chapter Eighteen

I needed to meet and know a Céline in my life, especially during those dark times when the choice of life or death hung so prominently and heavily in my head. She pulled me back into life simply by being there and needing me. She was proof that I was drawn to women in terms of my sexuality. And, she showed me that I was good for her, not as a source of money, but as a man. Here was a young woman that made choosing light over darkness, life over death, easy choices to make.

Perhaps, more importantly, this young woman's presence in my life served to begin the severing process that would allow me to escape the spider grip of my mother. Allegiance to *Mother* was being challenged. With that challenge, I began the process of shifting from *boy* to *man*. I didn't realise until many years later that something else was at work. I had entered into a strange world of psychological dysfunction with this young woman. The entrance into her dark world would test me, test my will to life.

~

Céline was a small, very slim girl with dark hair that was cut short but not quite into a boy cut. She had just finished with her studies, had a job, and dressed well in skirts which usually had a very high waist and high hem which would be considered almost too short. In seeing her, I was definitely aroused and breathed a sigh of relief with the feelings that touched me physically as well as emotionally. I finally knew that I was "normal" and that I was sexually attracted to females, not males.

I was wearing my light gray herringbone-patterned stove pipe pants and she wore a grey tweed skirt with shoulder straps that outlined her small breasts. I forgot all about Peter when she danced with me.

That first dance turned into all of the dances that remained in the evening. I changed from my usual pattern of dancing with any girl who sat or stood quietly on the sidelines hoping for someone to ask them to dance. It wasn't long before the dance was over and we were standing outside the dance hall. I got her name and her phone number and her address. She lived across the river in Gatineau. As we said goodbye with a kiss and hug, I could feel her heart pounding as hard as mine, her holding on to me as hard as I held onto her.

We were together at every opportunity, and we didn't hesitate to talk on the phone during lunch hours while we were at work. Some days she would come to the city to meet me during my lunch hours. On weekends I would go to her home where I met her mother, sister and step-father. They had a nice home, a place that said "we are not poor, never have been on welfare, and we are normal." I liked her step-father, George who was a strong, rugged looking man who had a new Mustang car that he was proud of owning. I didn't like Céline's sister who was the obvious favourite in the house. Carmen was light in contrast to Céline's darkness, soft in comparison to Céline's thin sharpness. Céline's mother looked like Céline in terms of body shape and size, but like Carmen in terms of colour. And, Céline's mother drank a lot.

Our first months together were both painful and a time of joy for me. I learned about Céline's passion for art and studied her charcoal drawings and her paintings which riveted my attention. There was so much darkness and torture in those works of art. I recognized so much of myself in her art. I thought that finally someone could see inside of me, see what was really there and not flee in horror. I didn't know that it wasn't really what I thought. The darkness and horror in her art was about what haunted her, not an understanding of what haunted me.

Neither of us knew this. In return, she would lose herself in my music and I would write for her, about her. I also drew, but this I kept hidden not wanting to compete, to have Céline doubt her own art. I was learning that she was quite fragile, that her feelings of self-worth were very low. I made it my mission to bring her joy and light, to make smiles appear in her eyes.

~

Now, I see that Céline had acted as a substitute for my own mother. I had abandoned my mother out of fear of being consumed, and filled in the empty space with the same role of caretaker that I had not quite yet abandoned at that time. I still gave my mother half of my paycheck at that time, but nothing else. The unspoken sexual component was buried under layers of denial. I had substituted a safer zone with my sexual response and interest in Céline.

~

The bond between us grew closer and tighter, obsessively too close. In late September, 1968 I bought a black pearl ring for Céline, a simple ring, from a jeweler's on Sparks Street. I had introduced Céline to Mémère and Pépère by then, as their apartment was close by to my workplace. Mémère began to think of us as a couple and was proud that I had chosen a French-Canadian girl, one who spoke French and whom she said was beautiful as well, though in Mémère's opinion, she could use a bit more weight. But time, as she pronounced with a smile on her face, and babies would fix that. I was happy that Céline was so warmly welcomed and began to find the courage to introduce her to my parents in Carlsbad Springs. Since I didn't have a car, I chose a time when we could make it an outing for Mémère and Pépère as well with Pépère doing the driving.

It was a sunny day when we got to the farm. Dad wasn't there, and in a way that made me feel better.

I didn't want his attacks, his character assassinations which might have given Céline the wrong idea of who I was. Mémère and Mom talked with Céline and there was a lot of laughter, especially with Mom telling Céline about some of my quirks. Mémère was already thinking of Céline and I as if we were getting married in the near future. Mom was quiet in response to that idea. Pépère had been quiet as usual throughout the discussion and spent his time with the young ones in the house, taking advantage of the time to be a grandfather with them. He loved his grandchildren without any question, and I knew that I was included in his love. Céline sat primly doing her best to answer questions, but didn't have a lot to say about herself. She did talk about her family and her home in Gatineau, about being finished school and her job as a store clerk. She talked about becoming a secretary someday as that was what she studied in high school.

We left later in the afternoon with me promising Mom that I would be coming home that night. Once back in Ottawa, I took Céline to the bus station so that she could get home and so that I could return back to the farm as promised. We talked about being together the next day, Sunday, at her home. Her mother was having supper for us and for Carmen and her boyfriend. Then when her bus left, I began the trip home. I took a bus to the Alta Vista shopping centre and began the hitch-hiking journey to the farm. Since it wasn't yet dark, I caught a ride that took me most of the way leaving me only a short walk to the farm.

When I finally got home, it was only to be greeted with Mom's anger that seemed to be flecked with spit and spite. The first barrage had to do with me being like my father, screwing every woman I could get my hands on, especially the skinny ones. I didn't have a clue what she was talking about. I wasn't like Dad, screwing around with women; I was still a virgin and assumed that it would stay that way until Céline and I got married.

It took a while for me to calm her down. I had learned to listen to her rants and now found out that Dad spent all of his time away from the farm living with another woman, someone she imagined to be young, thin and pretty. Dad disappeared for days at a time, only coming back for clean clothing and a quick screw according to Mom. Mom cried telling me that no one could love a fat woman like her, that no one really wanted to make love to a cow. I made her tea in her favourite cup and listened. She then told me she thought that I was abandoning her as well. After all that she did for me, I was leaving her to screw a beautiful, young woman who wasn't really all that beautiful in her opinion.

I told Mom that I wasn't screwing Céline, that there was no sexual activity between us, that I hadn't betrayed or abandoned her. I reminded her that I still came home and gave her most of what I earned so that she could raise the kids. And then, darkness. The darkness was heavy, something that I knew would have to forever live in the deepest pits of darkness. I left before dawn broke heading to the city then on to Gatineau feeling like a thief fleeing the scene of a crime. I felt as though I was somehow betraying my mother as I left to be with Céline.

Supper at Céline's was a noisy affair. Carmen and her boyfriend dominated the talk. As usual I sat quietly listening to the others speak. I was becoming familiar enough at the house that I began to see things I had before missed. Carmen was at the center, obviously the favourite child of the two girls. Céline's mom was drinking as the meal went on, occasionally talking to Carmen's boyfriend who had a good job in the government. When she made a comment to George, it was usually sarcastic. Céline tried hard to contribute to the conversation and get her share of attention but the only attention she got was either put-down from Carmen or no response at all, as if she had said nothing.

As expected, the conversation at the table was all in French which was okay with me as I was used to similar conversations with my aunts and uncles and cousins in the Laflamme clan.

At one point in the meal, Céline tried again to be heard. Carmen got upset at being interrupted and retaliated with a vicious insult. Carmen's comment to Céline had to do with the way that Céline had dressed, again in a very short skirt, dressed like a slut, "une putaine." Without thinking about it, I broke my silence in anger and called Carmen a cow, "une vache!" That was a mistake, Carmen ran from the table crying. No one batted an eye when Carmen called Céline a slut, but with my saying that Carmen was a cow, I had stumbled upon something buried deep, something that had both George and Céline's mother start screaming at me. Céline told me that I had better leave before it got worse for her. And so I quickly left the house not really knowing what had happened.

Céline called a few days later while I was at work. She told me that all was now okay at home, that the worst was over. Carmen was ready to forgive me and that I would be welcome back into her house.

During those few days of no contact, I had thought long and hard about where I was and where I was going. I knew that I needed a real job with a real future, not a job at Canadian Press where the successful people were drunk most of the time and where even that success was short lived. I had found out about the next sitting of the exams to become a civil servant and decided that I would get a good government job that would ensure that I had work for the rest of my life; and that with a good job, I would somehow be good enough to marry Céline. I didn't want to drift forever like the way I grew up, always hungry for food, for friendship, for a home.

~

The life I had experienced growing up had made its mark on me. Like any other person who becomes an adult, I could either replicate the early patterns of my life, unconsciously, or I could make a determined conscious effort to live my life differently. The thought of separating from my family of origin and eventually making my own family served as a catalyst to look at my own life differently. I had a job but knew that it wasn't a career job for me as it didn't *fit* into my hopes and dreams as a writer. I began to think that my dreams of being a writer were not what needed to be considered when choosing a career path. What I needed was a career that would offer me stability in place as well as in employment. At this point of my life, this was a critical understanding as it convinced me that I had choices and that my life would unfold because of my choices. Life wasn't about being a victim and not being able to make choices. I was finally growing up, growing independent and becoming responsible.

~

For the rest of the fall and winter, I fell into a pattern of heading to Céline's home most Friday and Saturday evenings with an occasional Sunday lunch thrown in. I never took Céline again to the farm, in fact, I went home as little as possible, mostly on Sunday evenings and a few more times during the week. Dad was never at home whenever I did go home, and Mom seemed to always be in bed and the house in a disaster. I don't know who was really taking care of Heather; somehow I think it was Béatrice. Kevin was almost never there either. Somehow, in spite of our closeness as children, we had become strangers. I would clean up the house as much as I could, sometimes doing the laundry upon seeing the piles of dirty clothes left near the machine, evidence that Mom had no energy to do any of this work. And always, I would leave early, before anyone woke up so as to make it to work on time.

On Fridays and Saturdays, I never went home to the acreage. I didn't always get to Mémère's and Pépère's though. Sometimes I found other places to sleep. At times, it was too late and the trip was too long of a journey to travel from Céline's back to the farm or even to my grandparent's place. Usually, I used buses in order to get to Céline's and back to the city. Occasionally, if it was too late, I would be forced to walk the whole way back into Ottawa. A few times, I found an all-night restaurant where I would hang out and listen to music from the juke box. And twice, with not enough money for a taxi or for an all-night restaurant, I would slip into a Laundromat simply to stay warm while waiting for morning and the first bus back into Ottawa.

In November, I finally got to write the Civil Service exam and I passed it. All that was left to do was to wait for an opening and get my first temporary posting. I was told that it could take up to six weeks; and even then, when a position opened, typically a person was put into several temporary postings from six weeks to three months postings until a permanent position became available.

In late November the call came. The postal unions had just negotiated a settlement and there was a lot of work that needed to be done to calculate individual back pay for carriers and letter handlers in time for Christmas. I took the job knowing that I needed to do this if I was to be able to have a career. Céline agreed even though it meant that I would rarely see her during the week which was much easier to do when I worked across the street from Parliament Hill.

Friday and Saturday evenings with Céline continued as normal though we didn't get to see each other during the week. In between, we would take turns calling each other using the public pay phones. When we were together, we spent it mostly sitting on the sofa and watching TV, or pretending to watch TV while we kissed and held each other when we were alone in the living room which was most of the time.

When Carmen was at home she was usually in her bedroom with her boyfriend. Céline and I would often talk, just being together without kissing. The desire for intercourse was strong, but I was learning about Céline's childhood and her abuse by her father now long gone. The stories she told me helped me put my sexual desires and needs into the background.

I began to suspect there was a lot Céline wasn't telling me about her past. All I knew for certain was that she loved me. However, that love wasn't enough for her to get passed her terror of sex, she couldn't manage to have intercourse with me. She wanted for us to be married first, that way she would know that she was safe.

~

The art of self-denial, of swallowing internally my needs and my emotions were reinforced during this part of my life. I was motivated by what I considered to be love, much like I was motivated as a very young child to focus on the needs of my mother and siblings rather than be *selfish*. Guilt played a strong role in convincing me I was doing the right thing. A true knight in shining armor, a true hero – and I was Céline's hero – would not give in to his base feelings that would hurt those for whom he was responsible. And yes, I did see myself in those terms, as being like Sir Lancelot, a man of honour who could be trusted.

~

Once the temporary job at the post office was finished, I was transferred to another temporary position at Energy, Mines and Resources. My ability to use a calculator and solve complex problems which had been my focus at the post office had led to my being assigned to work on more calculations involving inland water studies. That posting lasted for about three weeks before I found myself working for the Department of Vital Statistics at Tunney's Pasture.

My job for Vital Statistics was a new challenge. I was to take large registers that contained data of births, deaths and marriages, into a large room which held two big microfiche cameras. I was to transfer these registers onto film for more efficient storage.

It was late January and the job was to last about six weeks. It was a boring job to say the least, standing at a camera stand, turning the pages of the registers and then activating the camera with foot-operated switch. While working on this project, I did meet some other young people working at Tunney's Pasture. I met them during the lunch hours and the breaks as people gathered in one of the cafeterias. In the cafeterias the air was usually heavy with smell of burning marijuana, a smell I was very used to though I had yet to try smoking it. Grass was freely available, often a joint could be found stashed under the napkin holders. I was too afraid of smoking grass, not of the marijuana itself, but afraid that I would get caught, that Dad would find out. I didn't want to go to jail and see my life totally fall apart with no hope for the future. And even more threatening was the thought that I would also lose Céline. I could not protect her or provide for her in the future if I was in jail.

Unexpectedly the job didn't come to an end after six weeks. I was told I would be continuing in the job until the end of the maximum three month term for temporary postings. My work was proving my worth as a civil servant. I was told that at the end of this job I would become a permanent status civil servant and get my first posting with that status. My probationary period was coming to an end.

At the beginning of April I was assigned to a work at the National Headquarters of the R.C.M.P. I was to work in the filing department.

By this time, I was living almost full time with Mémère and Pépère though I was diligent in taking money home to Mom every payday. Mémère and Pépère were living on the first floor of an apartment building where Pépère was the apartment building manager, responsible for handling all the small jobs and finding service people for the rest of the needed work. They got to live rent free and had a small salary added to it. Because I lived with them, I got to see Céline a lot more often, having money now for taxis when I stayed too late at her house. Sometimes she came for an evening to sit in the coffee house and watch me play guitar.

The job at RCMP headquarters meant that I had to be fingerprinted and pass a security check. I gave Mémère's and Pépère's place as my place of residence. And as a result, was asked a few weeks later to pay attention to the comings and goings of people in two of the apartments. Apparently the residents of these apartments were Russian journalists. I refused the request saying that I was not often in the building and that I didn't know who they were or what they looked like. I was a filing clerk, not a spy. It turned out that the files I was working with had everything to do with the threats of communism, everyone who travelled to and from communist countries had a file in this section. Those who had a voice that others might listen to in matters of politics at the national and provincial level also had a file in the department, even if there was no association with socialism or communism, regardless of the fact that they had never been to a communist or socialist country. I was more than surprised at the names I saw in the files. Of course I wasn't supposed to look at what was within the file folders I handled, I was just to file them.

I guess I had proved my integrity enough as my next posting came earlier than expected. By the middle of May, I was placed in a more sensitive section under the control of the Justice Department. I was assigned as a filing clerk to the Narcotics Control office.

Here it wasn't simply a matter of handling file folders. There was also a safe which contained seized drugs which were being kept in security for criminal cases. This was my first job that seemed to have a bit of intelligence required for the job description. I was happy with this placement as it came as spring turned into the summer of 1969. Only one thing was marring the general level of satisfaction that I was feeling.

One payday I went to the farm as usual to give Mom her share of the paycheck. Yes, that is how I understood the world at that point. For some reason, I saw that this was just the way it was in our house. On this day, it was still daylight because of the season even though supper was done for.

Whatever kids may have been around, were either outside playing or watching TV in the living room. As usual I took the money to Mom's room in order to give her the money. She seemed to always be in her room and not downstairs. It was as if she didn't have the health or the energy to go downstairs. As I got to the top of the stairs and turned toward her room I saw my father in the room, on his knees with his head buried between my mother's thighs. I didn't say a word but Mom saw me and gave me a knowing and defiant smile. She was proud and happy now that she had Dad back, and glad that I had seen the proof that he loved her, that he fed on her. I turned quickly and went quietly down the stairs, left the money on the dining room table and then left the house.

Céline was plunging into a dark depression. She had lost her job for some unspoken reason. As Céline's depression deepened, she would call me at work. I would get the message and go at the quickest opportunity to the payphone to talk with her, promising to call again at the next opportunity, my next coffee break time or during my lunch hour. And, as soon as work was done, I would rush to her house and hold her.

I took to giving her a little bit of the money I had kept from Mom so that she would feel less powerless. I needed her and she needed me. We clung tightly together. The deeper she fell into her depression, the more depressed I became and the more I was sure that this was love as it was meant to be – two people desperately holding onto each other.

~

I was changing and beginning to see the world differently. Having finished school and finding a career for myself through my own efforts, my self-confidence as a young man was beginning to replace the insecure-self that had characterised my youth. Having a girlfriend that I had full intentions of one day marrying had put to rest my agonies over sexual identity. I was beginning to feel like a normal person, or what I thought a normal person felt like as he moved through life. I didn't expect life to be all sunshine and so I didn't panic with the appearance of extreme neediness in Céline, a neediness that in turn triggered something buried deep within me. I had a good job, security, and I held onto it perhaps too tightly from this vantage point of almost five decades later. The world had changed with that walk on the moon and it seemed my life had changed as well. I relaxed feeling that I had finally done with all the drama. I was felt safe.

~

Work kept me grounded and Céline gave me purpose. I was on a mission. One day one of my co-workers came around with one of those pyramid schemes that were always circulating, the kind where you pay so much money to the person on top of the list and your name goes into the queue with the eventual promise of getting oneself to the top of the pyramid and seeing your original investment become a gold mine. I always had the same response, "No, thanks." But this time the chart caught my eye.

I saw my Dad's name on it, just about at the top. If I bought then he would be only one more level away from the jackpot. I immediately took out the money that I needed and wrote my name in the open spot at the bottom of the pyramid. I told the co-worker about what I had seen, my Dad was getting close to winning it all. My co-worker, a male unexpectedly denied the possibility of the name being my father's name. The Laurent Laflamme that was on the list was too young to be my Dad in his opinion. He went on to tell me that he knew this Laurent Laflamme as he was his sister's boyfriend. They had been going out for a few years so for a few years. He also told me that they had two little kids together. I looked at the pyramid chart again. Perhaps I was mistaken. But no, there it was – Laurent William Laflamme – my father – the father of two more kids I had never heard about, the father of two kids in Bow Island and who the hell knew how many more spread between Gatineau and Calgary.

That same afternoon, I got a call from Céline at home. George had left her mother. He had had an argument with her Mom and now her mother was drunk and hitting her. I heard the panic in her voice and knew she needed me to help her. I was already upset with the thought of my father and his girlfriend and two new half-siblings. I was in no shape to focus anymore at work.

I decided to quit work early and rushed to the hospital where Dad was having some sort of treatment. As I walked into his room, I saw that he had an IV line inserted into his arm and that he was in a hospital dressing gown. He didn't look or sound well. But, in spite of what I saw, I had to have it out with him. Did he have a girlfriend named "X"? Did they have two kids? I didn't give him any time to answer, I just had to attack him with words and let out all the anger and sense of betrayal I felt. His only response was to take a swing at me with his fist, a weak swing that was far from being able to reach me because of the IV lines.

If he hadn't been weakened or tied up with his IV line, he would easily have dropped me where I stood. I stood there, out of range of his fists and glared at him. He then lashed out at me with words, a more powerful way to punish me:

"And who in the fuck are you to judge, you sick little pervert? You pretend that you are so fucking holy when you are worse than I am. At least I don't go around sucking priests' cocks or my grandfather's cock or my mother. You're a dirty, sick, disgusting little pervert."

I ran out of the room, out of the hospital and kept running and running and running. Dad was crazy. What the hell was he talking about? I had blocked out all of the sexual abuse and only remembered feeling how Dad had always hated me, how he was always finding a reason to hit me, insult me and shame me.

When I stopped running, I found myself at Céline's house. Carmen had just come home from her job. Carmen was consoling her mother who, I could see from the bruises on her face, had obviously been beaten by George. I found Céline in her room, bruised as well and hiding in the darkness. When she saw me, she fled into my arms and asked me to take her away; she couldn't take it any more in this crazy house. And so we left. I took her to Mémère's and Pépère's for the night.

Chapter Nineteen

This moment with my father in the hospital was a pivotal turning point in my life. My anger at my father, an anger that had accumulated over the years with the physical beatings, the shaming and belittling, and so much more, had crested to overflowing. The shock of hearing him tell me about *my* participation in incestuous relations with my mother and grandfather had me flee from his hospital room. I didn't leave out of fear that he would hit me in spite of his situation. Rather, I was running from the shadows of my own life experience that his words brought out of hiding. I had been denying to myself anything and everything I could that hinted at incest. I was twenty years old and I had no more excuses left. In fleeing from the hospital room, I did what I could to banish all the images that welled up, all the guilt, the fear and the weakness. I was running away and it wasn't long before I didn't even know what I was running from. Everything was buried and barricaded so deep that it would take decades before some of the buried images would begin to push their way back into my life. There was no other way to survive.

~

Céline and I left Ottawa at the end of July. Neither of us had a plan of where we could or should go. All we knew is that we had to escape our lives in the Ottawa valley, lives that were sucking us into darker and darker spaces. This urgency to flee meant that I didn't even think to wait until the next payday. Logical thinking and planning flew out the window. Common sense should have enabled us to be better prepared for leaving. However, our minds had shut down as we got caught up in fleeing. Céline had a small suitcase with a few of her clothes, her folder of art and things she considered essential. I had my guitar and a change of clothes.

It was strange to leave the city, to leave life as we knew it.

It was as if the only thing that existed was the pavement that stretched out in front of us when we got off the bus at the edge of the city, pavement that showed us that we were heading west, away from rather than going to. We just followed the road as we took our first steps taking us to the highway and then sticking out our thumbs in hopes that someone would stop.

The road ahead led to Toronto. It didn't take too long for someone to stop and give us a ride south-west to the town of Perth. Another ride was quick to come along and by late afternoon we found ourselves on the 401, the super-highway, headed for Toronto.

In Toronto with the guitar in one hand and Céline holding my other hand, we searched for Yorkville, the sector of the city where other young, lost people gathered. The guitar was like a passport of sorts that opened a few doors, allowing us to find a floor to sleep on and meals to be shared while we stayed in Toronto. While I played, sometimes earning a bit of money, but more often than not I played for free, Céline drew pictures. We were one couple of many young couples doing the same thing, running away from sad stories without a map or a plan.

~

Emerging from this last part of my story is the realisation that this was beginning of my own gypsy-like travels. Was I escaping uncomfortable reality or was I seeking out a new story for myself? It wasn't many years ago I would have answered that I was heading west in search of my own story. Now, the answer isn't so simple. Already only a few days away from life in Ottawa, I had buried the drama that had precipitated the flight away from the city. In Toronto, I began to lose more of the past. There was only the present and the mantra of love that could be heard from that generation now called Flower Children.

I notice from this position in time more than forty years later and through the eyes of a psychotherapist that this young version of myself had already begun to forget so much of his own past. Life was centred on Céline. She needed so much because of her childhood and adolescent wounds, deep wounds that left her incapable of looking after herself. Already at the age of twenty, I knew that my role was that of caretaker. Somehow or other, I had to find a way to protect her and provide for her. There was no space left for what I needed. Whatever lurked in my own dark corners had to be shoved aside and forgotten. This became my quest, my early search for the Holy Grail. I bit deeply into the mythology of a knight and pilgrim in search of a world that didn't exist. But that story, is a tale to be told at some other time. It was enough that I had broken away from the chains that bound me to the sins of my father, my mother and the generations upon generations that came before them. I abandoned Benjy and embraced the new man I was creating, Robert.

Afterword

As this story was written, or should I say as it was writing itself through me, I became aware of how this story of an individual became a story of a culture. One could read this story as a tale of a number of individuals that serve as stereotypical examples of that culture. Or, one could read this story as one in a long line of fairy tales that talk about how the human psyche is transformed with each character standing in the place of various human complexes and archetypes.

The year I was born, Joseph Campbell wrote a book called The Hero With a Thousand Faces, which traces the same descent into darkness that then propels a person onto a long journey, a heroic journey, where the forces of darkness are overcome. Campbell looked to the stories that have been with us for millennia and sifts through them to trace out the universal, or the archetypal, journey that individuals take to become conscious beings, mature beings.

One of the things I learned from Campbell, and a depth psychologist called Carl Jung who wrote Symbols of Transformation, a psychological study of the hero, a hundred years ago, was that once the journey has reached its end, it is somehow transformed into yet another journey. This story finds itself in the same position once one reaches the last page, the realisation that "happily ever after," is not what comes next. But rather, a new beginning with another complex journey for the hero or the heroine to follow.

And so, I leave you with this – I will return with the journey that follows the one you have just read.

Robert G. Longpré, November, 2014

Acknowledgments

No story can come into existence without the direct and indirect influences of others. It is with the guidance of Marvin Haave and Doug Glazer, two mental health counsellors that helped me at the beginning of my heroic journey of healing; as well as Mae Stolte and Zeljko Matijevic, two Jungian analysts for their guidance as the journey unfolded, that I managed to build a compass to make my way along this journey of soul healing. The story had been buried, unspoken and unwritten for many years other than sporadic attempts. Now, in my retirement, I have no more excuses.

I must thank my wife who gave me the encouragement to write this story. My need for quiet time in my study was honoured and protected by her. Of course, as I gave her bits and pieces to read as the story unfolded, she was honest in her opinions, something any writer needs if a story is to be worth reading.

I want to thank as well, three people who have read all or parts of the novel, pointing out various errors in grammar, logic and spelling while also encouraging and supporting along the way. Thank you, Dustin, Simone and Germaine.

And finally, I want to thank you, the reader, for making it to the end of this journey down a broken road. That more than anything else, is what motivated me to write the story, and motivates me to continue the journey, the story that follows this one.

About the author

Robert G. Longpré is a retired educator and psychotherapist who lives in Elrose, Saskatchewan, Canada with his wife of more than forty years. He is father to three children, and grandfather to six incredible grandsons and a beautiful granddaughter. The question of what to do with the shift from working for a living to retirement left the question, 'Now what?' to be answered. The answer grew out of a lifetime of writing on the side for pleasure, and sometimes (perhaps too often) for personal self-therapy.

Robert began writing and publishing while a teenager in Ottawa, the city of his birth, with the co- production of a literary journal called, *Left Center*. Poetry and essays of protest found a ready audience during the late sixties. A few years later, Robert turned to publishing small editorials in small town newspapers in Saskatchewan before turning to writing social history. In 1977, Sakitawak, a bi-centennial history of Ile-a-la-Crosse was published providing the first paid writing experience.

Through the early nineties, various chapters of educational books that focused on computer-mediated communications, educational reform, and strategies for learning a second language took care of the compulsion to write. Since retirement, a number of books that has formed a series called, Through a Jungian Lens, were published focusing on Jungian psychology and photography. As well, Robert has maintained a prolific body of blog posts.

This book begins a new series, Journey of Healing. One doesn't heal if one buries trauma under layers of denial. One has to expose trauma and come to terms with that trauma as it has shaped one's life and will continue to shape that life in spite of conscious intentions. Hiding and denying leaves one crippled in spirit and soul. Through making oneself vulnerable, one is able to move past the fear that paralyses and leaves one stuck in the past as a victim.

Robert can be contacted at:
rglongpre@gmail.com

Robert's blog sites are:
http://rglongpre.ca
http://rglongpre.com